THE WINNING OF THE WHITE HOUSE 1988

BY THE EDITORS OF TIME MAGAZINE
WITH AN INTRODUCTION BY GARRY WILLS

Edited by Donald Morrison

A TIME BOOK
Distributed by New American Library

Copyright © 1988 by Time Incorporated

First Edition

Published by Time Incorporated
Time & Life Building
Rockefeller Center
1271 Avenue of the Americas
New York, New York 10020

Cover design: Robert Potter
Text design: H. Roberts
Composition services: Ken Baierlein, Judith Ryan, Claire Conte Worley

Front cover photo: P.F. Bentley

Printed in the United States of America

10 9 8 7 6 5 4 3 2 1

ISBN Number 0-451-16165-3
Library of Congress Card Number 88-051735

5·3·89

Contents

Introduction: A Moral Derailing   1

1. The Mood   15
2. The Reagan Legacy   25
3. The Republicans   50
4. Bush: The Loyalist   78
5. The Democrats   103
6. Dukakis: The Loner   133
7. Jackson: The Spoiler   152
8. Atlanta: In Search of Unity   179
9. New Orleans: "A Kinder, Gentler Nation"   197
10. The Reckoning   213
11. The Media: Tools and Targets   244
Index   264
About the Authors   267

Introduction:

A Moral Derailing

By Garry Wills

THE CAMPAIGN WAS KINDER AND GENTLER WHEN IT BEGAN. The candidates—seven Democrats, six Republicans—appeared on separate two-hour sessions of William Buckley's *Firing Line,* where the languor and jocularity of the host made for some wit and civility in his guests, qualities that would be wrung out of the contenders as they went along. Looking back at tapes of those first encounters, when the candidates, still fresh, were just exploring themes their managers would later exploit, one regrets what they had to go through. Joseph Biden was relaxed and convincing, unaware of the fall ahead of him. Gary Hart was already gone (he left the race like Dorian Gray) and not yet returned (he came back like Dorian Gray's portrait on traveling exhibition). Paul Simon was everybody's funny uncle, not yet the scolding maiden aunt.

The candidates were still trying to distinguish themselves from the crowd, somewhat coy about their differences, like contestants on the old *What's My Line?* show. Bruce Babbitt's line seemed to be doing fish imitations in the invisible bowl he wore around his head. Richard Gephardt was all insect-lizardy alertness, more energetic than his words seemed to justify, but engagingly so. Albert Gore was the stiffest of the candidates, though he told the best joke. Buckley's own specialty, at the moment, was David Frost impressions.

It was when Buckley had the six Republican candidates on his show that George Bush started shedding his wimp image by calling Pete du Pont by his given name, Pierre. (Later Bush would feign horror that Michael Dukakis' campaign called Dan Quayle by his full moniker, J. Danforth Quayle.) The transition from the gentle mocking of the early days to the later meanness of little accusations is a gauge of the campaign's souring process.

What happened to those 13 attractive men? The Democrats were called dwarfs back then, though none of them looked any less plausible than du Pont, Al Haig or Pat Robertson. Seen again on the tapes, they all seem larger than the finalists who fought their way down to the dreadful end of this campaign. The Dukakis and Bush on display after Labor Day were cheaper versions of those earlier, more generous selves. As Jesse Jackson likes to say, their grapes have turned to raisins.

It was not supposed to happen that way, even in the view of cynical prognosticators. The first maneuvers were supposed to be aimed at true believers, who vote in primaries, while the general election would open them up to a broader, less fanatical audience. Sure enough, the Republicans were as dependably right wing at that first stage as the Democrats were open in their liberalisms. Alone of the six Republicans, Bush—who was stuck, in any case, with the Reagan Administration's position—vigorously defended the proposed INF treaty. (Haig, by contrast, called Mikhail Gorbachev "the most cunning, the most sophisticated Soviet leader since Lenin.") Every Republican but Bush felt surprisingly free to criticize Reagan in his post-Iran-*contra* weakened state. Haig pointedly excluded Reagan from the pictures of former Presidents he would hang in the Oval Office, choosing Eisenhower instead because "he never brutalized his Secretary of State." Robertson attacked the Reagan deficit, saying, "We are the first generation [of Americans] ever to consume the patrimony of our unborn children."

But the real charge made during the fall of 1987 would not be about the nation's economy. In the most surprising development of the whole campaign year, two candidates briefly caught fire with the charge that Reagan's America was *morally* bankrupt. Appropriately, both candidates were religious figures, and they tapped a yearning for moral rebirth that Reagan was supposed to have brought to America already. Yet Reagan's rhetoric, unable to re-create the America he remembered, just made that America's absence more haunting for those who saw a Sodom around them instead of the Eden they had been promised. Pat Robertson and Jesse Jackson deplored the loss of family values, the irresponsible sexuality of the young—what Jackson called "babies making babies." They said that drugs were hollowing out the country's moral center. They called for greater discipline in the schools. Both wanted to get tough on crime, Robertson with harsh penalties for drug dealers, Jackson by deploying the military against drugs coming into the country. Each used his church network while trying to reach out beyond it. Robertson presented himself as a corporate executive and university president. Jackson became a diplomat-negotiator, who had brought back hostages, kept factories and farms from closing and transcended racial divisions. Robertson offered a right-wing populism that had shed the overt racism of George Wallace's campaigns. Jackson represented a left-wing populism that had gone beyond the black base of his 1984 effort.

It was surprising, in a time of apparent peace and prosperity, to find such personal anguish welling up in response to Robertson's lament for a nation sliding into evil, or to Jackson's claim that white as well as black Americans were being victimized by corporations and a system that favored "merging corporations, purging workers and submerging our economy." This was a populism not derived so much from present economic distress as from uneasiness about the future, about the world of debt, of drugs, of illiteracy, of poor jobs or no jobs, that Americans will be leaving their children.

Robertson's effort seemed to flame out earlier. He mobilized his evangelical troops to show up in disproportionate strength at the Iowa straw ballot and the Michigan pre-caucuses. But his appeal went beyond the true believers (important enough in themselves) and had a lasting impact on the shape of the Republican race. By coming in second in Iowa and beating George Bush, Robertson gave Bob Dole, the winner in Iowa, a chance to derail Bush in New Hampshire; and the hard core of the right that Robertson had pre-empted was unavailable to Jack Kemp when he needed it. Robertson's early success, and Kemp's plight, helped prevent other right wingers (like Patrick Buchanan and Jeane Kirkpatrick) from getting into the race. But Robertson's campaign staggered from one kookiness to the next as the candidate not only professed he was opposed to abortion, but argued that Americans are committing genocide against themselves by depriving the country of all the wages unborn babies would be earning in the 21st century. (This was an implicitly racist argument, reflecting the fact that whites resort to abortion more readily than blacks.) He also made a wild claim about Soviet offensive missiles remaining in Cuba. He finally became a laughingstock when he suggested that Bush's people had engineered the Jimmy Swaggart sex scandal to damage his campaign.

Yet Robertson proved there was an unassuaged moral yearning that Reagan had stimulated without quite satisfying. Robertson's agenda of prayer in public schools, harsh penalties for drug dealers, a return to patriotism, opposition to abortion and an attack on liberalism in the form of teachers' organizations and the Council on Foreign Relations set the model for Bush's campaign in the fall. Robertson issued the marching orders in his speech at the Republican National Convention in

New Orleans: "Criminals are turned loose and the innocent are made victims . . . I submit to you tonight that Michael Dukakis is the most liberal candidate ever put forward for the presidency by any major party in American history."

Roger Ailes, Bush's media adviser, and his campaign allies are credited with inventing three of the campaign's most powerful issues: the Pledge of Allegiance flap, which involved Dukakis' veto of a 1977 Massachusetts bill requiring teachers to lead their classes in saying the pledge; the Willie Horton scare, so named after a convicted murderer who, after temporarily leaving jail under a Massachusetts prisoner furlough program, terrorized a Maryland couple; and the American Civil Liberties Union attacks, in which Dukakis' membership in the group was referred to in McCarthy-esque tones. Yet these were all modified leftovers from the Robertson campaign. Bush had been criticized as a "lapdog" early in 1987 when he courted the party's right wing, calling himself a "born-again" Christian. It was assumed that he had to do such things for the sake of expediency, but that he would move to the center after surviving the Kemp challenge. What Ailes and his allies did was take the Robertson base and build on it, incorporating all its major themes, sometimes in subtler form.

It was a brilliant stroke to run the incumbent Vice President, who was boasting of his own Administration's success, as the candidate of *grievance*—of affronts localized in a liberalism that is soft on crime and defense, exotic as a Harvard boutique yet stealthy enough to win an election by misrepresenting itself to the American people. Populism is supposed to be an appeal to the powerless. Populism of the powerful is a contradiction in terms; but Ailes and Lee Atwater and James Baker made it a successful contraption for garnering voters.

The Jackson story is almost the reverse of Robertson's. He went further, gained more votes, commanded more attention and remained an important factor in the race right up to the convention. But his themes were not incorporated into the

Democratic campaign after the convention. Robertson's cadres would be a quiet but key element in Bush's campaign, while Dukakis treated Jackson as an embarrassment, something he had to cope with, placate, keep a healthy distance from. This would lead Dukakis into his worst mistake, the renunciation of ideology, the attempt to build a middle constituency from scratch in the name of "competence." In effect, he fled his base instead of building on it.

This was not a bold decision but a cautious one, based on the conventional wisdom Jackson had been undermining all through the primaries. Before the 1988 campaign Jackson was regularly discussed as a threat to the Democratic Party, one who would damage the nominee, as he is supposed to have damaged Walter Mondale in 1984. Jackson is the most vivid symbol of those "special interests" (blacks, women, gays, teachers, unions) that were supposed to have trammeled the Democratic Party, making it their captive. (As Studs Terkel points out, the really powerful lobbies—for gun owners, doctors, lawyers, corporations—are not called special interests. They are just average citizens, the privileged again posing as populists.) The Democratic Leadership Council was created to free the party from the "encumbrance" of special interests and move it to the center. A centrist candidate strong on defense was thought to have the best chance to win the 1988 election, and Super Tuesday was created in the South to give such a candidate a boost. There was even talk for a while of "Atari Democrats," managerial types who would forget past labels and leap into the next creative age of Government-inspired technology. Democrats, while trying to build their dream candidate (an Atari Gary Hart or a Southern hawk like Sam Nunn), were unconsciously fashioning that Frankenstein's monster of "competence" and computer-friendly conduct, Michael Dukakis.

But while the experts were thinking in these terms, political reality was shifting under their feet. The Democrats had run for and won congressional majorities and statehouses with the help of the special interests that were supposed to burden them at the national level. And then in 1986 something striking happened: black voters, many of them registered during the Jackson campaign of 1984, turned out in large percentages—in some places larger than that of their white counterparts, defying historical patterns. These new black voters helped elect whites in states like Alabama, Georgia, North Carolina and California, returning control of the Senate to Democrats.

That shift in control meant, among other things, that liberal Joseph Biden became chairman of the Senate Judiciary Committee, rather than conservative Strom Thurmond. And moderate Howell Heflin, sitting on that committee, was one of the Southerners elected in 1984 with the help of black votes. So when Robert Bork was nominated for the Supreme Court in 1987, the man, a conservative whose intellectual qualifications seemed indisputable, found himself facing a panel that would respond to the special interests. Those interests felt that Bork's constitutional scruples did not reflect the changed realities of American society. Bork, by sticking to his record, was in the position of denying rights of privacy to gays and those using contraception, of opposing civil rights and women's rights. Yet a majority of Americans agreed with the special interests on respecting those rights. Even the South did not want to go back to the days before the civil rights decisions that Bork had criticized.

What took shape in the alliance formed to reject Bork was a liberalism that could prevail in 1988. The rights of women— the majority of the population—are not a special interest in the sense that the National Rifle Association or the American Medical Association is. Even many of those offended by homosexuality agree that the Government has no place in the bedroom. Jackson realized that the "rainbow coalition" he had tried to call into being in 1984 was knitting itself together in the effort to defeat the Bork nomination. If Jackson could keep those elements united, his 1988 campaign would be far more compelling to far more people than his 1984 race had been. He spent the summer of 1987 studying economic solutions to the trade imbalance and the budget deficit with Carol O'Claireacain, a New York–based labor economist. She says they spent hours discussing the various issues and came up with plans like the use of labor-union pension funds as Government-guaranteed capital for programs to rebuild the decaying infrastructure of America, the roads and bridges neglected for years. "Sure, some of the projects would go into default," she says, "and the government would have to pick up the tab on those. But meanwhile the bridges would be repaired, the jobs created, wages earned, taxes paid. It is more than we could accomplish by direct taxation, even if we could impose taxes. This would cost less, even with the worst scenario for defaults, and it would more than pay for itself." Jackson also proposed gradually lowering the federal deficit by taking away Reagan-era tax breaks for the upper brackets.

When Jackson took his message of economic populism to Iowa at the beginning of 1987, it elicited an astounding response. Several hundred people in Greenfield passed up the Super Bowl to hear him talk farm economics. He adopted the town as his Iowa campaign headquarters and won 66% of its caucus delegates a year later. He began showing up at farm auctions and factory closings. In Wisconsin he urged Lee Iacocca to keep a Chrysler plant open in Kenosha, a town that supplied some of his most enthusiastic delegates at the Atlanta convention. The improbable romance between Jackson and aggrieved whites was heating up—he would win three times as many white votes in the 1988 primaries as he had won in 1984, and white populists as diverse as Jim Hightower of Texas, John Jay Hooker of Tennessee and disc jockey Casey Kasem of the *American Top 40* said his message was the same as theirs. While Jackson was reaching out, party brokers like Ann Lewis and Bert Lance were taking his cause to Democratic regulars, saying Jackson was a player this year, one who meant no harm to the party and could do much good.

Dukakis, like most other Democrats, was careful not to criticize Jackson. Republicans had given Robertson the same polite treatment, thanking him for broadening the party's appeal. Yet Dukakis thought of himself as self-sufficient and did not actively seek partnership even with powerful white politicians in his fall campaign—people like Sam Nunn and Edward Kennedy. The Massachusetts Governor was certainly not going to let himself be seen as indebted to a black man with heavy baggage from the past. Dukakis had profited, after Super Tuesday, by the narrowing of the race to two candidates, of which he was the only white left running. Tuesday after Tuesday, he won victories over his more liberal opponent, taking on the aura of a moderate and defining himself as the alternative to Jackson.

At the convention Dukakis was, among other things, declaring his independence from Jackson when he said, "This campaign in not about ideology. It's about competence." Jackson was the most prominent of the party's progressives—and Jackson, not coincidentally, had never held office or managed anything with generally acknowledged competence. Dukakis, instead of recruiting the energies of his party's most zealous wing, as Bush had included Robertson's troops, was telling them in effect to get lost, or at least to lose their labels, while promoting his own credentials as a manager. It was a weird rallying cry: "Let Michael be Michael."

Dukakis' convention speech gave Roger Ailes the opportunity he was hoping for. Moderate in the context of Massachusetts, Dukakis is a liberal by national standards. He is undemonstrative by temperament in any case, but for him to forswear at least part of his own progressive heritage made him look positively furtive. He seemed to be hiding secrets as well as his smile.

That impression would help Ailes in the crucial assignment he had given himself—turning the unrelentingly nice George Bush into a vicious campaigner. In the past Bush's affability had come across as slightly sappy. To get him serious enough, Ailes had to convince Bush he was being roughed up. The manager programmed his man to launch an ad hominem assault on Dan Rather during a live interview on the CBS *Evening News.* Ailes persuaded Bush that there was a dastardly plot to eliminate him from the campaign. In the limousine on the way over to the network's studio, Bush protested that he could answer questions about the Iran-*contra* affair; he had been doing so all along. Ailes said, "You don't understand something. This is a hit squad . . . They've got you up against the wall. They're putting the blindfold on you. It's all over, pal." It was all a plot on the part of Dan Rather, who in this view was not a newsman but an ideological hit man. Ailes would say later in the campaign that Rather should be on the Democratic payroll.

Ailes saw his job as that of a fight manager animating his contender with energizing drafts of hatred for the foe. Before Reagan's second debate with Mondale in 1984 (Ailes had been called in because Reagan did so poorly in the first one), Ailes sent the President into the ring with these words: "When you see Mondale, remember this guy had twelve years as Senator and Vice President, and it was a mess. And what he wants to do is get your job so that he can undo everything you spent your entire life doing."

Roger Ailes had to make George Bush, who is not very good at hating, hate Michael Dukakis. Ailes went around spreading the word that Dukakis is "Mr. Elbows and Knees" when it comes to dirty campaigning, that Kitty was behind the release of the Biden tape, that Dukakis had mental problems he was hiding, that he "is a classic narcissist."

The clincher, so far as convincing Bush went, was the fact that Dukakis was being deceptive about his past, trying to deny his liberalism, to mask the menace to the nation presented by his softness on crime and defense. If Ailes could make that case to his principal, then the Pledge of Allegiance issue, the Horton horror stories, the A.C.L.U. membership would make sense to

Bush as defensive actions against the broad assault of Dukakis' lie.

The Governor made such absurd accusations credible by his refusal to take them seriously. In the eyes of many voters, that is just what he would do if he had something to hide. For weeks Dukakis took the position that it would be undignified even to notice the attacks being made on his patriotism, his opposition to crime, his feeling for the average citizen. Actually, given the opportunity to reaffirm all those qualities loudly, his refusal to do so confirmed the suspicion that Dukakis might after all be a bloodless ideologue. ·

The contrast between the two campaigns' response to attacks was made clear at the Republican Convention when a furor broke out over the nomination of Dan Quayle for Vice President. The day after that announcement, delegates found waiting for them on their seats in the convention hall statements from veterans' groups and National Guardsmen saying it was no disgrace to serve in the Guard. By the time the convention session began, each floor whip had a set of quotations from military spokesmen defending Quayle's patriotism.

The Republicans anticipated attacks. The Democrats ignored them. When Dukakis was hit with the Pledge of Allegiance issue, he should have appeared with such patriotic icons of the Democratic Party as astronaut-Senator John Glenn to declare that the flag was being cheapened by such attacks. On the Horton question, Dukakis should have convened a panel of penologists to explain furlough systems and compare the various state and federal programs with the Massachusetts version. On the A.C.L.U. issue, Dukakis should have appeared with officers of that organization and joked about all the times they had disagreed in the past, while asserting that what makes America great is the preservation of free discussion and advocacy. This is what Christopher Matthews, the onetime aide to Tip O'Neill, calls seeking to "hang a lantern on your problems." But Dukakis' problem was that he did not know he had problems.

With Jackson, instead of trying to hide him for a while, Dukakis should have shared the platform with him, saying the Democratic Party has nothing to hide—unlike the Republicans, who were smuggling Dan Quayle into small-city high schools, where the questioning was likely to be gentle. By the time Dukakis began to respond, it was with desperate imitations of Bush's first flag-studded rallies and with mean imitations of the Horton ad, substituting victims of a *federal* furlough program—a step Dukakis had earlier said he would not take.

The result was a dreary spectacle. Not only were two fundamentally decent men acting in foul ways, but they were being impelled in part because of their decent traits. Bush's reluctance to attack meant that he had to be overstimulated. Dukakis' self-containment was read as a form of acquiescence that stirred the other side to greater boldness. While describing all the "tough choices" he was going to make as President, Dukakis let himself be pilloried by the Republicans. That was hardly a recommendation for his ability to stand up to Mikhail Gorbachev!

Apportioning guilt for this unhappy outcome is not a productive exercise. The Bush operatives were swift and ruthless in attack. But Dukakis' renunciation of ideology left a vacuum that was bound to be filled with something more than his endless incantations about "good jobs at good wages" or "decent affordable housing." Dukakis could not talk meaningfully about the deficit, since his only response to it was the laughable proposal to collect more of the taxes due (a plan that had worked in Massachusetts, where state revenuers had previously not achieved the efficiency of the IRS). Having deprived himself of the liberal network that defeated Bork, he tried to appeal to a purely cerebral group of Americans who wanted things better done, a managerial élite that does not exist in large numbers.

The lost opportunity of 1988 is indicated by the early responses to Robertson and Jackson. The Robertson people were asking for substance to be added to Reagan's rhetoric. The Jackson people were saying Reagan's rhetoric was of its nature insubstantial, made up of nostalgia about "the market" as a magic restorer of God and country. The truth, under all the campaign charges and patriotic bluster, is that America is now a frightened empire. Outdated commitments, based on postwar U.S. superiority, have become a drain on the country's strength rather than an exercise of it. American successes in rebuilding the world economy have made rivals of former dependents, turned the country's debtors into its creditors and lured productive capital toward cheaper labor markets. More and more people are working, but often at lower wage levels. Parts of America are turning into little Third Worlds, squalid and crumbling, reachable only by obsolete equipment, moving on or through ill-tended bridges, rails and tunnels. America, while still No. 1 in ways that can lead to the self-hypnosis of the Reagan years, has entered a glide-down, an era of shared responsibilities and mutual dependencies—and it is the whole tendency of American electoral politics to disguise this fact from the citizenry. Nothing is more identifiably self-destructive in a modern campaign than any touch of pessimism. Smiley-faced promises never to raise taxes are the touchstone of "realism." What are candidates to do but berate each other once the people have forbidden them ever to speak of serious things?

In the first appearance of the Democratic candidates on the Buckley show, Bruce Babbitt said there was a "disconnect" between Reagan's TelePrompTer and the real country "out there." The lack of connection between American politics and actual conditions is even more fundamental than Babbitt suggested. A symbol of that occurred when Dukakis went to speak with workers at an automotive-parts factory in a St. Louis suburb. He was preceded on the platform by Richard Gephardt, the Congressman from Missouri who had made the threat of foreign competition his specialty. Dukakis, in a prepared speech, congratulated the workers at the factory for escaping foreign ownership, ad libbing such encouraging notes as, "I do not need to tell you this—you are among the survivors." Titters

at the back alerted the national press to the embarrassing fact
that the company's parent was owned by a European firm. The
multiple disconnects involved in this gaffe—between Dukakis'
Boston headquarters (where some managers knew very well
who owned the company), the speechwriters, the advance team,
the candidate, the local Congressman and the public relations
officials of the company and its union—all these indicate the
condition not only of this particular campaign but also of the
country. The campaign was not the solution. It was part of the
problem. The winner of such a contest fully deserves the problems he will be facing. That does not mean we should not feel
sorry for him.

1
The Mood

The idea was to follow a campaign from beginning to end. It would be written as a novel is written, with anticipated surprises as, one by one, early candidates vanish in the primaries until only two final jousters struggle for the prize in November.

—Theodore H. White,
on *The Making of the President 1960*

WHEN TEDDY WHITE BEGAN HIS FIVE-BOOK *THE MAKING OF the President* series—and thus invented a new genre of political journalism—deciding where to start the story was reasonably simple: the snows of New Hampshire. That state held the year's first primary, on the second Tuesday in March.

Nowadays life and presidential politics are more complicated. Any White-inspired, quasi-novelistic account of the winning of the White House 1988 must face the problem of where the story begins. In the snows of New Hampshire? In the frozen cornfields of Iowa, a state whose midwinter caucuses have been gaining in prominence in recent elections? In the 1987 strategy sessions of fund raisers and imagemakers for the handful of men and women who thought they had what it takes to win the White House?

No, the campaign for the 1988 presidential election began much earlier than 1987. Even as the votes were still being counted on the night of Ronald Reagan's thundering 1984 re-election victory, professional politicians were talking openly—and journalists were writing for the next day's edition—about the presidential contest four years down the road. Was George Bush the legitimate heir to Reagan's legacy? Or did that mantle now fall elsewhere, perhaps on the shoulders of New York Congressman Jack Kemp, the former Buffalo Bills quarterback and flag bearer of the New Right? Had New York Governor Mario Cuomo's inspiring keynote speech at the 1984 Democratic National Convention catapulted him into the role of his party's front runner? Or could former Colorado Senator Gary Hart claim that title by virtue of his second-place finish in the primaries? In America, the next campaign begins before the current one has ended.

So where did the 1988 campaign begin? On the July 4 weekend of 1985, when, amid the usual parades and fireworks, the American press noticed that a few presidential aspirants were behaving as if they were presidential aspirants. The Fourth of July holiday is a big one every year for politicians, though not traditionally as a vehicle for launching campaigns to win the presidency three years hence. This July 4, George Bush, just back from an eleven-day official trip to Europe, found himself sitting in a reviewing stand in Bristol, N.H. Asked if the trip had anything to do with the state's 1988 primary, Bush replied somewhat coyly, "I don't seriously have to address that problem until after the 1986 [congressional] elections." Jack Kemp, who usually spent the July 4 holiday at an annual Kemp family barbecue in upstate New York, skipped it this time to march in a parade in Clear Lake, Iowa. Asked whether the visit had anything to do with the state's 1988 caucuses, Kemp replied, not at all coyly, "Absolutely." Kemp, after marching in a procession that included fez-wearing Shriners on motorcycles, was approached by a woman who pleaded, "Let me shake your hand, just in case you're President some day."

A more complete list of presidential hopefuls—many of whom were busy shaking hands and reviewing parades that day—would have included, for the Republicans: Bush, Kemp, Senate majority leader Robert Dole of Kansas, former Majority Leader Howard Baker of Tennessee, Senator Paul Laxalt of Nevada, ex–Delaware Governor Pete du Pont, televangelist Pat Robertson and onetime Democrat Jeane Kirkpatrick, newly retired as Ambassador to the United Nations and the toast of the conservative dinner circuit. For the Democrats: Cuomo, Hart, 1984 vice-presidential candidate Geraldine Ferraro, Senators Joseph Biden of Delaware, Albert Gore Jr. of Tennessee, Jesse Helms of North Carolina, Edward Kennedy of Massachusetts and Sam Nunn of Georgia, Representative Richard Gephardt of Missouri, Arizona Governor Bruce Babbitt, the Rev. Jesse Jackson of Chicago, and, from outside the realm of politics, Chrysler chairman Lee Iacocca, who was also claimed by the Republicans.

How did such names get on such lists? In some cases the designees themselves suddenly and inexplicably began pumping hands and frequenting parades far from their home districts. In other instances, the ill-defined community of Washington journalists and political professionals found themselves speculating out loud about the next election, and could not help overhearing one another. Columnist Russell Baker once blamed it all on the Great Mentioner, a mysterious figure who flitted about the country bestowing candidacy on various people simply by mentioning their names. Some names, notably Bush's, were tossed into the hat by virtue of their bearer's current job—in his case, as sitting Vice President to a second-term, about-to-retire President. Bush, however, was doing little that summer of 1985 to dampen speculation about his future. Bob Dole, with characteristic wit, chided the Vice President for trying to emulate Reagan's macho image by visiting the President's California ranch to "chop horses and ride wood."

As the election of 1988 drew nearer, and the field of candidates began to narrow, some Americans may have wondered why anybody would want the job. After eight years of Reaganism, the country seemed on the surface to be in good shape. The economy was in the midst of a long and steady expansion. According to the University of Michigan's Survey Research Center, more Americans felt good about economic conditions than at any time since the late 1960s. The Soviets under Mikhail Gorbachev had been behaving themselves overseas and even adopting vaguely capitalist economic reforms at home. Democracy was breaking out in various parts of the Third World. Though U.S. troops had occasionally been dispatched to foreign trouble spots, the country was at peace.

Yet beneath that blanket of undeniable well being, the electorate looking toward 1988 could not help feeling a frisson of anxiety. Times had been good, but there was a gnawing expectation that a day of reckoning was at hand, that the bills piling up during the Don't-Worry-Be-Happy Reagan years would eventually have to be paid. In a 1988 CBS/New York *Times* poll, more than half of respondents believed that the next generation of Americans would be bogged down by problems left behind for them.

As if to demonstrate what terrors might lie ahead, the stock market on Oct. 19, 1987, took a header. The Dow Jones industrial average fell 508 points that day to 1738.74, a drop of 22.6%. Some $500 billion in paper value, a sum equal to the gross national product of France, vanished into thin air. Markets around the world collapsed in reaction. Though they recovered somewhat in the following year, Black Monday, as that chilling day was known, had sent a shiver through the body politic. The financial community had cast a vote of no confidence in the country's economic future. The high-flying, junk-bond-fed, Reagan-era dream of painless prosperity had been punctured. A more sober age of realism and contrition beckoned. No matter who became President, the next four years would be no picnic.

The problem was simply that the country had been living beyond its means. Under the Reagan Administration, the national debt had nearly tripled, to $2.6 trillion. The federal budget deficit for fiscal 1988 widened to $155 billion. One enterprising inventor, Warren Dennis of Pasadena, Calif., developed a desk clock that displayed the time, date and, at the touch of a button, an up-to-the-second tally of the national debt, programmed to rise $8,000 a second. Said Dennis, whose item was priced at $39.95 and aimed at the 1988 Christmas gift market: "Maybe when people see the national debt like this, right in front of them, they'll take an interest in the issue."

Not that the next President could do much about it. More than 80% of the federal budget consisted of such hard-to-cut items as defense, interest on the national debt and entitlement programs like Social Security and Medicare. Even without any policy changes, federal spending would rise 24% in the subsequent five years because of various provisions for automatic increases. No matter who became President, a top priority would be to hold down such increases through further unpleasant spending cuts and help attack the budget deficits by raising taxes.

Perhaps even more distressing, America had lost its competitive edge in the world. In the first eight months of 1988 the country imported $92 billion more in goods than it exported. At that rate the 1988 trade deficit would hit $138 billion. The figure was less than the previous year's, but by all rights the decline should have been steeper: the value of the dollar had fallen sharply, making U.S. goods comparatively cheaper. (The dollar's drop, meanwhile, had prompted foreigners to buy up alarming amounts of American companies and real estate.) The inability to meet foreign competition had virtually wiped out some U.S. industries. The share of the domestic consumer-electronics market held by U.S. companies had plunged from almost 100% in 1970 to less than 5% in 1988. American firms, for instance, pioneered VCR technology but decided to sell Tokyo's models rather than try to make their own.

While America's position as the world's leading economic power was eroding, voices could be heard in the 1980s warning of a larger decline. In *The Rise and Fall of the Great Powers,* a book that aroused considerable debate among policymakers, historian Paul Kennedy argued that great military powers tended to decline once their overseas commitments became too taxing, as was allegedly the case with the U.S. In another much discussed book, *The Birth Dearth,* demographer Ben J. Wattenberg warned that a declining birthrate was undermining the country's global eminence and that the free Western nations would soon account for only a tiny fraction of the world's people.

Doubts about the nation's economy and global power were not the only ones nibbling at the corner of the electorate's consciousness. Many Americans were beginning to fear that the very fabric of the nation was unraveling. Drugs had become a problem of frightening proportions, especially with the emergence of crack, a potent, cheap and highly addictive derivative of cocaine. In 1982 the U.S. Customs Service seized 5.2 metric tons of cocaine; in 1986 it seized nearly five times that amount. Princeton professor Ethan Nadelmann estimated in 1988 that federal, state and local governments were spending $8 billion a year on drug-enforcement activities. But the cost to society was incalculable.

Government corruption flourished at high levels, and scores of Reagan Administration officials left office under a cloud. The specter of AIDS was haunting the nation; by October 1988 at least 75,000 Americans had contracted the disease, which so far had no cure.

America's beaches and waterways were increasingly polluted; in the summer of 1988, beaches in the New York City area were closed to bathers when hypodermic needles and other medical wastes began washing ashore. Accidents and radiation leaks at nuclear-weapons plants, covered up for decades by the government, were brought into the public eye in 1988; no one knew how many people had contracted radiation-caused cancer as a result of the leaks. The nation's schools were turning out millions of young people who could not keep up with the intellectual demands of an increasingly technological economy. American universities were turning out armies of would-be lawyers and investment bankers, but graduate engineering programs had trouble filling vacancies. As many as 1,500, or 7.5%, of the engineering faculty posts at U.S. colleges were vacant. In his 1987 best seller *The Closing of the American Mind,* professor Allan Bloom of the University of Chicago excoriated American education for maintaining low academic standards, failing to teach values, turning out a generation of ignorant youth and leaving the culture mired in mediocrity. One of Bloom's more vivid images was of a hypothetical 13-year-old doing his math homework while listening to "orgasmic rhythms" on his Walkman. Declared Bloom: "In short, life is made into a nonstop, commercially prepackaged masturbational fantasy."

A new national concern had pushed its way into the headlines during the Reagan years—or rather, an old problem had gained new urgency: the homeless. On any given night in 1988, an estimated 735,000 people in the U.S. did not have a home. During the course of the year, as many as 2 million people were without shelter for one night or more. Many were mentally ill, on the streets because of a long-standing policy of deinstitutionalization. Many were drug or alcohol abusers. But a growing number were the working poor and entire families. Federal spending for low-income housing had been cut sharply by the Reagan Administration. Meanwhile, prices of new and existing nonsubsidized housing had zoomed by double-digit percentages in some parts of the country, freezing many first-time buyers out of the market.

For that reason, among others, many younger Americans

were beginning to wonder whether they would ever enjoy a living standard as high as their parents'. College tuitions were soaring, but federally subsidized tuition-loan programs were being slashed. Though inflation had largely been tamed, real hourly wages had declined 2.6% since 1981, and nearly 1 million factory jobs had disappeared. Real per capita income had risen $1,500, to $12,287 a year, but median incomes for younger and less experienced workers had fallen substantially. More women were working than ever before. There were also more two-paycheck families, and the median income for those households hit $40,422. But in many families, both parents had to work just to stay even. Nearly 57% of all mothers with preschool children had joined the work force, and surveys indicated that most of them would prefer to stay at home.

On balance, women had made some impressive gains during the Reagan years. The gap between women's and men's pay had narrowed five percentage points, to 65%. The number of women in management jobs had increased about 48%. More new businesses were being launched by women in 1988 than by men. Female equality was marching forward on many fronts, from children's athletic teams to the U.S. Supreme Court, where Sandra Day O'Connor became the first female Justice in 1981.

Economically, however, it appeared that America was becoming a nation divided. The top fifth of the population received nearly 44% of all income, and the bottom fifth less than 5%. That gulf had been widening since 1969. The rich were getting richer and the poor poorer.

The poor were also growing more numerous. In 1987 13.5% of Americans were living below the poverty line ($11,611 for a family of four), up from 13% in 1980. Almost one-third of blacks were poor, as were more than one-third of single-parent families headed by women. Between 1980 and 1987, the proportion of Hispanic poor increased from 25.7% to 28.2%. Among whites, the figure rose from 10.2% to 10.5%.

For blacks, who made up roughly 12% of the population in

1988, the picture was both better and worse at the end of the Reagan era. Unemployment among black teenagers was down sharply and the black middle class had gained ground; median incomes among black couples working full time rose a real 10%, to almost $40,000. Still, of the many black families headed by single women, over half were poor, vs. just over a quarter of single-parent families headed by white women. Other problems also ravaged the black community: the leading cause of death among young black men was murder by another young black man; in the inner cities, drug use and its related problems had grown to tragic proportions.

Many Americans were ambivalent about the poor. In the self-absorbed 1980s, with its emphasis on entrepreneurial vigor and market solutions to problems of all sorts, few Americans could be expected to stay awake nights worrying about income distribution. In the earnest 1960s, poverty and its attendant ills were considered a responsibility of society as a whole. But in the 1980s, it was important to be rich. In a 1987 poll by the American Council on Education and the Cooperative Institutional Research Program, 76% of college freshmen said that one of their most important goals in life was to "be very well off financially," up from only 41% in a similar poll two decades earlier.

Poverty was increasingly blamed on the system of government support designed to ameliorate it. Welfare programs survived in the 1980s, of course, but there was growing concern about their ability to create dependency. Conservative theorists like Charles Murray contended that Aid to Families with Dependent Children, a major federal program, provided an economic incentive for women to have babies out of wedlock and for men to avoid supporting their children. An exaggeration, perhaps, but persuasive enough to become part of the national debate on government social spending. Even some liberals had begun talking about the wisdom of government not trying to do more than it could afford, of the need for unsentimental pragmatism and hardheaded realism.

Yet voters in 1988 seemed ambivalent about what their government should be doing. In a poll by the Gallup organization for the Times Mirror Co., more than three-quarters of respondents agreed that the Federal Government should run only those things that cannot be run at the local level. Other surveys, however, showed that people did want government to take a major role. In a TIME/Yankelovich poll only a year earlier, some three-quarters of respondents believed that federal spending should be increased on such items as health care for the elderly, cleaning up the environment and aid to the homeless. Americans wanted things to stay the way they were, but they also wanted them to change.

As the presidential campaign of 1988 got under way, that ambivalence was lending a sense of mystery and suspense to the proceedings. Would Americans choose a candidate who would continue the small-government ethos of the previous eight years, or someone who would lead the nation into a new, more activist age? Would the economy be the dominant issue? Or would it be a foreign policy crisis, like the seizure of American hostages by Iran, an issue that hobbled Jimmy Carter in the 1980 election? Or perhaps a social concern like education, drugs or the environment?

One issue appeared likely: Ronald Reagan, who had set the tone, changed the course and dominated the public imagination during the 1980s. No matter what burning national questions would surface, the election of 1988 would almost surely be a referendum on Reaganism.

2
The Reagan Legacy

"We are the change."
"Go out there and win one for the Gipper."

TWO SPARE DECLARATIVE SENTENCES, JUST 13 WORDS, ONLY 14 syllables, were all the verbiage Ronald Wilson Reagan needed to describe both his mission as President and one secret of his method. He delivered those words to the 1988 Republican National Convention in New Orleans while helping, like a good constitutional monarch, to anoint George Herbert Walker Bush as the Grand Old Party's new champion. The assembled barons and squires of the party loved both lines, and for good reason.

Change, once a Democratic monopoly, evoked the Republican transformation Reagan had led from narrow, conventional conservatism to a broader, bolder variety. *The Gipper* reminded the crowd of the personal brand of leadership Reagan had made to work after a quartet of failed presidencies. That distinct persona, built on its owner's ability to articulate and symbolize cherished American values, had been critical to Reagan's stewardship. Now, though Reagan himself was graciously receding, his large shadow lingered over the battle for succession.

Seen from the floor of the expansive New Orleans Superdome, Reagan seemed a small, distant figure. The acoustics on the convention's opening night still needed refinement. As a result, the familiar throaty baritone was less mellifluous than usual. That diminution of oratorical wattage gave literal-minded listeners a metaphor for the inevitable shrinkage suffered by any leader whose departure from power is imminent. Seen through the prism of his Administration's record during the previous two years—a period in which Reagan's revolution had suffered severe stall-out, intellectually and politically—he was indeed a figure whose time had passed. But seen on television, his chosen medium of persuasion, Reagan was little diminished. And seen, most important, in the sea of Campaign '88 and to the shore of the Administration beyond, Reagan continued to look impressive.

Liberals still choked on that fact to the point of denying it. Early in 1988, when the residue of the Iran-*contra* episode clung like mildew, when Edwin Meese's impersonation of an Attorney General reminded the nation yet again of the inadequacies of so many other Reagan appointees, when memory of the October stock-market bust was fresh and frightening, when U.S. intervention in the Persian Gulf appeared feckless, it was easy to ridicule the staying power of Reaganism. Of course the President had never made good, in the literal, box-score sense, on his evocation of Tom Paine at the 1980 convention: "We have it in our power to begin the world over again." Modern Presidents are not in that business. Rather, the goal is to alter the old world effectively enough to keep it rotating under new conditions. But there were times, early in the election year, when even that aim seemed grandiose. Arthur M. Schlesinger Jr., the Democratic historian, spoke for many critics as he told a seminar at Harvard University's Kennedy School in February 1988: "When the smoke of neoconservative rhetoric drifts away, it will become obvious how little difference Reaganism has made."

Someday that prediction may turn out to be true. In the here, now and likely tomorrow, the rhetorical smoke of Reaganism still lingered and the policy embers continued to glow. How could it be otherwise? For better and for worse, Reagan's stewardship had brought about, blundered into or at least witnessed some of the most dramatic changes in decades. When the boy from Dixon, Ill., made what amounted to his valedictory address at the 1988 Republican Convention, it was still too early for a final assessment of the Reagan legacy. But consider three items beyond argument:

▶ In 1980 Soviet troops tightened Moscow's vise on Afghanistan, acting out the most virulent phase of the Brezhnev Doctrine, which asserted the Soviet Union's right to intervene to preserve Communist rule in its satellites. Meanwhile, in Iran, a fanatic fundamentalist in turban and robe humiliated America with no fear of retribution. What was to have been a monument to Jimmy Carter's diplomacy, the SALT II arms treaty, lay dormant in the Democratic-controlled Senate, never to be revived.

Eight years later, the Soviets were trooping out of Afghanistan, mission decidedly unaccomplished, and the Reagan Doctrine—under which the U.S. would aid anti-Communist freedom fighters around the world—could justly be accorded much of the credit. A treaty eliminating an entire class of nuclear weapons was safely ratified. Further, the U.S. Chief Executive now had a counterpart in the Kremlin who labored, in Reaganesque fashion, to get the commissars off the back of Soviet enterprise. In the Persian Gulf, American sea power helped to throttle, finally, Iran's ambitions. Elsewhere, to be sure, American aims were still frustrated, and Reagan's performances on the world stage were occasionally awkward and even dangerous: dispatching a cake and a Bible to the Ayatullah's henchmen, for instance, or agreeing at Reykjavík to give up the entire U.S. nuclear deterrent. But the realm of national security, both in political terms during the campaign and in policy terms for the next President, regardless of his political party, could not be the same.

▶ In 1980, at home, the dominant economic facts were inflation, high interest rates and unemployment. It would take a shattering recession and disguised doses of Keynesian medicine during Reagan's first term to reverse those trends. While Reaganomics revolutionized the tax code not once but twice, it also created a new set of problems, as daunting as any experienced in the Carter years. From the viewpoint of most voters, however, the federal budget deficit, the trade imbalance and the anemic national savings rate were theoretical worries rather than real ones. Except for those who lived in the several regions of the country left behind by the great economic expansion that started in late 1982, or who had the misfortune to be poor, Americans generally felt less threatened by hard times in Reagan's last months than they had in Carter's. In a September 1988 TIME poll, 73% of probable voters, when asked "How well do you think things are going in the country?", responded "very well" or "fairly well." That was the most positive reading registered in the magazine's surveys in four years. And even with the Democrats back in control of both houses of Congress after the 1986 elections, there was a great reluctance on Capitol Hill and on the campaign trail to embrace anything like the liberal-spending programs of old. Reagan had altered the country's fiscal priorities. All this had impact on the politics of 1988 and delineated the choices for the next White House occupant.

▶ In 1980 not many Americans had heard of a newly incorporated organization called Moral Majority. Nor was the Reverend Jerry Falwell a household name, except among the faithful of televangelism. When the Republicans assembled in New Orleans eight years later to choose Bush, the only other candidate who could still claim any delegates was not Bob Dole, Jack Kemp or some other established party leader but the Reverend Marion Gordon Robertson, Pat to his friends and enemies. In fact, he brought only a few score delegates to the convention but enough to show he still had a following. Robertson had transformed Falwell's agenda into a political movement. Robertson was too controversial ever to be nominated by a major party, let alone elected, but he was skillful enough to construct durable political cells in a dozen states from Florida to Washington. They would be heard from in the future, thanks initially to Reagan's embrace.

True, the President did not deliver on a single major policy pledge to the religious right. Abortion, for instance, was still legal in 1988, while prayer in public schools was still outlawed. But Reagan had bestowed legitimacy on the Moral Majoritarians that could not be measured by acts of Congress or amendments to the Constitution. He had invited their leaders to the White House, appointed a few of their supporters to sub-Cabinet posts, told the country that their goals were his goals. Most important, he had added three staunch conservatives to the Supreme Court and more than 360 to lesser federal benches. These jurists, more numerous than any lot ever appointed by a single President, were likely to exert a socially conservative influence for decades. The politics of all this elaborate homage to the right could not have been more obvious in 1988. Bush, an alien and an enemy in the minds of conservatives eight years earlier, now paid homage to each of the movement's sacred cows at every opportunity. In Dan Quayle he found a running mate who passed every conservative litmus test. The religious right had not taken over the Republican Party, not by any means, but it had found an influential seat at the G.O.P. table.

Besides those achievements, Reagan was leaving less visible though no less important contrails as he faded from the sky. He had no competitor as a personage during the 1980s, no rival when it came to expressing the feisty, upbeat mood that was so welcome after the dour ambiguities of Carter and the stolid tedium of Gerald Ford. "Reagan luck" was an easy, simplistic way

of explaining his political survival, but it was also a phenomenon that could not be ignored. Fortune smiled on Reagan in
many ways. During his first term, the Soviet leadership suffered
serial decrepitude, slowing Moscow's adventurism and allowing
Reagan to set his own priorities at his own pace. At home, the
Democratic leadership during those early years was almost as
attenuated as the succession of Soviet dictators.

Certainly one of the major pieces of Reagan's good fortune
was the timing of accession. The country, including the national
press corps, was ready for a sunny success story in the White
House. Four Presidents had left in varying conditions of failure.
The institution itself showed frightening signs of wear. If ever
there were a time for the cavalry to ride to the rescue of national
morale, the 1980 election was it. And central casting could find
no better captain, at least in public relations terms, than the old
celluloid soldier who had learned his horsemanship as a reserv-
ist in the 14th Cavalry Regiment and his amiable composure as
a radio sportscaster.

Optimism, the mood-altering substance Reagan brought
to the White House, was a decidedly mixed blessing. Eventually
his adamant refusal to confront unpleasant realities—whether
in economics, in the quagmire of Lebanon, in the inadequacies
of some of his subordinates, in the scandals that came to be
known collectively as the "sleaze factor"—set Reagan up for
unnecessary failures. But the public ignored or forgave some of
these as jobs became plentiful and his cheerfulness habit forming. His pollster, Richard Wirthlin, observed toward the end of
his client's term: "There are no bitter pills among Ronald Reagan's jelly beans." All too true, even when bitter pills were the
correct prescription. The mood change for which Reagan could
be credited, or blamed, can perhaps be summed up by the contrasts between his and Carter's tastes in country singers. Carter
liked Willie Nelson, with his wistful evocation of earthiness and
protest, as in *The Troublemaker*. Reagan liked, and occasionally appeared with, Lee Greenwood, whose thumping rendition of

God Bless the U.S.A. suited Reagan's brand of patriotism.

That brand rested in a reaffirmation of American particularity in a troubled world and in a reassertion of individualism in an era of huge, faceless institutions. Reagan played on these themes relentlessly, managing always to tie them to his image. Toward the end of his pugnacious yet nostalgic valedictory in New Orleans, he did it again. Don't talk to him, said this 77-year-old, about "the twilight of my life." He elaborated:

Twilight? Not in America. Here, it's a sunrise every day—fresh new opportunities, dreams to build. Twilight? That's not possible, because I confess there are times when I feel like I'm still little Dutch Reagan racing my brother down the hill to the swimming hole under the railroad bridge over the Rock River . . . We [Republicans] lit a prairie fire a few years back. Those flames were fed by passionate ideas and convictions, and we were determined to make them burn all across America. What times we've had! . . . We can never let the fire go out or quit the fight because the battle is never over. Our freedom must be defended over and over again. And then again . . .

Schmaltzy? Of course. More than a little phony? Sure. Reagan at the first opportunity had fled the poverty and tedium of Dixon, Ill., and its swimming hole. Yet evoking the rose-tinted memory was a comforting exercise, a relaxing warm bath in nostalgia. Reagan would do that repeatedly, overfulfilling the ceremonial responsibilities of the presidency. Though he had only played at soldier himself, his ode to the "boys of Pointe du Hoc" during the 40th anniversary observance of D-Day in early June 1984 was a classic and moving evocation of the country's citizen-soldier tradition. Even today, watching reruns of that performance, it is difficult to keep one's emotions in check. Later, when Reagan eulogized the lost crew of the *Challenger,* he managed in five minutes to make pride in the astronauts' courage supersede shame and indignation over the disrepair of the multibillion-dollar U.S. space program.

The "Gipper" tag, which Reagan hugely enjoyed, was also emblematic of his high skill at manipulating emblems. As a young actor he had portrayed George Gipp, the Notre Dame football star, in the 1940 film *Knute Rockne, All-American*. The real Gipp died young, and on his deathbed is said to have enjoined his teammates "to win one for the Gipper." As Reagan later observed about the movie, "It's hard to tell where legend ends and reality begins." In his ceremonial and inspirational roles as President, the vagueness of that boundary was often apparent but really did not matter much. In his role as Chief Executive, it mattered a great deal. Despite his affection for myth, perhaps because of his skillful use of it, Reagan remained a political success in terms of his own popularity and his continued capacity to touch the American people. Reagan's approval rating, though brought low by the 1981-82 recession and again during the Iran-*contra* debacle, rebounded in 1988 to a robust 58% during the general-election campaign.

More than luck and adroit public relations were at work. Reagan had, after all, survived an assassin's bullet, two bouts with cancer, assorted scandals, a variety of unfulfilled promises, and a few abrupt changes of course. Yet he had stayed true enough to his basic tenets to still be regarded as a strong leader. The simple fact of longevity in the White House—since World War II only that other benign patriarch Dwight Eisenhower had served as long—gave Reagan an aura of substance. Younger voters in the late 1980s had known no other Presidents besides Reagan and Carter. What they had heard of Gerald Ford, Richard Nixon and Lyndon Johnson was heavily negative. No wonder then that pollsters conducting focus groups discovered a presidential-popularity gap. Americans born after 1963 nonetheless "remember" John Kennedy admiringly, and despite the political cleavages, they like Reagan too. Presidents between Kennedy and Reagan come off poorly by comparison.

This effect raised obstacles for all the contenders early in the 1988 cycle. For the first time in 20 years, no incumbent would be running. While Bush, Gary Hart and Jesse Jackson had high name recognition, no one in the field except Jackson had a well-defined political profile (and even Jackson performed plastic surgery on his image in his quest for white supporters). Jackson excepted again, none of the contenders possessed Reagan's evocative powers. Senator Joe Biden of Delaware knew the music pretty well, and Congressman Jack Kemp of New York had the lyrics straight, but neither could master the whole song. With no single figure dominating the arena in either party's contest, Reagan's shadow stretched further and lingered longer than that of a lame duck would be expected to do.

The problem was more complex for the Republican field. Each G.O.P. contender had to play to Reagan's continued popularity in the party while at the same time seeking ways to talk about his own future intentions in a distinctive way. Most afflicted in this regard was Bush. In the comic strip *Doonesbury*, the Vice President was caricatured as a brainless preppy so insubstantial that he was literally invisible. In other depictions, he was some species of slavish wimp, unwilling even to try to sever the umbilical cord tying him to Reagan.

The weight of the Reagan legacy on Bush hit its peak of oppressiveness in May, when Michael Dukakis was well ahead in the polls and Bush—though already the de facto Republican nominee for two full months—seemed unsure of how to address the general electorate. Ritual demanded that Reagan formally and publicly endorse his heir. After some verbal scuffling between the White House and vice presidential staffs, date and venue were set: a party fund raiser in Washington's Convention Center on May 11. Trouble was, the event was designed with Reagan, not Bush, as the star. The ubiquitous "expectations game" of the moment centered on the question of just how enthusiastic Reagan's blessing would be. By this stage Bush cautiously had begun to cite a few subjects in which his administration would go beyond Reagan's. As any candidate must, he was trying—gently, tactfully, slowly—to talk about the future, his and the country's, while of course basking in the successes of the previous seven years.

Somehow Reagan did not get the word on that occasion. After Lee Greenwood had worked the crowd into a suitably patriotic mood, the President committed a tactless joke about "almost" wishing he could serve four more years. It was not lost on the party centurions and the political reporters in attendance. Both groups knew that, if the Constitution did not bar another term, a large segment of the G.O.P. would opt for Reagan rather than Bush. Then the President delivered a lengthy defense of his record in office. He dealt with change, expectably enough, but with changes already accomplished rather than those still needed. Of course, he delivered a reprise of his basic credo, that government is the problem, not the remedy. "There may be no easy solutions," he said in paraphrase of many earlier speeches, "but there's a simple solution: get government out of the way, and let free people in a free economy work their magic . . ." Those lines had worked their magic well enough in Reagan's first Inaugural, when he was the rebel who had just captured the citadel. By 1988, however, Reagan *was* the government. Further, his preferred successor had spent more than 20 years in a variety of federal offices and was trying to tell voters how a Bush government would serve them.

Bush, sitting nearby, could be forgiven for feeling uncomfortable. In his own formal announcement speech months earlier, he had declared boldly (for him): "I do not hate government . . . I've met some of the best people in the world doing the people's business in the Congress and the agencies." Later, in New Orleans, he would use that formulation again, and it would have some resonance as part of the separation process between the old order and the aspiring new. But in mid-'88, it appeared that the strong-willed father was keeping the restless offspring in check.

That impression gained even more credence on the occasion of the May 11 endorsement, when Reagan waited until the end of his speech even to mention Bush, proceeded to mispronounce his name, then devoted all of one paragraph to describing Bush's credentials. The political press, naturally, pounced on the President's eccentric performance as yet another example of Bush's predicament. Luckily for the candidate, the electorate at large was not paying much attention yet. By convention time, when voters were tuning in, Reagan had perfected his baton-passing act.

In more sustained and serious ways, Reagan's legacy was having other kinds of impact. One of the most obvious, and paradoxical, was a gradual transformation of national security into a political issue. Though he had originally campaigned for the presidency in 1976 and 1980 as a bellicose hawk, and though he had brought about the largest military buildup in the nation's peacetime history, Reagan finally managed to attain a degree of stability in Soviet-American relations. The fear of nuclear holocaust hovered over two generations. Now Reagan, with a large assist from Mikhail Gorbachev, was lessening that shadow to some extent.

In other situations abroad, Reagan was usually a cautious hawk. He overcame the Viet Nam syndrome that had inhibited the projection of American force overseas, though he did so more in symbolic gunboat-diplomacy terms than with sustained intervention. Sometimes the effort worked, as did the invasion of Grenada, the dispatching of U.S. ships to the Persian Gulf and the covert U.S. support for the anti-Soviet *mujahedin* in Afghanistan. Sometimes the effort failed, as in the ill-fated decision to send U.S. Marines to Lebanon. Sometimes it produced protracted deadlock, as in the case of U.S. support for the *contras* in Central America. Occasionally, his policies led to agonizing humiliation, as in the arms sales to Iran and the failure to oust General Manuel Noriega from Panama. In following that zigzag path, Reagan demonstrated that there was enough latent nationalism surviving in the U.S. for a President not merely to rattle a saber when needed but also to draw it on occasion. Irving Kristol, the neoconservative scholar, had it right when he said, "People want to see America assert itself again in successful ways." But Reagan, despite his flag-waving fervor, seemed unsure as to how far he could push. Certainly in Panama he pulled back, though Noriega had entered the same rogues' gallery, in American minds, as Fidel Castro, Muammar Gaddafi and Ayatullah Khomeini. Said Kristol, referring to Noriega: "We could send troops into Panama, and people [in the U.S.] would say, 'Great, get rid of the bastard.' "

Fascinating as these Third-World adventures and misadventures were, dealings with Moscow remained, as they must, the main arena of U.S. foreign policy. The how and why of the evolution in Soviet-American relations were destined to become the subjects for shelves of history books. But the domestic political implications were clear enough. Achieving the Intermediate-Range Nuclear Forces (INF) Treaty and staging more or less amicable summits in Moscow and Washington significantly offset the dead weight of Reagan's handling of national security affairs. Here was a President, after all, who had to fire one Secretary of State (Alexander Haig), change his National Security Adviser five times and attempt to explain away the Iran-*contra* mess. Puny dictators in Nicaragua and Panama defied him. Terrorists in Beirut blew up American diplomats and Marines and seized American civilians as hostages for bargaining purposes. As fireman in the Arab-Israeli tinderbox, Reagan performed poorly compared with Carter. But the favorable trend on the Soviet-American fever chart had a soothing effect at home—so much so, in fact, that the Republicans were in danger of losing an issue that for several elections had worked for their benefit. Bolshevik-bashing was out of style.

Dick Cheney of Wyoming, chairman of the G.O.P. House Conference, put it starkly after the fourth Reagan-Gorbachev summit, the 1988 meeting in Moscow: "Ronald Reagan chopped off that conservative limb." A unique series of public opinion polls called Americans Talk Security described the phenomenon in more detail. Financed by a wealthy political activist, Alan Kay, the surveys were conducted by a consortium of four firms: one Republican, one Democratic and two nonpartisan. The polls showed that the public, while still suspicious of Soviet intentions, was becoming significantly more optimistic about negotiating with the Kremlin. As recently as October 1986, only 24% of those surveyed believed that Soviet-American relations were improving. That number rose dramatically in succeeding months, reaching 68% in June 1988. By the end of that period, neither political party enjoyed a generic advantage on the issue of managing dealings with Moscow. Majorities of almost identical size said that neither a Republican nor a Democratic victory would have much impact on future relations between the superpowers. Other surveys demonstrated, predictably, that Bush was seen as more capable and experienced than Dukakis in foreign policy. But that evaluation rested on the candidates' résumés much more than on competing policy positions or philosophies.

Another finding of the A.T.S. series was that the public's definition of external threat was changing. The international drug trade, terrorism and economic competition became larger sources of worry and anger as more traditional fears of military confrontation receded. This evolution, along with Reagan's ability to shove Iran-*contra* off the front pages by concluding the INF Treaty, became a subplot through the election year. On the Republican side, Bush was initially on the defensive as several of his rivals attempted to out-hawk the Administration. Bob Dole sought to score points by charging that the White House was moving too fast on the nuclear pact. Jack Kemp agitated for sterner measures against the Sandinista regime. But Reagan's credibility as an anti-Communist—even as he photo-opped his way around the White House and Red Square with Gorbachev—remained too high for such arguments to succeed. Southern Republicans, the most militant bloc in the country, were not bothered by the signing of the INF Treaty. In fact, they provided Bush with the margin of delegates he needed to secure the nomination by voting overwhelmingly for him on Super Tuesday, March 8, just three months after the signing ceremony, while humiliating his most bellicose opponents, Kemp and Robertson.

Among the Democrats, it appeared during the early rounds of the primary campaign that peace-movement politics would dominate once again. Reagan's manifest frustrations in Central America, Iran and elsewhere—along with increasing disillusion over Pentagon spending—made the Administration's national-security record an irresistible target. Thus the Democratic candidates, Al Gore and Joe Biden excepted, competed for position as paramount dove. But as the campaign broadened out beyond the narrow confines of Iowa and New Hampshire, where antimilitary sentiment remained strong among Democratic activists, the tenor of the argument changed. Only Jesse Jackson clung defiantly to the dovish line, while the rest of the party shifted toward the center. Dukakis, once his nomination was secure, sought to prove that he was neither a pacifist nor a patsy. At the Democratic Convention in Atlanta, his forces quickly defeated a proposal by the Jackson faction to have the party pledge that under its rule the U.S. would never use nuclear weapons first, regardless of the threat.

The no-first-use argument carried great symbolic and strategic freight. Though his most liberal supporters favored it, Dukakis could not afford to be branded a philosophic peacenik; Reagan had totally discredited that ilk. Rather, Dukakis tried to steer his campaign against Bush toward the question of pragmatic competence. The Democrat would shelve the mega-billion Strategic Defense Initiative, the antimissile shield popularly known as Star Wars, not for philosophical reasons but because, he insisted, it simply would not work. He would abandon the *contras* not because he liked President Daniel Ortega's repressive Marxist government, but because the *contra* policy had failed and was illegal. He would not gut the defense budget; he would rearrange it to give higher priority to conventional forces. The party platform, drafted by Dukakis' allies, proclaimed that Democrats believe "in standing up to any American adversary whenever necessary and sitting down with him whenever possible."

Bush and his surrogates declared all that Democratic pragmatism to be a sham. They sought to brand Dukakis & Co. as closet McGovernites who would disarm America while bedding down with its evil adversaries. The essence of the Democratic response was that Bush represented the gang that couldn't shoot straight. Still, the tenor of the foreign policy debate had changed drastically since 1980. Though Bush would later make an issue of Michael Dukakis' patriotism, he did not base his successful attack heavily on the Democrat's foreign policy positions. Rather, Bush relied on symbols, such as the Pledge of Allegiance. It was a flattering emulation of Reagan's style. Nor would the Democrats make the usual charges of reckless Republican warmongering. Eight years of Reagan incumbency had drained much of the passion and venom from the argument.

That was quite an irony, considering Reagan's large role in injecting those juices into public discourse as early as his 1976 challenge to Gerald Ford. These changes seemed certain to carry over into the next presidency. Either a Democrat or a Republican would have considerable leeway on the home front in dealing with Moscow, just as Nixon's successors had concerning Beijing. Further, the INF Treaty, even though it covers only one category of lesser weapons and thus represents only a modest step toward arms reduction, nonetheless raised the stakes for the next nuclear agreement. For that pact to appear meaningful, it too would have to bring about an actual net reduction in arms rather than a mere curb in the growth rate of each side's arsenals.

In 1988, however, voters were not focusing on foreign policy or military affairs. When the fall campaign opened, TIME
sponsored a comprehensive poll of attitudes. One open-ended
question asked Americans to name the "single most important
issue in the election that the presidential candidates should address." Of those who said they were likely to vote in November,
40% answered by citing economy-related matters, such as the
federal deficit, the possibility of recession or fear of unemployment. Another 22% mentioned social problems or programs:
the traffic in drugs, the quality of public schools, the plight of the
homeless. Only 17% responded by mentioning any aspect of national security or foreign policy. As always when war neither
raged nor threatened, the public's eye remained fixed on family
finances, current and prospective.

Beneath the surface of the political landscape, a fascinating shift was occurring. While survey after survey showed
Americans to be relatively content with their current level of
prosperity, there were subtle signs of anxiety about tomorrow.
Further, definitions of "national security" were changing. As
the Democratic pollster Stanley B. Greenberg wrote at midyear,
"The events that strike Americans as national humiliations are
not military defeats but economic failures, like our burgeoning
trade deficit and the eclipse of many of our most valued industries . . . By nearly three to one (62% to 22%), voters believe that
'economic power' is more important than 'military power' in
'determining a country's influence in the world today.' "
Whether the Democrats could exploit that sentiment without
seeming to be churlish naysayers would become one of the tantalizing questions of the election year.

Reagan, with his customary gift for hyperbole, liked to say
that journalists and his opponents gave up using the term "Reaganomics" when prosperity returned after the 1981-82 recession. On the contrary, the label did continue to show up now
and then. To both commentators and critics, it was a handy

caption for the wild contradictions amassed during his Administration. Bush, like Reagan before him, could have great sport
with the Democrats by flailing them with a whip of their own
invention, the "misery index." Carter used this measure, the
simple arithmetic sum of the inflation and unemployment rates,
to dramatize Ford's failings in 1976, when the index stood at 14.
But in 1980 the figure was at the even more painful level of 20, a
telling symbol of Carter's troubles. By the time Reagan passed
the baton to Bush in New Orleans, the index had been cut
roughly in half.

The taming of inflation was among the major accomplishments of Reaganomics. The annual rate of price increases bottomed out at 1.9% in 1986 and by mid-1988 was still at a relatively comfortable 5.2%. The Federal Reserve Board deserves
much of the credit for that feat by maintaining a tight-money
course in the early years of Reagan's first term, though federal
spending cutbacks were also a factor. Whatever the cause, the
U.S. in the later Reagan years enjoyed its longest period of unin-
terrupted economic growth since World War II. Thus Reagan
had given George Bush a reasonably healthy economy on which
to run in 1988.

Reaganomics, however, had several bottom lines. The economic expansion about which the Republicans bragged so loudly was cruelly uneven in its effects. While the Northeast, parts of
the South and the West Coast prospered, several states lagged
far behind. In large swatches of Texas, Colorado, Louisiana,
Arkansas, Oklahoma, Iowa and Oregon, for instance, talk of
boom times was a bad joke. True, unemployment in September
1988 was only 5.3%, and the G.O.P. made much of the creation
of roughly 17 million new jobs during the Reagan Administration. But the base period for that latter statistic is not the whole
of Reagan's tenure. Rather, the comparison is from November
1982, which happened to be the nadir of the recession, to mid-
1988. A more apt comparison would use January 1981, Reagan's Inaugural, as a starting point. In that case, the net gain in

jobs is 15.2 million. That is fewer, on an annual average, than the number of jobs created during Carter's four years.

One promise of supply-side economics was that expansion would benefit all levels of society. "The best welfare program is a job," Reagan loved to say. Yet throughout the 1980s, government figures would show that the affluent were doing quite well while the poor were not. The poverty rate in 1987, for instance, was 13.5%, a touch higher than in 1980, when it was 13%. One-third of all blacks lived in families officially classified as impoverished, as did one-fifth of all children, black and white. Where Reagan was able to cut domestic spending as a proportion of the federal budget and the gross national product, the reductions were felt primarily by the poor. Construction of low-income public housing diminished to the vanishing point, food stamps became harder to obtain, and Americans holding marginal jobs found it more difficult to obtain supplemental welfare payments. Programs of benefit to the middle class, such as farm subsidies, veterans' benefits and Social Security, fared better.

Periodically, TV networks and major publications produced heartrending reports on the plight of the homeless. It became almost a cliché to depict the disinherited huddled a few hundred yards from the White House, or in the shadows of glitzy office towers and luxury apartment buildings in other cities. What to do about beggars—to give or not to give, to put them in custodial institutions or to let them roam free—received a flurry of attention in 1988. But as political issues, such motes in the eye of a prosperous and presumably enlightened society did not seem to affect the body politic decisively. After all, if it was still morning in America, as Republican TV commercials asserted, these matters could not be that serious. And after all, little more than half the eligible population, generally the more affluent half, bothers to vote, even in presidential elections. From the Great Depression through the economically ebullient 1960s and into the troubled '70s, the widespread assumption was that Americans could indeed spare a dime. Increasingly, government was the collection and distribution agency, taking trillions of dimes from taxpayers and handing them out to the poor. Reagan did not end that practice, nor could he if he wanted to. He merely slowed its growth, and did it with at least the tacit applause of the middle class.

The process had started in California, during Reagan's governorship, when rocketing tax rates and the cumulative burden of government waste fed a taxpayers' rebellion. Welfare abuses became the single most vivid symbol of middle-class indignation. Eventually, rebels such as Howard Jarvis put through Proposition 13, which imposed limits on the rate of real estate tax rises, and later crimped government spending for a variety of services. Other states began to experiment with similar tax-limiting devices. Reagan did not himself ignite this fire. As one of his most loyal policy advisers, Martin Anderson, points out in his 1988 memoir *Revolution,* neither Barry Goldwater nor Reagan was the creator of what amounted to a popular uprising. "It was the other way around," says Anderson, himself a Californian and populist conservative theorist. "They contributed mightily to the movement, but the movement gave them political life, not the reverse." In Reagan's case, that contribution included helping Americans stop feeling guilty about selfishness.

By the mid-'80s, the damage inflicted by Proposition 13 on public services in California was becoming manifest. The Los Angeles *Times* observed in a retrospective editorial that "in subtle ways, Reagan made it acceptable to resent assistance to poor people. No longer was there emphasis on citizens fulfilling their collective responsibility to society through the vehicle of government."

Some of the presumed beneficiaries of this new ethic, particularly skilled working families in both manufacturing and service industries, were having their own problems. Wage stagnation, an unfamiliar phenomenon that had begun in the 1970s, appeared to become ingrained in the 1980s. Significant sectors of the middle class had to run faster simply to stay in the same place. Median family income rose only marginally during this period, and did so at all primarily because millions of women went to work to supplement their spouses' earnings. According to the Council on Competitiveness, employed Americans have enjoyed a much smaller increase in their standard of living than their counterparts in other major industrial democracies. While Reaganomics did not start the erosion of living standards, it failed to check the trend. In fact, the purchasing power of average annual wages in the U.S. fell 1.5% between mid-1985 and mid-1987, despite relatively low inflation.

Perhaps the most enduring legacy of Reaganomics was the budget deficit. Reagan's initial success in slashing tax rates while greatly increasing defense spending propelled total U.S. indebtedness toward the $3 trillion level, in contrast to $1 trillion in 1981. By 1988 the proportion of federal tax dollars devoted to paying interest on the debt had hit 15%, up from 8.5% when Reagan took office.

The idea behind the original supply-side tax reduction of 1981, along with the cut in marginal rates embodied in the tax reform act of 1985, was that incentives to creativity would be enhanced. Irving Kristol, who views those changes as a major, positive part of Reagan's legacy, argues that "strong economic growth is incompatible with egalitarian fiscal policy." Why? Because "activists" in the economy, the people who make things happen, need incentives to do so. Assure them a greater yield after taxes and they will invest creatively, the economy will grow in more durable fashion, and everyone will have a better chance of living happily ever after. The theory sounded reasonable enough, but it did not work out that way. Corporations in the early 1980s did not respond by investing in new plants and equipment with the zeal hoped for by the Administration. Donald Regan, then Treasury Secretary, complained, "It's like dropping a coin down a well. All I'm hearing is an empty clink."

The wave of corporate mergers, the Administration's

fondness for new weapons systems, consumers' love of imported gewgaws and other factors combined to keep savings and useful investment low. In the 1970s the country had an annual savings rate—including private and public assets—averaging 8% of net domestic product. From that, the U.S. was able to export a tiny fraction in the form of overseas investment. By 1987 the national savings rate had plunged to 2.2%, and the country had to import $157 billion, net, in foreign capital. Said Barry Bosworth of the Brookings Institution: "We simply have not been saving enough to finance our own needs."

The list of those needs had grown long by the opening of Campaign '88, and voters did not have to rely on Jesse Jackson's speeches or other voices from the left to hear them. The Committee for Economic Development, a nonpartisan research group of business executives and educators, appealed for greater public investment in the education and medical treatment of impoverished children. The motivation was not merely humanitarian; American business needed better-trained workers. A Republican-controlled commission assigned to study the nation's public works concluded that "the quality of America's infrastructure is barely adequate to fulfill current requirements, and insufficient to meet the demands of future economic growth." An alumnus of Reagan's White House lamented, after being assured of anonymity, that "the pile of unpaid bills coming due is everywhere you look. It's air-traffic control, it's education, it's applied civilian R. and D., it's housing." This Republican analyst speculated that the next Administration *might* find the courage and the revenue to reduce the deficit. But he doubted that the means could be found to address domestic needs as well.

That relatively simple math problem became one of the great obfuscations of 1988. Reagan had charged the atmosphere with relentless happy talk for so long—and prospered politically by doing so—that attempts to deal in cold candor seemed as risky to most candidates as advocating satanism. He had ignored, even ridiculed, the forecasts of sourpuss economists, including a few in his own employ. He had promised that economic growth would satisfy all needs, any minute now. He had equated liberalism with statism with tax-and-spend irresponsibility. He had told the folks, except for the poor, that they could pretty much have it all: lower taxes, prosperity, a bigger military machine, less government involvement in their lives and all the luxuries their credit cards could purchase. In short, Reagan had created a free-lunch illusion and invited the electorate to dine on it indefinitely. Though sharp realities occasionally pierced this fantasy, though Reagan's own Administration had been hobbled by scandal and lame-duck torpor in its final years, the myth was hardy enough to color the '88 campaign.

Because politicians, like generals, are wont to fight old wars, most of the candidates in 1988 were haunted by the ghost of Walter Mondale. In an excess of frankness, he had told the American people four years earlier that their taxes would have to go up, that the bills would have to be paid. He lost 49 states. Though many other factors were at play in the 1984 election, Mondale's mistake weighed heavily on Michael Dukakis and his fellow Democrats, as well as on the Republicans, throughout the 1988 campaign.

George Bush had some special, highly personal problems with the Reagan legacy. In cultural and stylistic terms at least, Bush represented the very forces in the party that Reagan had challenged in 1976 and finally defeated in 1980. He was a remnant of the old G.O.P. establishment, closer in many ways to Gerald Ford and Richard Nixon than to Ronald Reagan. And Bush, veteran entrepreneur that he was, could read a balance sheet. Hence his description of Reagan's fiscal program, during the 1980 primaries, as "voodoo economics." So Bush was a Reaganite by Reagan's fiat. In order to win the 1988 nomination, he had to prove to the arch-conservatives who dominated the nominating process that his conversion was genuine and enduring. The clearest, largest test for that was the tax issue. Thus his declaration early in the fray: "I am not going to raise your taxes, period." This is what is known in politics as immunizing yourself against the toxins of a controversial issue. From time to time Bush gave himself a booster shot, just to be sure. In the process he created a credibility problem.

Because he could not simply stand pat on Reagan's record, Bush had to begin citing some specific things he would do differently and presumably better. Well, he would be the "education President." He would wage war on drugs. He would protect the environment in the spirit of that great conservationist Republican, Teddy Roosevelt. And of course he would proceed with Star Wars and otherwise protect the Pentagon's budget. Yet he would also impose a "flexible" spending freeze that would somehow save money. Some of his more astute policy advisers winced at all this, at least in private. One of those counseling the campaign confided, "The next President will have to go for a tax increase during the first six months. Almost all the economic advisers on both sides believe that." What of Bush's oft repeated pledge to the contrary? Well, this adviser replied, "if he tries to be very honorable about it, there will be serious problems."

In fact there would be a variety of problems, and serious ones, regardless of which candidate succeeded Reagan, and many of the difficulties could be traced to Reagan's legacy. Determining a winner is only the most obvious function of a national political campaign. Another is to give the country an opportunity to decide on what course it wishes to take next. Whatever his later failings, Reagan in 1980 had presented a vivid alternative to the electorate. Not only did he stand for relatively drastic change, but he also laid out in unmistakable terms the main elements of that change. When he took office then, he owned as much of a mandate as the difficult U.S. system of checks and balances allows. Eight years later, Bush and Dukakis both found themselves prisoners of the unintended consequences of the intervening period.

Because Reagan was so successful in persuading a huge portion of Middle Americans that liberalism is poison, Dukakis felt it necessary to flee from what should be some of the core concepts of any Democratic candidate for President. Dukakis for a time took refuge in "competence," which should be a necessary but not sufficient qualification for the White House, and which is barren of inspiration. He waited until September to begin delivering a class-oriented message; even then he sounded tentative. To some extent at least, Dukakis had to campaign as something less than himself.

Reagan had redefined conservative ideology, interlacing social values, supply-side economics and other concepts, so Bush felt constrained to play the ideology game. Yet it was an unnatural role for one who at heart was a problem solver more interested in dealing with one tree at a time rather than whole forests. This dilemma would dog Bush throughout the year in his attempts to portray himself simultaneously as the loyal heir and as the agent of future change. In this regard, he had to campaign as something more than himself.

Because Reaganomics had so distorted fiscal affairs, neither candidate had flexibility in dealing with the kitchen-table concerns that clearly preoccupied the electorate. Further, in looking ahead to 1989, any sensible pol or economist had to fear the strong possibility of a recession that would finally yank the tablecloth—perhaps the whole table—from beneath the free-lunch illusion. In the event of recession, there would be precious little latitude for Washington to spend its way back to prosperity. To do that would send the deficit and the cumulative debt to still new heights and further undermine the country's competitive position in world trade. Recession or no, the country needed a variety of reforms that would be neither cheap nor simple. Yet as candidates, Bush and Dukakis both lacked the courage to tell voters explicitly that the bill was coming due, and that it had to be settled, quickly, on a Dutch-treat basis in which everyone contributed something. In that kind of candor vacuum, the winner could not expect to start his presidency with much of a mandate.

Speculation on what might have been is as tantalizing in politics as in other arenas. Could Reagan have repudiated his smile-button myths and still have maintained his own political standing? Could he have given up his wondrous habit of soaring above problems on a magic carpet woven of his own illusions? That Reagan declined even to try may be the most negative part of his legacy. The time to have made the attempt was immediately after his 1984 re-election triumph, when he stood atop a huge pedestal of credibility. That was the moment when he might have refreshed his agenda, acknowledged some of the shortcomings of his first term and used his formidable powers as Great Communicator to enlist constituents both in a repair job and in new efforts to push forward. Instead, Reagan pretty much stood pat. When he campaigned to retain Republican control of the Senate in 1986, his appeal included that favorite chestnut, "Win one for the Gipper." But he neglected to reaffirm in any persuasive way that he was still an enthusiastic agent of change. So the G.O.P. lost control of the Senate that year. In domestic affairs at least, the President then invested most of his energy defending Reagan I rather than in making Reagan II a strong second act. Reagan luck being what it is, that historic omission became a far heavier burden for his would-be successors than for Ronald Reagan.

3

The Republicans

A stuffy, sterile ballroom in Houston's Hyatt Regency
holds 2,000 or so prosperous-looking Texans, most of middle
years or older, nearly all of them white. The lapel button of
choice this morning reads TEXAS IS BUSH COUNTRY. If there are
rural folk or others who work with their hands present, they are
well disguised. The decibels emanating from a brass band make
conversation difficult, though several women pass the time by
recalling their volunteer work in George Bush's campaigns for
Congress two decades earlier. Anything approaching excitement in this crowd has dissipated gradually, because most of the
spectators have been standing patiently for an hour by the time
Milo Hamilton, the Houston Astros' TV announcer, begins the
political pregame show.

Half a dozen Republican stalwarts from around the country, Governors and congressional types, explain why Bush

should be President. Illinois Congresswoman Lynn Martin, for instance, declares that "he is the legitimate heir to Ronald Reagan—an independent man, but the legitimate heir." Finally Bush takes the lectern to give a cautious elaboration of Martin's introduction. He pays filial respects to his patron, drops hints of how he would be a different incumbent, describes his own virtues in what might be called anticharismatic terms: "I am a practical man. I like what's real. I'm not much for the airy and abstract. I like what works. I am not a mystic . . ."

Behind the TV-camera riser, Bush's media adviser, Roger Ailes, paces restlessly. He uses earphones to hear his candidate via the network's audio feed. For weeks Ailes has been coaching his client on delivery, trying to improve Bush's broadcast quality. "It's great, just great," Ailes stage-whispers, hoping to persuade reporters within earshot. The press pack, usually tough on Bush, decides on its own that the speech, in which Bush formally announces his candidacy, is well above par for the Vice President.

Snapshot from the same album, Nov. 9, 1987, Main Street in Russell, Kans.:

Traffic has been blocked off; most of the shops are closed; thousands of farmers, oil-patch workers, factory hands, shopkeepers and schoolchildren let off for this celebratory morning mingle happily in the cold sunshine. Great quantities of coffee and doughnuts are consumed. Dream Cinema's marquee hawks a new program: HOT DOGS—BOB DOLE—APPLE PIE—AMERICA'S HOMETOWN COMBO. Near the sign saying "Thank you for shopping in Russell," the local high school marching band belts out a fight song as pom-pom girls in white tights provide the cheer: "Go Bob Dole! Go Bob Dole!" Lucynda Raben, a dentist, shows reporters her unusual handiwork: on her front teeth she has laminated the letters B-O-B-D-O-L-E. She will keep that adornment, she promises, until Dole wins.

On the platform, the object of all this adoring hope for once shows some emotion. He taps his feet in time to the music, then turns somber as Russell's newspaper editor, Russ Townsley, recalls for the crowd the day in 1945 when the telegram arrived announcing that Dole had been wounded in combat. Dole himself mines the small-town nostalgia vein for several nuggets, allows his voice to quaver slightly as he notes the recent death of Huck Boyd, an early political mentor. Then, in the familiar voice as hard and flat as rolled steel, delivered from pipes that need no training, he describes his strong suit: "I *can* make a difference. I *have* made a difference. I *will* make a difference." The event, staging and performance both, is boffo as official announcements go. Even the crustiest of the Washington-based reporters are moved at least a little. And they are warmed a lot by the prospect of covering a tough and perhaps long contest between Dole and Bush.

The end would in fact come suddenly, telescoped into a manic month of caucuses and primaries in 1988, between Iowa on Feb. 8 and Super Tuesday on March 8. The pace would be furious, with critical decisions made by tired operatives working under cruel deadlines. But that outcome was a distant prospect the previous fall, when there was still time for parsing tactics and evaluating style.

Of the several rituals in presidential politics, the Announcement is usually the most tedious. The very term is a misnomer. By the time the formal tableau is staged, the candidate has been running for months, his organization is in place, his position papers drafted, much of his campaign coinage amassed. Still, the clear contrasts in atmospherics and the more subtle similarities of nuance in the Bush and Dole announcement ceremonies spoke volumes about the state of the Republican contest in 1987. At the symbolic level, the Dole camp triumphed. It was attempting to depict its man as the candidate of Main Street, the one in touch with the real heartland, the striver who had conquered hardships to live the American Dream of upward mobility. Bush, in this formulation, was the scion of privilege and the exemplar of the stagnant Establishment. Repeatedly, in speeches and broadcast commercials, Dole implored voters to think of him as "one of us." Bush, in the arid setting of his announcement and in other bumbling ways, cooperated by coming across as one of *them*, the privileged minority at the top. If Dole could sustain this cultural contrast, he might overcome the strong advantages Bush enjoyed as the incumbent Vice President.

Only millimeters below the surface, however, the competing rituals emitted a more fundamental message about the G.O.P.'s 1988 contest. The Announcement receives more media attention than any other single act up to that stage of the election cycle. Thus the content represents what the campaign organization wants to get across to the broadest of audiences. Both Bush and Dole carefully crafted their pitches to show relative moderation rather than the rough edges of conservatism. Bush, for instance, talked about "prosperity with a purpose," a code phrase for modest public altruism. He did not talk at all about abortion, school prayer, the Strategic Defense Initiative or several other hot-button issues for ultraconservatives. The only important sops thrown to those factions were his pledge of support for the *contras* and "freedom fighters" elsewhere, along with a renewed oath not to raise taxes.

Dole did not even give the Reaganaut faithful a binding tax promise; he cunningly stated opposition to an increase in "tax rates," allowing some room for maneuver. Instead, Dole emphasized compassion for the poor and an austerity approach for combating the federal deficit. Among insiders, both of those items were translated as anti-Reaganomics. Contrary to earlier expectations, this primary contest had become a fight staged in the center of the Republican spectrum.

There would be no re-enactment of the ideological passion plays of 1964, 1976 and 1980. In those three primary campaigns, right-wing purists—"wingers," they were sometimes called—

crusaded against the party's two other factions, the Eastern progressives once led by Nelson Rockefeller and the orthodox conservatives who congregated around Gerald Ford in '76 and Bush in '80. After Reagan's triumph, the progressive remnant went out of business as an effective political force except in the U.S. Senate and a few statehouses. So it seemed logical, to the early scenario writers contemplating 1988, that the wingers would fly to one neo-Reaganite ideologue or another. Congressman Jack Kemp seemed the likeliest prospect. That ideological heir to Reagan was expected to emerge as the main challenger to Bush, the institutional heir.

Virtually from the time of Reagan's second Inaugural onward, the competition for recognition as the next high priest in the temple of Reaganism was intense. Kemp, who had few peers in politics as a generator of raw energy, talked from California to New Hampshire in his Gatling-gun style about pushing supply-side economics further, about putting the country back on the gold standard, about simplifying the income-tax code to the point where "you would be able to file your tax return on a postcard." In foreign affairs as well, he out-Reaganed Reagan. Secretary of State George Shultz should be retired, Kemp argued, for lack of militancy. The *contras* should be not only armed and fed, but formally recognized as the legitimate government of Nicaragua. Kemp retained a bit his pro-football glamour. He also had a better knack than most Republicans for relating to working-class families and minorities. When he reminded white, upscale audiences that the G.O.P. was the party of Lincoln and that it had unmet obligations to the descendants of those whom Lincoln emancipated, Kemp spoke from the heart (and over the heads of most of his conservative listeners). To see Kemp tour a black public-housing project, mixing it up with residents as naturally as if he delivered mail there every morning, was to watch a pol with a genuine Everyman touch.

Unfortunately for Kemp, Everyman has little to say about bestowing the Republican presidential nomination. By 1987

neither Reagan nor most of his aides took Kemp seriously.
What had once been a warm relationship between Kemp and
the President cooled as the younger man repeatedly tried to tu-
tor the elder on the fundamentals of the 1980 Reagan program.
Kemp had converted to supply-side economics in the 1970s,
somewhat earlier than Reagan, and had a much better grasp of
its theory. Further, as a prominent member of the House minority, Kemp was free to express a purist line on many subjects.
That he did, loudly and often. Reagan, like any other incumbent Executive, was frequently forced to compromise with
opponents.

Besides, Kemp had competition for the designation as
Reaganism's high priest. Pierre (Pete) du Pont, the former Governor of Delaware, had been first into the arena. Du Pont attempted to run to the right of Bush, Dole and even Kemp, on
positions that were vaguely libertarian. The Rev. Pat Robertson
bid strongly, and for a while successfully, for the support of
those whose paramount concerns were moralistic and religious.
Paul Laxalt, former Senator from Nevada and Reagan's oldest
friend in politics, toyed long enough with the idea of running to
draw off campaign contributors and advisers who otherwise
would have helped Kemp. When Laxalt's prudence finally
overcame his ego, restless conservative sectlets prowled for other champions. Pat Buchanan, the conservative commentator
and former White House aide, had a few moments of specula-
tive attention, only to demur. Jeane Kirkpatrick, a onetime U.S.
Ambassador to the United Nations, felt a weak draft, but allowed common sense to prevail.

"We Republicans were balkanized," John Buckley, a top
Kemp adviser, would lament after the issue was decided. "Every faction had its candidate. The supply-siders had Jack. The
libertarians had Pete du Pont. The religious right had Pat Robertson. Different parts of the Establishment had George Bush or
Bob Dole." And patrolling the battlefield's periphery, allied
with no one in particular, Alexander Haig sought to capture

Republican stragglers. Balkanization of the party during the
early stages was even more severe than the presence of six active candidates and a few contenders manqué would suggest.
One reason was the pervasive sense that Bush, despite his prox-
imity to Reagan and despite relatively good economic times,
was a leaning tower of weakness. Any severe blow might topple
him, it was thought. The Iran-*contra* scandal, which seemed for
a time to impugn both Bush's judgment and his veracity, could
have been that blow.

That early time of the nominating process, still in the stage
often called the underground or invisible primary, is an insiders'
game. The broad electorate during the winter of 1986-87 was
paying little attention, and public-opinion polls measured name
recognition rather than genuine support. The "voters" during
the underground period consisted of perhaps 200 Washington
cognoscenti—campaign consultants, fund raisers, journalists—
plus a couple of thousand activists around the country. Their
judgments, though often insular, help establish the competition's initial structure. Bush's strategists wanted that structure
to be the Vice President against an undifferentiated field for as
long as possible. That way, Bush would not have to risk much in
direct competition until later. The initial contest would be
among the second-stringers to determine who would become his
principal adversary.

Dole managed to frustrate that strategy by early 1987. He
did so partly because of his stature as Senate Republican leader
and as a onetime candidate for Vice President (in 1976, running
with Gerald Ford). More important, Dole conveyed a sense of
gritty independence and gravitas that set him apart from
Kemp, du Pont and the others. When the Iran-*contra* fiasco
broke, Dole shrewdly sculpted a persona that was neither Administration cheerleader nor Republican apostate. In his frequent appearances on network talk shows, Dole took the scandal seriously enough to demand a prompt, thorough
investigation. This added to his reputation as a common-sense

realist, an image based heavily on Dole's efforts over several years to forge a deficit-reduction compromise acceptable to the White House and Congress.

One measure of Dole's success at this point was the straw polls taken periodically by CBS political director Martin Plissner and his wife Susan Morrison, former CBS assignment chief in Washington. Now and then Plissner and Morrison entertain a substantial stratum of Washington's insiders. Guests are expected to mark printed ballots predicting political outcomes. In February 1987, they split between Bush and Dole, 35-35, with only ten picking Kemp. Though totally unscientific, that nose count was a reasonably accurate reflection of the contest's structure. Dole, essentially a centrist in the Republican spectrum as redefined by the Reagan reign, would duel with Bush. Few policy differences worthy of the term separated them. Instead, the competition would hinge on personal experience, character, judgment—and what Dole would attempt over and over to define as that intangible quality called leadership. Dole had even named his dog Leader.

And where were the fierce ideologues who had served as company commanders in the Reagan Revolution? A surprising number of them were choosing sides between Bush and Dole rather than picking among the second-tier candidates. None of the latter could command a broad following. Just as important, many of the New Right rebels of the '70s had become the incumbents of the '80s. Being in power has a tranquilizing effect on zealots.

Take, for example, Senator Chuck Grassley, a star member of the New Right class of 1980 and conqueror of moderates in his home state of Iowa. By 1987 he was working hard for Dole. Occasionally he even sounded downright pragmatic. "Those of us in office," he told a reporter, "don't have the liberty to be purists, unless you're willing to be a do-nothing person."

Or take Tommy Thomas, a successful Chevrolet dealer in Panama City, Fla. Thomas claimed proudly that he was the only politician in the U.S. who headed his state's Reagan campaign three times (1976, 1980, 1984). He observed jocularly: "If everyone were as right-wing as I am, the world would be a screwed-up place." But looking to 1988, Thomas signed up early with Bush and reactivated his old network of Reaganites down to the county and town level. Why? Because Bush had been so loyal to Reagan. "I know the Vice President is more moderate than I am on most issues," Thomas said. "But I can live with that."

Such allegiance, typical of Bush's recruitment in many key states, was hardly serendipitous. Bush worked hard for several years cultivating right-wing groups. His pollster Robert Teeter described that effort as a typical front runner's strategy. "You don't let anyone else become the 'anything' candidate," said Teeter. It would have been dangerous for Bush if one rival had emerged as the sole conservative champion. Preventing that sometimes required Bush to digest his pride. He even spoke at a memorial dinner for William Loeb, the bombastic publisher of the Manchester (N.H.) *Union Leader* and a fierce Bush hater.

Such pandering carried a price tag. Loeb's widow Nackey continued to criticize Bush in editorials, accusing him, for instance, of "acting the part of the spoiled little rich kid who won't play ball with the rest of the gang." Later her paper formally endorsed du Pont. Bush's strategy seemed to ratify the satire by cartoonist Garry Trudeau, who had already coined the line about Bush having "put his manhood in a blind trust." George Will, the country's most influential conservative columnist, uncorked a devastating critique that became part of the anti-Bush lexicon: "The unpleasant sound Bush is emitting as he traipses from one conservative gathering to another is a thin, tinny 'arf'—the sound of a lapdog." That sort of commentary strengthened the negative "wimp" image that, well, dogged the Vice President through mid-1988. But the need to divide and conquer the conservative factions overrode other considerations. Ultimately, it would pay off handsomely, particularly in the Southern primaries.

Waiting for those dividends was a long, nervous ordeal for the Bush team. While it signed up operatives and raised vaults of campaign funds with impressive efficiency, the view from inside Bush central was often downright pessimistic, well into the fall of 1987. Dole, who was getting far more positive press notices as he emerged from the pack of challengers, was a special source of anxiety for Bush. Ironically, the mood inside the Dole organization was just as troubled, though for different reasons. Bush during this period was a weak candidate kept ambulatory by a well-financed crew of veteran retainers. Dole appeared to be a strong candidate personally who nonetheless was unable to marshal sufficient money or the right combination of operatives to mount an effective, sustained campaign.

In one of numerous counseling sessions Richard Nixon held with Dole's advisers, the former President tried to sound encouraging. In a written summary, obtained by TIME, Nixon's thoughts were relayed to the candidate: "Dole is an interesting person. In politics, the only thing worse than being wrong is being dull. Bush is dull. And when he tries to be interesting, he is a little silly." Nixon's words were true enough, but they consoled the Dole people only slightly.

Other confidential memorandums generated within each headquarters—and obtained by TIME—showed parallel anxieties that would have given heart to the second tier, had those fears become known. Meetings of Bush's principal advisers, including campaign manager Lee Atwater, pollster Robert Teeter, chief of staff Craig Fuller and former Senator Nicholas Brady, who became Treasury Secretary in 1988, constantly reviewed the campaign's progress, or lack of it, and produced rafts of papers. Most of them were drawn up at Atwater's direction by one of his deputies, Ed Rogers, and by issues adviser James Pinkerton. One recurrent theme was the need to overcome Bush's image as a weak leader. Another was that after the G.O.P.'s defeat in the 1986 Senate elections and the still raging furor over the Iran-*contra* affair, Bush would have to accelerate his effort to appear somewhat independent of Reagan.

A strategy document dated Feb. 20, 1987, observed judiciously, "Whatever lingering illusions we may have had about the invincibility of the Reagan mantle or the permanence of a broad-based G.O.P. realignment must be put on the shelf." In conversation with his colleagues, Atwater sounded downright alarmist. One participant noted in a personal journal, "Lee says we're going to die of a thousand cuts if this keeps up. We can't control Iran, but on the things we should control . . . we are killing ourselves." Another Atwater metaphor: "The Bush effort is in a tailspin on ice. The last thing you do is slam on the brakes. We've got to ride this out for a while and hope for the best."

What tormented Atwater and a few others most was the drumbeat of negative publicity. Bush was unable to explain in a politically satisfactory way exactly what his role had been in the original decision to sell arms to Iran. Nor was it clear why one of his aides, Donald Gregg, retained cloudy ties with an operative involved in supplying arms to the *contras*. News story after news story implied that Bush knew more than he was saying. His denials, while not totally convincing, reinforced the image that he had really not amounted to much in the Administration.

The problem would plague Bush well into the general election campaign. Among his Republican rivals before the primaries, Alexander Haig took particular pleasure in twisting the Iranscam knife. In one televised debate, Haig picked up on Bush's claim to have been Reagan's "co-pilot" in the White House: "Were you in the cockpit, or were you on an economy ride in the back of the plane? The American people want to know precisely what you advised the President, and if you did not, why not." In another encounter, Haig struck again: "If you can't answer your friends, what in heaven's name is going to happen next November, if you are our standard-bearer and these Democrats get after you on this subject?"

The real answer, of course, was that Bush hoped public interest in the Iran-*contra* affair would subside, which it eventually did. But in the interim, such assaults, together with Bush's reluctance to distance himself from Reagan in any significant way, heightened the search for a "defining event" to turn the tide. One novel way to depict Bush as muscular, an Atwater-Rogers paper proposed, was to have him receive credit for a reorganization of the White House staff in the wake of Iranscam. Using capital letters for emphasis, the memo argued, "THERE IS ONE WAY TO CURE THIS MISPERCEPTION [that Bush lacks clout] DRAMATICALLY AND ONCE AND FOR ALL. LET THE VP BE SEEN AS THE MAN WHO FINALLY SWUNG THE AXE AND GOT RID OF DON REGAN!!!" At the same time, the younger advisers urged that by mid-1987 Bush begin taking the initiative with policy proposals that would clearly separate him from Reagan. Among the possibilities: that the Veep take a page from Gary Hart's script by endorsing a civilian national-service program for young people and that he come out with his own bold program for combatting AIDS.

Bush would have none of it. He was often skeptical about the alarms from Atwater's shop. After the formal announcement in Houston, for instance, Atwater and Rogers reported to the chief on his declining poll numbers and on soundings among field organizers, who fretted about defections to Dole. How could this be? Bush replied. After all, we had such good reviews after Houston. Atwater's reaction was to have Bush make a round of phone calls to state coordinators so that he could hear the bad news directly. As to Don Regan, Bush was rather sympathetic to the stricken chief of staff and reluctant to be seen as the one who fired him. Further, Bush had never meddled much in White House staff matters and was not about to begin. Ultimately it was Nancy Reagan who swung the principal ax. After Howard Baker had replaced Regan as White House chief of staff, Bush complained privately about how the change had affected his own standing. Baker, he felt, was inconsiderate of Bush's interests. Several times the Vice President remarked to aides, "It's not like we still had Don Regan there."

Nor was Bush prepared, during 1987, to wave a new-policy flag very energetically. He might have been persuaded to do so if his advisers were unanimous. However, Fuller and Teeter were both less alarmed and more cautious than Atwater. Teeter, the savvy pollster and strategy adviser, had worked in presidential campaigns since 1968 and seen assorted crises come and go. He argued that Bush had ample time to draw distinctions between himself and the President. Fuller, always concerned about Bush's comfort level, was reluctant to urge any tactic that made Bush uneasy. Occasionally James Baker, from his perch at the Treasury Department, would be called on to referee. But Baker was reluctant to get involved too regularly until he moved to the campaign full time.

Tension between Fuller, representing the office of the Vice President, and Atwater, representing the campaign apparatus, would remain a constant undercurrent until the summer of 1988, when Baker took firm control of the entire outfit. Atwater, ever aggressive, had a paper drafted on *The Vice President and the Vice Presidency,* dated Feb. 19, 1987. The document argued that "the real problem lies in the fact that the VP has never really carved out a major, defining role for himself in the Administration." Further, Atwater described Bush's assistants as "guilty of letting themselves be treated as second-stringers. Worse, they have allowed themselves to think like second-stringers, content to gnaw on the bones tossed to them by the first string in the West Wing." The point of this argument was to seek specific White House assignments for Bush that would put him in a bright, favorable light. Yet such plums remained scarce.

That scarcity played right into Dole's attack strategy, which emphasized from the beginning that Bush was an empty suit, lacking a record of firm accomplishment and hard decisions. Bush's campaign aides sought ways to retaliate. In a document labeled a "strategic overview," dating from January 1987, they emphasized the need to "counter Bob Dole's surge" in Iowa, where the first critical encounter of 1988 would take place

13 months later. A set of notes from these strategy sessions indicated that Atwater, who owned a well-deserved reputation for using political brass knuckles, talked of the need to debunk Dole's favorable image, particularly in the Hawkeye State.

This led to recurrent proposals—only partially implemented, as things turned out—that insiders labeled "I.D.F." (In Dole's Face). A six-page memo in June outlined a sub rosa media strategy that would seek to "bracket" Dole's activities with negative stories. "We have the opportunity to knock Dole off his stride," one ambitious passage read. "No Dole appearance, no Dole press conference, no Dole broadcast or print story should appear without some form of criticism from surrogates or some tough questions from reporters." This document proposed identifying and spoon-feeding journalists who were working on stories about Dole. The fare, obviously, would be thoroughly sour.

Another paper, 14 pages long and dated Nov. 24, drew parallels between the "dark side" of Dole's personality and Lyndon Johnson's. The point, made laboriously in a psychohistorical vein, was that someone so driven by ego and lust for power is "not motivated by a desire to do good for the sake of doing good."

Bush's spear carriers in Iowa did jab at Dole whenever opportunity permitted. They circulated a memorandum, for instance, that belittled Dole's effectiveness in protecting farmers' interests. Later, when a small Kansas newspaper did an exposé on some of Bob and Elizabeth Dole's personal financial transactions, Bush's managers promptly distributed photocopies of the stories to national reporters. Bush's circle quietly accused a Dole adviser, David Keene, of fomenting salacious gossip about the Vice President. Both the accusation and the rumors proved unfounded.

Incidents like these provided interesting news blips, but they affected the course of the campaign only marginally. While many skeptics waited through the long preliminaries for Bush's manifest weaknesses to destroy his candidacy before the first real participation by voters, the Vice President managed to plod on. A principal reason for his survival, much clearer in retrospect than at the time, was Dole's inability to capitalize on his rival's vulnerabilities either in 1987 or early 1988.

Dole labored under severe handicaps of his own throughout this period. He insisted on retaining his demanding post as Senate Republican leader, which gave him high visibility but also drained his energy. Further, Dole could never shake his habit of attempting to micromanage his campaign organization. Always hard on subordinates, he had trouble inspiring many of them to treat his candidacy as a cause rather than an interesting activity that might advance their careers. Most of all, Dole could never fully articulate—perhaps not even to himself—any grand design for his presidency, any thematic rationale beyond a successful politician's desire to step up to the next rung of power. This weakness he shared fully with Bush. In both camps it came to be known as "the vision thing." But Bush, as the sitting Vice President and as the G.O.P.'s nominal crown prince, had an institutional claim on the succession. A party with mildly royalist instincts needed strong reasons to reject the natural heir. Dole's struggle to provide that rationale, based on the inchoate assertion that he had already somehow proved his bona fides, kept falling short.

For his initial campaign chairman, Dole chose someone of his generation whom he trusted as much as he could trust any adviser: Robert Ellsworth, a fellow Kansan, a former Congressman and Ambassador to NATO and a thoughtful soul of gentle mien. But Ellsworth was neither a world-class campaign strategist nor an aggressive tactician. For months the organization lacked operatives with those credentials. Meanwhile, Ellsworth fulfilled Dole's confidence in one critical respect: he was totally candid in their private communications.

On June 19 Ellsworth informed the candidate, "Conceptually, as you know, we do not actually have a campaign, a strategy, a plan for winning the nomination away from Bush. Or from keeping the 'lesser lights' from catching fire." A week later he implored Dole to begin "looking into your heart and soul to decide what you believe you want to do for this country as President. Not only your brilliant and powerful political skills, but what you want to do with those skills . . . Above all, I ask you to begin. It is the only way you can win."

A month later, still seeking to recruit a master strategist, Ellsworth wrote to Dole about the tortuous efforts to sign up John Sears. A veteran of Nixon and Reagan campaigns, Sears enjoyed a superb reputation as an independent political thinker with high credibility among the national press. (He was too independent for some former colleagues. In 1969 Sears was forced out of the White House by Nixon's disciplinarians. Though he had almost won the nomination for Reagan in 1976, he was dismissed from the 1980 organization because of staff disagreements.) For months semipublic negotiations to find a suitable role for Sears stumbled along. Now, in a memo dated July 21, Ellsworth tactfully used what he called Sears' "reservations" to prod Dole again. Sears, Ellsworth wrote, "knows our organization is weak because many of our political operatives lack punch. This is true; you already know it; I know it . . . He [also] senses that you are not yet fully, internally, heart and soul, committed to be President (not that anyone else is either) . . . He senses that you are holding an important part of yourself back. I have told him this is still true, though you are gradually breaking through the walls toward a commitment to being President, to lead this nation." From his home in Saddle River, N.J., Nixon sent word via a lobbyist close to Dole: "I agree with Sears. Dole should keep away from the nitty gritty of the daily campaign. Tell him to start thinking big." Sears never came aboard. Dole never explicitly answered Ellsworth's challenges. "His life itself was his response," Ellsworth later told a reporter. That is, Dole did attempt to personalize his approach to the electorate. But when in one major speech he specifically mentioned his "vision," he talked about sharing one with Harry Truman and

Dwight Eisenhower. It boiled down to being "willing to make the tough choices needed to preserve opportunities." When reporters brought up the vision question, Dole either expressed mild impatience or joked about it. "The last person I saw when leaving Russell," he said of one visit home, "was my optometrist, Arch Glenn. And I said, 'Arch, they're always after me on this vision thing. So I may have to get a new prescription.' "

In private communications to his subordinates, Dole showed none of that humor. On June 11 he sent a stinging admonition to Bill Lacy, who was running the headquarters. "The organization has to catch up with the candidate one of these days," Dole wrote. "We cannot ward off the press much longer on the issue of organization, or lack thereof. They won't buy for very long our story that we have more support than we can catch up with . . . Finance is not your responsibility, but it is just short of being a disaster. The entire finance operation must be thoroughly reviewed, revised and whatever else it takes to make us competitive." Ever suspicious that money was being wasted, Dole wanted a "complete listing of all staff: who they are, what they do, who they answer to, what they're paid and who sets their goals and monitors their performance." In other notes to Ellsworth and Lacy, Dole repeated his complaints about excessive travel by underlings ("We're paying for all these people to fly back and forth; they have almost a free airline pass"). He also criticized the schedule devised for him, which he found wearying and unproductive.

While the organization improved to some extent, the basic problems remained unsolved. On Sept. 8 Ellsworth reported that "overall, morale is not good. Most people in the campaign are committed, but more to what's in it for them than to what's in it for Bob Dole. This is partly because they have not received inspirational leadership. There is no clear focus of authority or responsibility."

Ellsworth proposed a new organization table that would divorce Dole from micromanagement. As an alternative, Ellsworth offered to step aside in a "graceful" fashion. "We would remain friends," he assured the boss. Six weeks later Ellsworth did leave active management of the campaign, but not before he had arranged for Labor Secretary Bill Brock to be the new boss and Richard Wirthlin to serve as the campaign's chief pollster. Brock, a former Senator and G.O.P. national chairman, was a better fit for the job. Ellsworth, blessed as he was with a moderate ego, was the first to acknowledge that. Wirthlin had high-level experience in Reagan's service and dozens of elections. But by now the campaign was way behind in preparing for imminent combat. Wirthlin did a quick review of the long-range plans and confided to a friend, "There is no strategy." Settling into his new role in early November, Brock had dinner with a few reporters in Manchester, N.H. Normally a sunny, upbeat character, Brock remarked, "You look at it and feel a little insecure because there is so little time left. It's daunting."

Again, there were fascinating parallels between the fears felt by the two camps. The October stock-market slide had been bleak news for the Administration—and hence for Bush. Robert Bork's nomination to the Supreme Court was slipping away. These developments, among others, prompted Atwater to warn Bush that by the turn of the year, the Vice President might actually be running behind the Senate minority leader. One of the few bright spots for Bush was the first important Republican debate, presided over by conservative columnist William Buckley in Houston on Oct. 28. Though his rivals tried to gang up on him, Bush acquitted himself relatively well. Dole, by contrast, turned in a listless performance. By this point, attention was focusing on Iowa, which had been the cradle of Bush's political success in 1980 and which now threatened to be its hearse.

The ironies were succulent. Eight years before, a combination of Bush's arduous organizing effort, some mistakes by Reagan and the state's generally moderate cast of mind had allowed Bush to eke out a slim victory. (He ran two percentage points ahead of Reagan, but procedures that year failed to produce truly comprehensive results. Some precincts simply never recorded their totals. As the underdog, Bush scored a major psychological victory, but to this day no one knows if he actually won.) Nonetheless, a great deal had changed since then. Reagan was relatively unpopular in the Midwest, particularly in Iowa, because hard times had been excruciatingly slow to lift. In fact, Iowa was one of the few places where Bush's tie to Reagan was a clear liability among Republicans. Dole, as a neighbor who had been immersed in farm issues for decades, enjoyed a cultural affinity with Iowans that Bush could not match. Here, Dole's "one of us" approach was a natural. Iowa was also one of the few places in which Dole's forces were well organized. Tom Synhorst, son of an Iowa farm family and one of Chuck Grassley's young assistants, had pulled together an effective apparatus, county by county.

The extent of Bush's difficulties had already come through dramatically at a pseudo event typical of Iowa's eccentric caucus politics. Well before the caucuses, the state G.O.P. holds a large fund raiser and conducts a symbolic straw poll. Success in this media circus depends not so much on a candidate's popularity as on the ability of his organization to deliver a few hundred more bodies to the meeting hall than the competition can.

On this sunny Saturday in September, most Iowa Republicans had far better things to do than drive for several hours to the Iowa State University campus at Ames. But Pat Robertson's supporters, compensating in fervor what they lacked in gross numbers, decided to make Ames a declaration of strength—just as Bush's managers had in 1980, when they managed to pack the arena. In buses and vans and station wagons, sporting Robertson T shirts and straw hats, Robertson partisans converged on Ames. The same techniques had already worked well in Michigan, which for 1988 was using a convoluted, multistage caucus system susceptible to blitzes by small groups of zealots. At Ames, well before the 3,843 ballots were counted, it was clear that Robertson's forces had outnumbered and outshouted the opposition. The televangelist came in first with 34%. Dole was second with 25%, and the incumbent Vice President ran an embarrassing third with 22%. Robertson visited the press room later to declare, in the verbal italics he used so effectively, "The Vice President has been wounded *very* badly."

Bush was soon back in Iowa, announcing his determination to recoup. "They've unleashed a tiger now," he said as he accelerated his campaign pace. From Washington, Atwater dispatched his chief deputy, Rich Bond, to take personal command in Iowa, which had been Bond's assignment in 1980. Bush tried to explain away the Ames setback with a clumsy joke. Many of his supporters, he said, had been busy at "their daughters' coming-out parties." Again, Bush inadvertently helped Dole build the case that the issue was Main Street vs. the country club, the farm vs. the boardroom.

Dole argued that brief in one small town after another, recalling that his father went to work at the grain elevator or the butter-and-egg station in overalls "every day of his life." Over and over, Dole told the story of his climb from penury to prominence, and of his recovery from near fatal war wounds. And he told Iowans that they owed him one. At most of his stops he recalled his disastrous Iowa showing in 1980. "Everyone was very nice," he would say. "But they said, 'I'm for Reagan' or 'I'm for Bush.' They said, 'It's not your time; come back later.' Well, it's later and I'm back!"

The stakes could not have been higher. If Bush could somehow prevail in what had become hostile territory for him, Dole's claim to be the most "electable" Republican in November would be demolished. Some of Dole's most senior advisers admitted privately that defeat in Iowa would effectively end Dole's campaign. A Dole victory would be less conclusive, but could well start a domino effect. Though Bush's advisers still professed confidence that his Southern base would hold regardless of the earlier contests in Iowa, New Hampshire, Minnesota and South Dakota, their doubts were growing geometrically.

"Our grass-roots support is soft," Atwater warned his colleagues. "In every state, at every level . . . there is not enough enthusiasm for the Vice President's campaign." Ed Rogers said privately, "We really do not want to test the theory that George Bush can survive a loss in Iowa."

Bush, however, suffered from a shortage of ammunition in the opening battle. He had the remnants of the old Iowa moderate network, now fraying and out of power. But he did not have any fresh arguments, any compelling new concepts to add to his status as crown prince in a state where the aging king was unpopular. As Atwater had noted in yet another memo, on Oct. 7, "Our low-risk strategy has itself become risky." Dole could trade on his Kansas roots, his tactfully expressed skepticism about Reaganomics, his reputation as a no-nonsense leader willing to make difficult decisions. He also had the endorsement of the influential Des Moines *Register*. The continued frailties of Dole's national organization were not an important factor in this small arena, where Synhorst produced a workable machine and where Grassley personally labored for Dole.

On caucus night, the weather was mild as Iowa Februaries go, but the results rattled the Republican chessboard. Not only did Dole win with 37%, but Robertson's followers produced a surprise second-place showing at 25%. Bush ran third with only 19%. The outcome appeared to be disaster for Bush, fulfilling his camp's worst fears about the softness of his support. With the New Hampshire primary only eight days away, the political world was sure that another defeat would be terminal for the Vice President.

But Dole's victory came with its own caveats. While Robertson was not widely considered to be a serious candidate for the nomination, his showing in Iowa detracted from coverage of Dole's success. Further, Dole still had to prove that he could do well in a place where Reagan was popular. Suddenly the Granite State, which had been somewhat overshadowed by the press's obsession with Hawkeye State politics, became the focal point of all the contenders' energies.

In New Hampshire, Bush enjoyed some advantages. His loyal ally Republican Governor John Sununu had recruited sheriffs and county clerks and other local centurions who could get out the vote. By trade an engineer with a fine mind for detail, Sununu personally screened nearly all of Bush's 299 precinct captains. Through his associate, party chairwoman Elsie Vartanian, Sununu maintained a strong hold on the G.O.P.'s statewide apparatus. When Bush canvassers weeks before the primary ran across a couple who were strong supporters of the Vice President, they would ask whether the family had children away at college. If so, those presumably pro-Bush offspring were sent applications for absentee ballots. Dole's principal local backers, Senator Warren Rudman and a veteran political organizer, Tom Rath, could not match that kind of depth. More important than organizational differences, New Hampshire was a conservative, prosperous, low-tax state in which Reaganomics—and Reagan himself—remained much admired.

Dole hurtled into the state well aware of that circumstance, giving as his major opener a hawkish speech on foreign policy. But the Bush camp knew that Dole's principal vulnerability was the tax question. So it invested heavily in aggressive TV commercials intended to depict Dole as tax happy. The most prominent of these was a 60-second spot that came to be known as the "straddle ad." The commercial, while visually dull, listed several issues with a repetitive punchline: "Bob Dole straddled . . ." On the most significant passage, the announcer concluded in an ominous, knowing tone, "He just won't promise not to raise taxes. You know what that means." In the final weekend before the vote, Sununu and Atwater personally persuaded Manchester's WMUR-TV to sell the Bush campaign even more airtime than had been reserved. So, during a single hourlong newscast over WMUR, the straddle spot was shown five times. Later, when Wirthlin did a postmortem poll, he discovered that during the seven days leading up to the vote, Bush's advantage over Dole on the tax issue had increased from 12% to 27%.

Dole, meanwhile, was broadcasting his "nothing to do with it" commercial. This 60-second spot started with shots of Dole and Bush side by side. As the narrator listed three subjects—the 1983 Social Security compromise, the INF nuclear treaty and Reagan's original tax cuts—he repeated a refrain, "George Bush had nothing to do with it." Meanwhile, Bush's likeness gradually faded until Dole was seen alone as the candidate who "will make a difference for America. The difference is leadership."

During that long, blurred week between Iowa and New Hampshire, it appeared that Dole was making progress. Bush's lead, which before Iowa had been as wide as 20 points, disappeared in new spot surveys of New Hampshire voters. One poll by the Gallup organization during the final weekend even showed Dole eight points ahead. Wirthlin's tracking surveys, which measured movement from day to day, indicated that Dole was getting support from voters who had been wobbly in their allegiance to any of the candidates.

Dole, however, was not answering Bush's tax accusation effectively. Efforts to broadcast a new Dole attack ad over the weekend foundered. The spot was not in sufficiently polished form, his advisers would explain later. Nor was Dole able to counter a last-minute personal endorsement by Barry Goldwater, who answered an SOS from Bush. A private jet owned by Bob Mosbacher, a Bush friend and fund raiser, was sent to Arizona to fetch the retired Senator. Though feeling his 79 years, the New Right's godfather responded with brio, appearing on primary eve and even taping a commercial. The spot was a minor masterpiece. "I believe," Goldwater told the camera, "in George Bush. He's the man to continue the conservative revolution we started 24 years ago." Al Haig had withdrawn from the race the previous Friday, but not before throwing one last spear at Bush by announcing support for Dole. Haig, however, lacked a following in the state, so his gesture mattered little.

As voters went to the polls on Feb. 16, Bush was already benefiting from the perceptions game. The apparent erosion in his support following Iowa made him seem almost the underdog. Thus even a close result would not be a disaster. In the event, Bush came in first with 38%, ten points ahead of Dole. Kemp ran third with 13%.

Suddenly, Bush was the comeback kid. He had in fact demonstrated some personal resilience. But the more important message was that Bush's organization had held together well during a period of stressful challenge, while Dole's team was unable to capitalize on the opening provided by Iowa's caucuses. Intrinsically, the New Hampshire victory was hardly a stunner. For the incumbent Vice President to get just a bit more than one-third of the vote in a state where his Administration was so popular and prosperity so high did not signal overwhelming strength. But at least Bush had demonstrated that he was no Humpty-Dumpty. By primary night, Dole was surly and defensive, remarking foolishly in an NBC interview that Bush should "stop lying about my record." On the plane carrying Dole's party home, one of the Senator's senior advisers, David Keene, told a reporter, "If we learned anything, it's that we're going to have to knock [Bush] down. He won't fall down by himself."

The central question was where that knockdown could occur. The venue was not at all obvious. South Dakota and Minnesota were favorable to Dole for some of the same reasons Iowa had been. But the eccentricities of the nominating process—and the way the national press covered it—understated the importance of those two states. Dole got little benefit from carrying both of them.

What dominated attention now was Super Tuesday, March 8, in which most of the South would vote, along with a few other states. On the preceding Saturday, March 5, South Carolina would hold a primary. This string of contests was the big casino, with nearly 35% of the Republican delegates on the block between Saturday and Tuesday. Further, the South was Bush's strongest region, largely because of its fealty to Reagan and its traditionalist sentiments. Here, more than in any other area, Bush's status as the loyal, dutiful heir was an asset. Finally, Atwater, Rogers and several other Southerners in the Bush campaign had deep personal ties to the party apparatus in their home region. The G.O.P. establishment there was still relatively new, largely a product of the 1960s civil rights upheaval. Atwater, a South Carolinian who once played guitar with the backup group for soul singer Percy Sledge, had grown up in that ferment and had close associations with most of the talented activists. For them, he reinforced Bush's legitimacy.

Bush decided to stand, rather than run, on those advantages. He assumed a more cautious posture than ever, avoiding interrogation by the national press most of the time, staying away from new speech texts that might evoke controversy. His longtime press adviser, Peter Teeley, was now back in Bush's service, and occasionally prodded his candidate to take a stronger, more topical line. It was Teeley, after all, who had ghostwritten the phrase "voodoo economics" to characterize Reagan's fiscal program in 1980. But Teeley, along with Atwater, was usually held back by the amber lights being flashed by Fuller and Teeter. (Three months later, that friction forced Teeley out of the organization.) The reasoning behind this caution was simple: Southern Republicans, who would decide the issue, were orthodox loyalists. In this narrow arena, there was little to be gained by risky innovation unless circumstances forced the issue. Yet no threat was visible.

Robertson, though boldly predicting that he would win South Carolina and do well elsewhere in the South, was collapsing. His campaign had spent most of its large war chest. His personal credibility was damaged by a series of gaffes, including his unsupported charge that Bush had somehow engineered disclosure of the scandal that brought down fellow televangelist Jimmy Swaggart. The Kemp campaign was also fading, and showed no ability to capitalize on Robertson's slide. Dole's team was staggering as well, short of funds, short of strategy, short of unity. Bitter over what he considered bad advice from subordinates during the final days of the New Hampshire contest, Dole grew hostile toward Wirthlin, Rath and a few others. Then a serious rift became public between Brock on the one hand and Keene and Don Devine on the other. On a swing through Florida, with reporters near enough to hear him, Brock summarily fired the pair.

Dole's only hope was to pick off four or five states, such as Missouri, Oklahoma, North Carolina and Arkansas, where his personal standing was relatively high. Instead of concentrating his limited resources on important states, a strategy the pros call cherry picking, Dole allowed himself to be diverted into South Carolina. An endorsement by Senator Strom Thurmond, patriarch of the South's G.O.P., created the illusion that Dole might gain an upset there. But Bush had Governor Carroll Campbell doing in South Carolina what Sununu had done in New Hampshire. As the Republican candidates scampered across 18 states in three weeks, all of Bush's organizational strengths—and Dole's weaknesses—became ever more obvious. "What's the strategy?" Dole demanded of advisers in one private meeting. The question met only silence.

In that environment, Bush simply had to hold fast. The huge amount of real estate involved in Super Tuesday dictated that campaigning be superficial, with candidates hopping from airport to airport. Their differences on the issues, never really vivid, became virtually invisible in the South. Voter interest remained low. Atwater and Teeter realized that the earlier prospect of large numbers of conservative Democrats crossing over to vote in Republican primaries had evaporated. Heavy switching would have aided Robertson and possibly Dole. With that threat minimal, Bush was safe in emphasizing his narrow agenda, centering on his no-tax pledge and on patriotic themes. In the small arena of the orthodox Republican electorate, that proved to be more than enough.

In the South Carolina primary on Saturday, only 8% of the eligible voters showed up at the polls. But Bush captured 48% of them, more than Dole and Robertson combined. That was an omen for the following Tuesday. Bush won all 16 primaries, including the entire South, the border states, plus Massachusetts and Rhode Island. His only defeat was in the Washington State caucuses, which Robertson carried. No Republican candidate in an active contest had ever enjoyed so broad a victory on a single primary day. And Atwater was probably correct when he predicted, "There will never be another regional primary with this sort of conclusive impact." Suddenly, Bush—the man who had been branded a wimp, the candidate whose own retainers had worried over for so long, the model for so many derisive cartoons—sounded halfway credible when he told his supporters in Houston, "I'm now convinced that I will be the President of the United States."

Almost as suddenly, the Republican field narrowed. Du Pont had quit after New Hampshire. Kemp withdrew after Super Tuesday, and Robertson retreated to the status of a symbolic candidate, talking mostly about the future of his Christian political movement. Yet Dole sailed on, a flying Dutchman with no political base, no prospect for a comeback.

Illinois was the next big test. Once it had seemed a promising state for Dole, that paradigm of Midwestern Republicanism. Now, however, Bush led by 20 points. Dole's pride would not let him quit, not yet, so he flew on to Lincoln's state. Nothing worked right, not even his chartered Presidential Airways jet (the very same plane later leased by the Dukakis campaign). When it stalled on the ground in Peoria, Dole muttered, "Let's get another plane, let's get another plane." There was no other plane. When his aircraft finally got him to Chicago that night, it taxied to the wrong terminal. "I can beat George Bush," he said several times, "but I cannot beat Ronald Reagan." In fact, Dole could not overcome his own shortcomings as a candidate either.

He lost Illinois, 55% to 36%, and withdrew from the race on March 29.

With Dole's departure, George Bush became his party's de facto nominee. He had the luxury, if he chose to use it, of starting his general election campaign early. The Democratic hopefuls were still busy fighting it out among themselves. For a brief time, Bush even pulled ahead of their formidable front runner, Michael Dukakis, in national polls. But the largely substance-free campaign with which Bush captured the nomination had done little to make him attractive to a national audience. To make matters worse, his strategists chose to have the Vice President lie low while they regrouped and replanned for several weeks, rather than have him sally forth to exploit his advantage. In late April Bush was the underdog, according to a TIME poll and some other surveys. Once again he would have to confront the "vision thing" and find ways to explain what America under President Bush would be like.

4

Bush: the Loyalist

EVEN AS GEORGE BUSH REACHED THE PINNACLE OF HIS PO-
litical career, the power and glory of his party's nomination,
there remained about him considerable public skepticism and
unease. For eight years he had displayed a seemingly unquench-
able loyalty to Ronald Reagan. Yet in the process Bush had so
drastically subordinated himself, become such a presidential
cheerleader, that his own identity was almost unrecognizable.
Often he seemed a man with no mind of his own. One of his rivals for the nomination expressed it harshly: "Sometimes I feel I
can put my hand right through him." But there was far more to
the persevering Bush than that. His deferential exterior concealed an inner toughness. In private he was vastly self-assured,
opinionated, almost bullheaded in his views.

What happened to all that confidence when George Bush
was called upon to be his own man? Often he seemed out of control, too eager to please, a figure not certain of where he was going or even who he was. What did George Bush really believe

in? Whatever his convictions, would he stand behind them? The questions themselves were almost insulting. But there was about Bush the lingering perception that he was too weak and unsure to lead. More than most other politicians, he was a paradox. A brave war hero, he was mocked as a wimp. Modest and ingratiating, he was at times downright nasty. A Phi Beta Kappa student at Yale, he could sound incoherent and sometimes even goofy. What was one to make of George Bush? Did he possess the personal force and imagination for leadership, or was he just a sycophantic smoothy?

There was something curious and remarkable about the man. After a quarter-century in politics, Bush, at 64, was still largely an evanescent presence. White House aides who had attended hundreds of small sessions with the Vice President said they had no idea what he really thought. Old friends were puzzled about why the sturdy and witty Bush they knew so well became stiff and stilted on television. "I've heard exactly the same thing," he acknowledged in an interview with TIME during the 1988 campaign. "I'm 6 ft. 2 in., and when I go out on the campaign trail, people say, 'We thought you were a short guy.' I've been 6-2 ever since I was 18 years old. So I've got to do better, particularly on television."

The public, he allowed, still understood too little about him and his values. As he approached the fall campaign, the candidate made a few superficial efforts to correct that. People needed to know, Bush told reporters, that he was an enthusiastic fan of country-and-western music, that at home he liked to pitch horseshoes and eat pork rinds. Such desperate attempts to humanize his image only made the problem more visible. Bush had difficulty communicating his deeper feelings to the public.

His extraordinary job résumé was by now broadly familiar. But the interior Bush remained mostly unknown. As would-be biographers rushed to probe the Vice President's past, they found telltale signs of the Bush character and personality even in his early years.

The second son of wealthy and accomplished parents, young George grew up in a happy and privileged environment: private schools, Christmas vacations at his grandfather's South Carolina plantation, called Duncannon, summers on the Maine coast, where college friends remember being met following a late-afternoon swim by servants bearing large towels and cold drinks. George won friends easily, and adults especially liked him. "He knew how to get around them," said younger brother Jonathan. Truly generous, George acquired the name "have-half" because he was always ready to share. If older brother Prescott Jr. grabbed at his toys, George never demanded total return. Instead, he would say, "Have half, Pressy, have half?" He could show a tender nature. During an obstacle race at school, one overweight boy got stuck inside a barrel. As onlookers guffawed, George sprinted from the sidelines and helped pull him free. He could not stand the boy's pain, George told his mother afterward.

Bush favored his mother Dorothy, a warm, embracing woman who focused her energies on raising her daughter and four sons. Her father George Herbert Walker was a successful St. Louis investment banker and sportsman—he created golfing's prized Walker Cup, the British-Irish-American amateur competition—and Dorothy Walker was once a tennis finalist in the national women's championships. At Kennebunkport, Me., where the family had a huge compound on a peninsula named Walker's Point, friends used to stand and watch as Dorothy swam the cold water between her home and the Kennebunk River Club. She spent hours hitting tennis balls to her sons. Outgoing and vibrant, she inserted herself fully into her children's lives.

Her husband Prescott Bush was more formal and austere. Physically towering at 6 ft. 4 in., with a singer's deep voice, the senior Bush in his crisply tailored clothes had an air of outright authority. Without having to raise his voice, he commanded his children's respect. The son of an Ohio steelmaker who helped launch the nation's Community Chest movement, Prescott Bush went east to Yale University. There he played varsity football, baseball and golf, sang bass in the Whiffenpoofs and was tapped to Skull and Bones, the most exclusive of the university's secret societies. He saw combat as a captain during World War I, returned to start a business career and eventually rose to become managing partner of the prestigious banking house of Brown Brothers Harriman & Co. It was a glittering record. After serving for 17 years as moderator of the Greenwich, Conn., town meeting, Bush in 1952 ran successfully for the U.S. Senate. A moderate Republican, he was known as a man of high principle—at one point daring to oppose Wisconsin's witch-hunting Senator Joseph McCarthy—as well as a champion of civil rights. Unlike son George, who over the years was to swing between extreme and moderate conservatism, Prescott Bush kept his distance from the far right.

He made a deep and lasting mark on his children. "We were all a little afraid of Dad," remembered Jonathan Bush. The senior Bush was not one for long, heart-to-heart talks. Instead, after some particular achievement he would drop an approving note that might be signed "devotedly, Dad." Sparing with his praise, Prescott Bush seldom intervened with his offspring, but instead made clear his own set of high values. Within the family, remembers Dorothy Bush, there was little introspection or heavy analysis. After a hard week on Wall Street, Prescott Bush spent most weekends swinging a golf club at the nearby Round Hill links. His wife sometimes urged him to take the boys along. "Oh, Dottie," he would answer, "if they want to learn, they'll pick it up." Instead the father much preferred to gather his family around their shiny Steinway piano, his rich voice leading the way, and pound out songs by ear. Regularly he brought home a group of fellow crooners, nicknamed the Silver Dollar Quartet, or the better-known Merry Macs. On occasion the celebrated bandleader Fred Waring would drop by.

Around the house the older Bush never lost his temper.

Nonetheless he was a hard man to challenge. Prescott Jr., the eldest son, might argue back, family members recalled, but never George. Explained Dorothy Bush: "George was a peacemaker. He never instigated an argument that I remember." Years later, Bush the politician had the same conciliatory style. He rarely challenged authority. At the White House, Bush practiced absolute compliance. "George's operating principle," said one of his White House colleagues, "was 'Don't make anybody mad.' " That kind of upward deference had its roots, friends were certain, in Bush's respectful but wary relationship with his father. "George never really knew what his father wanted of him," reasoned one family friend, "except to do things well. But 'doing well' never had any context."

Despite their standing and money, the Bush parents worked hard to create limits, stressing where they could discipline and self-reliance. Prescott Bush provided for top private schools for his children but thereafter expected them to fend for themselves. Nevertheless, his highly placed contacts were always within reach of the Bush offspring. At home Dorothy Bush emphasized duties, no matter how small. She insisted that her children turn out lights in empty rooms, an ongoing task in the family's nine-bedroom Greenwich house. She circled personal calls on telephone bills and expected her children to pay for them.

Certain ironies existed, of course. A family chauffeur, Alec, sat ready each morning in a limousine to drive the children to school. Beds were always made by a maid and meals prepared by the family cook. "Life was easy in those days," recalled Dorothy Bush, "but we tried to create a sense of values." Rich-kid ostentation was firmly discouraged. Neighbors in Kennebunkport remember that the Walker side of the family was disposed to throw its weight around. When they showed up at the tennis club, for instance, the Walkers expected courts to be vacated. Recalled William Richardson, a friend of both families: "The Bushes would never dream of doing such a thing."

Thus when the Bush kids took to bragging, they were quickly squelched. "I couldn't bear to have them boast," said Dorothy Bush. Sometimes George would return home and declare that his tennis game was somewhat off. "You don't have a game yet," his mother would say, keeping things in perspective. "Get out and work harder and maybe someday you will." The children were urged to drop the first person singular. If George described one of his numerous sports exploits, Dorothy Bush pointedly asked if any other boys were on the team. Teamwork was valued over individual performance. Eventually George learned it was better to conceal his pride. Later, when he turned to politics, Bush was awkward with the self-promotional rhetoric that was part of the game. Dorothy Bush no doubt approved, but voters tended to squirm at her son's uptight and graceless style. Always Bush strained to play down his élitist background. So thin-skinned was he at being called a preppy that he avoided wearing button-down shirts as a presidential candidate. Bush even took to needling guests who wanted a glass for their beer instead of swigging directly from the can. From time to time his own buried sense of social standing showed through. To candidate Bush, paid political operators were strictly hired help. Volunteers, on the other hand, won his admiration.

George was born in Milton, Mass., but the family moved to Greenwich, Conn., shortly thereafter. Daily the Bush chauffeur drove Poppy, as young George was now called, after his grandfather, from the big house on Grove Lane to nearby Greenwich Country Day School. Years later, sitting in the White House Oval Office while a blizzard raged outside, he was surprised to hear Ronald Reagan burst out laughing as Bush described how during big storms in Connecticut his chauffeur made a point of getting him to school faster than anyone else in the neighborhood. The image of hotly competitive chauffeurs racing through the snow broke up Reagan, the small-town boy. At Greenwich Country Day, George was a diligent student and athlete and had numerous friends. "It was amazing that none of our children resented him for doing so well," said Dorothy Bush. "Everything came easy to George." In those days the school had a report-card category called "claims no more than his fair share" of time and attention. When grades were brought home, the Bush parents always made a point to ask about the claims-no-more entry. George's high marks gladdened them.

In 1937, at 13, he followed his older brother to Phillips Academy in Andover, Mass. George began to gain some of his father's height and was accomplished enough to make the varsity baseball and soccer teams. Bright but not intellectual, he earned his academic honors through hard work. Andover roommate George Warren remembered that during bull sessions in the dormitory, George mostly stayed on the edges of conversation. He listened hard and recognized a good concept when he heard one. If someone displayed conspicuous good reason, Bush later remarked on it. Always he identified more with the person than the idea, a pattern of thinking that stuck with him. In the years that followed, Bush the politician was motivated less by ideology than by people. One man interviewed for a senior post on his 1980 presidential campaign staff asked Bush what two or three issues mattered the most to him. The candidate paused, then answered in his own way: He would put the best people in charge and thus create a superb Government.

As a young man, and over the years, George preferred motion to reflection. Like his father, he had no enthusiasm for personal analysis. "You guys," he frequently chided reporters, "are always trying to stretch me out on a couch. I spent my whole life learning not to talk about myself from my mother." Bush invested little time in either self-pity or getting even. "There isn't a bitter bone in the guy's body," said former Ohio Congressman Thomas ("Lud") Ashley, a longtime friend. When Bush was troubled, he threw himself into physical overdrive. It was his way of dealing with anxiety. Action made Bush feel more in charge of himself. Once he identified a goal, he single-mindedly worked toward it. It was no great surprise that his first baseball hero was the New York Yankees' Lou Gehrig and not the more flamboyant Babe Ruth. Bush admired the way "Iron Horse" Gehrig plugged along.

From the time George was a boy, his attention span was short. He easily turned restless. Years later White House colleagues noticed that during extended staff briefings Bush often became edgy and started popping questions. "He lacks patience," explained one senior staff member, "for things that are not distilled." On the water around Kennebunkport, Bush preferred powerboats to sail. Power, he said, saved time.

The young Bush had an upright side. Roommate George Warren remembered that George would rarely accept an invitation to slip off and have a drink. Warren, who later joined the U.S. Marines, had a more daring streak. Sometimes he would abandon Bush to join up with a faster crowd. To buy some whiskey, the boys had to lie about their age. When Warren returned to his Andover room after a night of boozing, Bush upbraided him. "He'd go after me unmercifully," Warren recalled. "I knew he was right. George always had a strong set of values and was not self-conscious about expressing them."

His junior year at Andover, Bush dropped out because of a serious respiratory infection. "Our parents thought they were going to lose him," recalled brother Jonathan. George returned the following fall and subsequently spent a fifth year at Andover. A chipper, lighthearted achiever, now he became president of the senior class, secretary of the student council, captain of the soccer and baseball teams and a member of several other student groups. "He was a legend," recalled classmate Jack Greenway. "He was friends with scholarship students, with jocks, with academic types." Basketball captain Robert Furman remembered that his parents had been unable to attend a game in which he starred. Bush on his own wrote to the Furmans and described their son's heroics. By his last year Bush had reached his full adult height of 6 ft. 2 in. Greenwich buddy Vinnie Lynch recalled limousine rides to New York City during holidays to attend various debutante parties. The blue-eyed Bush, tall and slender, cut a handsome figure.

Summers Bush journeyed with his family to Kennebunk-port to a sprawling shingle-and-stone cottage, joined by assort-ed cousins and friends, who could always find a spare bedroom or an extra tennis racquet. Saturday mornings Prescott Sr. ar-rived by sleeper car from Manhattan. Days were crammed with sailing and tennis at the Kennebunk River Club, fierce games of backgammon and blackjack at night. George and his elder brother had a small 10-ft. skiff with a three-horsepower motor, and alone they took it past the breakwater and into the ocean. It was hard to imagine a better life, recalled childhood friend Bill Truesdale. Months ahead of time Bush and his chums would be-gin anticipating Maine. George did not miss a summer at the coast until 1944. He grew up surrounded by warm relationships, most of which he continued to hold close all his life. Bush was an inveterate writer of personal notes, and even boyhood chums have never stopped hearing from him. George Pfau Jr., a Yale classmate, related in an interview: "George generally calls on New Year's Eve. I don't hear from people in my family, but I hear from George Bush."

At the Andover commencement in 1942, Secretary of War Henry Stimson somewhat surprisingly urged graduates to com-plete their education before rushing off to war. Prescott Bush, who attended the graduation, asked his son about his plans. When George replied that he was enlisting immediately, his fa-ther simply nodded and shook his hand. It was a critical deci-sion, and the graduate liked the idea that he was making it on his own. A few years later, George would make another impor-tant decision on his own, rejecting his father's advice to follow him into the investment-banking business and instead taking off for Texas. Such unexpected moves, friends figured, were George's way of asserting independence from his father and making up for a life of privilege.

Bush volunteered for naval aviation and was trained as a

torpedo bomber pilot. He earned his wings at 18 and became the youngest pilot in the Navy. Assigned to the U.S.S. *San Jacinto*, a light carrier on a converted cruiser hull, Bush in 1944 was off to the Pacific. There he flew 58 combat missions. On the fuselages of his planes was painted the name of a good-looking girl named Barbara Pierce, daughter of a top executive of McCall Corp., whom Bush had dated when she was a student at Smith College. Four different planes either were shot out from under him or malfunctioned. On the morning of Sept. 2, 1944, the pilots on the *San Jacinto* were ordered to strike Japanese installations on the island of Chichi Jima. They were warned that the *San Jacinto* would not remain in the area to rescue anyone who went down. Bush, flying a TBM Avenger carrying two crewmen, was in the second wave. That day he had agreed to let a Navy buddy, William ("Ted") White, fly along in the gunner's seat. White had been begging to accompany him on a bombing mission. It was a decision that haunted Bush for years afterward. As the squadron approached the target area, he saw all around him puffs of black smoke from Japanese antiaircraft shells. While closing in on the target, his plane was hit, and smoke filled the cockpit. "I felt I had to finish the run," Bush said.

He hit his target, a radio station, and pulled out over the ocean, flames now licking at the wing tanks. As Bush bailed out, his body was swept back toward the tail, and he struck his head. Somehow the parachute pulled clear, and he fell toward the water, landing feetfirst. Ted White and Jack Delaney, his radioman, were dead. Bush inflated his tiny rubber raft and waited. Four hours later, a periscope broke the surface of the water. For an instant Bush feared it was a Japanese sub. When the U.S.S. *Finback* surfaced, Bush, his head still bleeding, was pulled aboard. For a month the submarine stayed at sea, during which time it was depth-charged and bombed by air. Finally the ship with Bush aboard tied up at an island base. Even though he had earned the right to go home, Bush chose to return to combat.

Toward the end of 1944, Bush, now only 20, winner of three Air Medals and the Distinguished Flying Cross, was assigned back to the States to train pilots. He returned home Christmas Eve and within two weeks married Barbara Pierce, 19. After he was discharged in September 1945, Bush started the fall term at Yale. The young couple lived off campus in cramped married-student quarters. Their first son George Walker Bush arrived the following summer. From the start Barbara—or "Bar," as George called her—was an active ally, usually at his side. Level-headed and more relaxed than her husband, she backed him fiercely and in the political campaigns that followed was less forgiving about personal attacks than her husband. Recalled second son Jeb: "We used to turn to Mom because she was always there. Dad was usually caught up in something. Our family has never been physically close, but we're close in every other way."

At Yale Bush mastered his studies, graduating Phi Beta Kappa in economics. He captained the baseball team that for the second year in a row made the N.C.A.A. championships. Like his father, George was invited to join Skull and Bones. Twice a week the prestigious secret society met in a windowless stone building. Partly because Bonesmen were encouraged to open up to one another, friendships became intimate and lasting. One night during his senior year, George related the story of Ted White's death and how much the episode stayed in his mind. The listeners were deeply moved, as they later told the Washington *Post*. Around the campus, the exuberant Bush was a magnet of attention. His goodwill was demonstrable. When he heard that a popular Andover professor who had taken a job at Yale was in the grip of a serious problem with alcoholism, George made room at his cramped quarters and helped him get back on his feet.

After graduation in 1948, Bush took the wheel of a red Studebaker and with his wife and infant son headed for the booming oil fields of West Texas to seek his fortune. It was one more cry of independence. "I wasn't going to live in the suburbs," he told a friend, "and be Pres Bush's boy." Nonetheless, influential family ties still helped. George's first job was in blue-collar Odessa, selling oil-field supplies for Dresser Industries, an equipment firm run by Neil Mallon, one of Prescott Bush's close friends from Yale and a fellow member of Skull and Bones. The senior Bush served on the Dresser board. In 1950, on the strength of $300,000 raised by his uncle G. Herbert Walker Jr., Bush started his own development company in nearby Midland, where drilling sites atop the Permian oil pool were being grabbed up by eager investors. Bush and his new partner, John Overbey, bought up and traded oil and gas leases. "I knew something about trading," recalled Overbey, "but was short on cash. Once we got going, George learned the business fast." Overbey remembered a trip back east to raise funds. On Wall Street the two partners walked into the splendid offices of Uncle Herbie Walker and his colleagues, lunched at the "21" Club and soon had the money they needed.

In Midland the tall lanky Easterner had the look and friendly manner—if not the accent—of a Texan, and he thrust himself into community activities. He taught Sunday school, served on the boards of the community theater and a local bank. He installed his family in a tiny frame house on a dirt road known as Easter Egg Row, because the houses were painted in various bright colors. By now a lot of other Ivy Leaguers had been drawn to Texas. New roads took on names like Princeton Avenue. "The only golf course," recalled John Overbey, "was a nine-hole sand trap."

Thrilled at the opportunities around him, Bush nonetheless kept his ties to home. Overbey remembered that his partner had a typewriter in the office and spent hours writing letters to friends back east. Always he labored to hold and strengthen his friendships. They seemed to sustain him. Stories about help from Bush during crises are numerous. He and his wife took in the five children of friends who were hospitalized for weeks.

Years later, Bush would be held in great affection by two friends, James Baker and Robert Mosbacher, for the emotional support he offered them as their wives were dying of cancer. Such friendships, according to son George, later provided his father a permanence that was missing in politics.

In 1953 Bush and two brothers, J. Hugh and William Liedtke, formed Zapata Petroleum and a year later a drilling subsidiary, Zapata Off-Shore. The first few years Zapata Off-Shore turned a small profit. Bush drew a salary of between $30,000 and $45,000 and created one of the country's first stock-option programs for employees, according to the Washington *Post*. In 1959 the two companies separated, with Bush heading Zapata Off-Shore. But while other Texas oil projects sprang into fortunes, Zapata Off-Shore only loped along. By 1966, after Hurricane Betsy destroyed the company's newest and largest drilling barge, worth $5.7 million, Bush had sold his share of Zapata Off-Shore for $1 million. The real oil boom was just ahead. Bush once said that selling Zapata when he did "cost me a bundle, but that's fate. I don't look back on it."

High-stakes oil took another toll on Bush: he developed a bleeding ulcer. On a trip to London in 1960, he passed out on the floor of the posh Savoy Hotel. "I was alone, naked, lying on the floor, trying to reach a buzzer on the wall," Bush said later. Back in Houston, doctors told him he could cure the ulcer by not worrying so much, and the hyperactive Bush tried to follow their advice.

That was a tall order. Bush now had a different, more absorbing challenge: politics. "George has this driving sense of accomplishment," Andover friend Ernest Obermeyer had told biographer Nicholas King, "and once he has achieved accomplishment, his tendency is to walk away from it. His attitude was, 'Well, I've done that, let's see what I can do next.' He wasn't willing to wait around. He was after the ultimate challenge, first the Senate, and then the presidency."

The striving Bush had another important goal. He struggled to find time for his growing family. Sometimes there was far too little. He did not meet his son Jeb's wife Columba, for example, until the day before the two were married. But Bush invested enormous emotion in his role as father. Nothing was more important to him, he told close friends. "After all these years, our kids still come home," the Vice President said years later. "The most fun I have today in my life is when I'm doing something with my grandkids or with our boys and Doro [their name for daughter Dorothy]. It's the most fun. Nothing else compares, nothing."

Son George, 42, graduated from Yale and Harvard Business School and then migrated back to Midland, where he ran a company that explored for oil and gas in the same Permian basin that had attracted his father. In 1987 he moved to Washington and joined his father's campaign. Jeb Bush, 35, was born during the family's years in Midland. As an exchange student in Mexico during high school, he met Columba, who just recently became an American citizen. A real estate developer based in Miami and for nearly two years Florida's Secretary of Commerce, he was also active in the 1988 campaign. Neil Mallon Bush, 33, received a master's degree in business administration from Tulane University, and has a small oil-exploration company in Denver. Marvin Pierce Bush, 32, graduated from the University of Virginia, and is a partner in the investment-advising firm of John Stewart Darrell & Co. Dorothy Bush LeBlond, 29, graduated from Boston College, became a travel agent and caterer, and later moved to Maine with her husband, who is in the construction business. The Bushes have a total of ten grandchildren. There are no divorces in the family. A daughter, Robin, died in 1953 at age three of leukemia. Her death was a shattering experience for the Bushes, who until then had known no real tragedy in their lives. Barbara Bush remembers that her husband could barely contain his grief, weeping openly at the funeral.

Even before he abandoned the oil business, Bush had his

mind on big-time politics. In the early 1960s Republicanism was springing roots in long-Democratic Texas. A group of moderate Republicans approached Bush and asked him to serve as the party's Harris County chairman. They were concerned that ultra-right members of the John Birch Society might take over the budding party. Bush, son of a moderate Republican Senator, was perfect for the job. The new chairman played adroitly to both sides. His ability to conciliate held things together, no small task considering the zealotry of Texas conservatives. Bush was free of such ideological fervor. Results, as always, were more important to him than creed. Eventually some of Bush's original sponsors began to change their opinion, viewing him as too accommodating to the Birchers.

Bush had other things on his mind. In 1964, at age 40, he took a giant step and announced his candidacy for the U.S. Senate, where his father had served for ten years until retiring in 1962. The move was typical of George's daring and ambition. He was still fairly new to Texas politics and had never before run for political office. His opponent, incumbent Senator Ralph Yarborough, was a populist Democrat with a rabid following. Bush was easily defeated, capturing 43.6% of the vote. But that was an impressive showing for a Republican. It convinced Bush to sell his Zapata Off-Shore shares and concentrate on politics.

Two years later, he won a seat in the U.S. House of Representatives as the first Republican ever elected from Houston's conservative 7th district. Through the influence of House minority leader Gerald Ford, the new Texas Congressman was assigned to the vital Ways and Means Committee, an almost unprecedented appointment for a freshman. Bush quickly established a conservative voting record. He backed controls on federal spending and supported the war in Viet Nam. The liberal Americans for Democratic Action gave Bush a rating of only 7 during his first term. He voted for setting limits on foreign aid and in favor of a $460 million cut in antipoverty programs. In 1968 the conservative Bush, who was unopposed for re-election, improved his record by batting zero with A.D.A. On one issue Bush surprised his many constituents: he voted in favor of using federal funds to build public housing. For years the housing vote was viewed as a measure of Bush's philosophical ambivalence— or his courage, depending on who did the viewing. Conservatives condemned him for it, moderates saw it as a sign of his humane side. In fact, Bush had originally been firmly opposed to the measure and switched sides only after he saw that the bill was sure to pass.

His reputation for years was one of political ambiguity. To many, Bush seemed a man of expedient positions rather than deeply held convictions, a suspicion harbored especially by far-right conservatives. "He's the dog that doesn't bark," said right-wing fund raiser Richard Viguerie in scorn. Bush played it safe. For years he endured whatever hand-dirtying chores were necessary to get the right wing off his back. In 1986, for instance, he accepted an invitation to speak at a dinner honoring William Loeb, publisher of New Hampshire's scurrilously right-wing Manchester *Union Leader*. Loeb had repeatedly abused Bush in print, calling him an incompetent hypocrite and, even worse, a wimp. So ingratiating were the Vice President's remarks about Loeb that even some of Bush's family members complained to him.

Politically, Bush knew how to settle for half. Sometimes he even courted the Democrats. In 1969 Bush, eager to run a second time for a Senate seat, was concerned that former President Lyndon Johnson—who had by then left the White House and returned home—might get in his way. Bush had started working on a strategy to neutralize Johnson. The day the former President departed Washington, while Republicans were celebrating at Richard Nixon's 1969 Inauguration parade, Congressman Bush turned up at Andrews Air Force Base outside Washington to say goodbye to the man Nixon was replacing. Johnson was startled by Bush's appearance but pleased nonetheless. Back in Texas, Bush made a secret trip to LBJ's ranch ostensibly to seek his advice about running for the Senate. News of such a visit could boost Bush's standing with Texas Democrats. Word of the visit did get out. The leaker, according to a 1988 Washington *Post* story based on information gathered from the Johnson library archives, was Bush. Later he sent a letter of apology to LBJ.

In 1970 President Nixon, trying to defeat a bloc of liberal Democrats seeking re-election, made a personal request that Bush try again for the Senate seat. Bush had already made up his mind to do so even though his father urged him not to. Ralph Yarborough again was the expected opponent, but in a surprise upset former Congressman Lloyd Bentsen defeated the incumbent Senator in the Democratic primary. Bush ran ahead of Bentsen for most of the campaign. But former Texas Governor John Connally managed through political allies like State Senator Barbara Jordan to spur a big black turnout that, coupled with a heavy rural Democratic vote, in the end helped topple Bush. Once again the Eastern achiever had been bested. Bush's children said they had never seen their father so dispirited. He even considered abandoning politics.

In his despondency, Bush turned again to a powerful sponsor, Richard Nixon. A month after Bush lost the Senate race, he was invited to join the Nixon Administration. For Bush it was the beginning of long and loyal service in the shadow of others. Until then, he had mostly made his own way. Now he was hooking himself to someone else's star. At 46, Bush was an attractive protégé. Nixon had considered offering him a White House job. Instead, Bush persuaded the President to make him U.S. Ambassador to the United Nations, convincing him that he could be useful not merely in putting the Nixon stamp on the U.S. mission there but also in enhancing the ever insecure President's standing in New York social circles. Nixon was impressed with the argument. For two years Bush served as ambassador, swinging through the delegates' dining room slapping backs and greeting ambassadors by their first names as if he were still prowling the back corridors of Congress.

At the U.N. Bush encountered figures who later came to power around the world. The experience heightened his passion for foreign affairs. He served faithfully and without complaint, even as his boss was secretly undermining his efforts. While Bush was publicly defending Taiwan's hapless efforts to retain its rightful seat among the family of nations, Nixon and Henry Kissinger were working behind his back to restore U.S. ties to Mainland China. Throughout his service at the U.N., Bush routinely dispatched warm notes of support to the President and his family. By now Bush was thinking of running for President, though he guessed that his time would not come until the end of the 1970s.

After Nixon won re-election in 1972, Bush hoped for a senior State Department job, as Deputy Secretary of State. But Nixon asked Bush to head the Republican National Committee, a less prestigious assignment. Reluctantly Bush accepted, after getting an assurance that he could attend Cabinet meetings. The new party chairman was unaware, of course, of the political ruin ahead. Within months Watergate erupted. A far worse event that fall was the death of Prescott Bush Sr., 77, who succumbed to cancer. In the next two years Bush took a mauling as he struggled to support the beleaguered President and still maintain the party's credibility, as well as his own. There were a few bright spots. As R.N.C. chairman, Bush strengthened his political connections around the country. He was an affable but not especially bold party chief. Colleagues at the national committee recalled that chairman Bush usually made decisions by counting pluses and minuses. When G.O.P. leaders around the country began to condemn the President and call openly for his resignation, Bush was trapped. He remained loyal to Nixon almost to the end, telling doubters that the President had assured him there was no cover-up. Only one day before Nixon stepped down did Bush finally urge in a letter that he quit. Wrote Bush: "I now feel your resignation is best for the country, best for this

President." All in all, it had been a miserable two years for the man who strove to please.

As Gerald Ford assumed the battered presidency, Bush once again sat expectantly in the wings. An appointed President now was to appoint his own Vice President, and Bush had reason to be optimistic. He radiated acceptability at a time when ethics were under assault. Besides, he was in good standing with the same party officials whom Ford now intended to consult before he made his Veep choice. Bush's spirit was buoyed by a private White House survey. By a count of 225 to 181, party leaders favored Bush over Nelson Rockefeller, according to the Washington *Post*. But Ford saw it differently. He wanted the more seasoned Rockefeller. Bush, waiting anxiously with Barbara in Kennebunkport for a phone call from the President, watched the event unfold on television. Minutes before Ford appeared on camera with his new Vice President, he telephoned Bush and told him the disappointing news.

There was some consolation for the party's top stand-in. Bush could have any ambassadorship he wanted. "George picked China," recalled a friend, "because he wanted to get as far away as possible from the stench of Watergate." Bush said he had other reasons. He liked a difficult challenge, and China represented the future. The Bushes landed in Beijing in the autumn of 1974 and plunged into the assignment with typical energy. On their bicycles, George and Barbara Bush became familiar figures pedaling through the streets of the Chinese capital. Eventually Bush's interest began to wane. As the political winds began to rise, so did his aspirations. Gerald Ford was certain to be the candidate, and Bush badly wanted to be his running mate. In the summer of 1975, after less than a year in China, Bush could begin thinking about the vice presidency again. First, however, he had to get out of Beijing.

Unexpectedly, Gerald Ford solved that problem for him by asking Bush to return to Washington to take charge of the Central Intelligence Agency. The CIA was demoralized. Intense congressional hearings had uncovered stories of assassination plots against foreign leaders, as well as spying on American citizens. In the President's view, the popular and untarnished Bush could help soothe Congress and restore CIA morale. Bush took a longer view. He was concerned that beginning such a difficult task just before the 1976 election might make it difficult for him to seek a place on the national ticket. He turned out to be right. Democratic members of the Senate Armed Services Committee—the panel that held hearings on CIA appointments—insisted as the price of confirmation that Ford rule out Bush as a running mate. Watergate still was in the air, and the Senators did not want to politicize the CIA. Ford acquiesced. The frustrated Bush, declaring that he did not like the idea of renouncing his political birthright as the price of confirmation, nevertheless went along.

It was the first time Bush, now 51, had ever headed a large operation. He was well received at the CIA and made no attempt to overhaul the agency. Instead, he worked to improve its image. "He did a great job with the Congress," said one agency veteran, who noted that Bush testified dozens of times before various committees. "No one could have done better." Bush's willingness to delegate responsibility on substantive issues to senior officials won him high marks. Morale quickly improved. Eventually Bush installed a few of his own people—a new deputy, a new director of operations and a new officer to coordinate activities with other intelligence agencies. But his tenure was too short for him to leave a deep imprint. From the start Bush loved the arcane ins and outs of spook talk. Later, as Vice President, he frequently chased down his old CIA buddies by phone in search of inside information. When Gerald Ford lost the 1976 election to Jimmy Carter, the eager Bush had no qualms about asking the President-elect to keep him on at the CIA. He had been director only 356 days. Bush even promised not to run for President in 1980. Carter, surprised by the proposal, wasted no time in saying no.

For the first time in ten years Bush was back in private life. He joined the boards of directors of several companies. One of them was Purolator, Inc., a manufacturer of automotive parts and provider of courier and armored-car services, whose chairman was his good friend Nicholas Brady. (More than a decade later, in 1988, Bush helped Brady secure the job of Treasury Secretary.) Within months Bush began assembling troops and money to make a run for the presidency.

By 1979, as the primaries approached, he was more than ready. He plunged into the campaign against Ronald Reagan with energy and a tendency to stress tactics at the expense of substance. When Bush won an upset victory over Reagan in the Iowa caucuses, top aides urged him to broaden his pitch. Now was the moment, they argued, for Bush to define himself, to lay out exactly how he stood on various issues and where he wanted to lead the country. Bush ignored the advice. Instead he filled the air with predictions of delegate counts and jubilant boasts of "big mo," Bush's term for momentum.

It was Bush at his compulsive worst. Even in his Texas campaigns, process seemed more important to him than ideas. While Bush surely understood the complexities of issues, he did not easily fit them into larger themes. This led to the familiar charge that Bush lacked vision, a judgment that rankled him. But he did seem unable to think or speak in broad and uplifting terms. "Ronald Reagan," declared one White House official who knew both men, "had his shining city on a hill. George just doesn't think that way." Idealized or abstract thinking was not his style. A few weeks later, he was defeated by Reagan in the New Hampshire primary, and in May he withdrew from the race.

The night of Ronald Reagan's nomination at the Republican Convention in Detroit, Bush sat nervously by a phone in a nearby hotel watching the event on television. There he was again, waiting. This time he had less hope than six years before. The former Governor of California, Bush knew, did not hold him in high regard. Their temperaments were drastically different. When Reagan late in the evening called and asked him to be his Vice President, Bush literally jumped off the floor in joy. Remembered Congressman Barber Conable, who was with him in the hotel room: "George was stunned. He never thought Reagan would pick him."

Once more Bush was back in loyal service. Cheerfully, he took on any assignment the new President gave him, sticking far in the background, leading the applause whenever possible for Reagan's programs. More than most Vice Presidents, Bush was aware of what was really going on around him. He lunched alone with the President weekly. His closest friend, James Baker, who had become White House chief of staff, looked out for the Vice President's interests. Both men understood that one day Bush might occupy the Oval Office.

In the past Bush had witnessed the slow undoing of other Vice Presidents. Nelson Rockefeller had told him personally how he was shut out of important decisions in the Ford White House. Early on, Bush decided he would maintain total silence regarding his dealings with the President. He would give his counsel to Reagan and no one else. When the aides who prepared Bush for his luncheon with Reagan, curious about the mealtime fate of their ideas, would ask about the President's reactions, the Vice President refused to answer.

Bush's solitary approach fit his upright nature. It was cautious and partly self-serving. In an Administration in which the President generally did what the consensus of his staff wanted, Bush—its most experienced member—had pulled back from the vital give-and-take of policy preparation. His chief mechanism for influencing decisions was a private relationship with the President, yet the President was not that important to the decision-making process. Thus it was difficult to tell where Bush stood on many policies, or to blame him if they failed.

The Vice President did have a few difficult moments. Two of Reagan's closest aides recalled Bush's clear discomfort with

Administration proposals aimed at rolling back civil rights legislation. After numerous meetings in the Oval Office, the aides
cornered Bush and urged him to confront Reagan. The President was making a serious mistake, they warned, and the Vice
President should tell him so. Bush was reluctant. Reagan, he
told them, had already made up his mind. Although no one truly knew how Bush handled the President alone, insiders say he
never made Reagan feel uncomfortable. The President from
time to time grumbled about overzealous associates like Defense
Secretary Caspar Weinberger and Secretary of State Alexander
Haig, but never about Bush.

Former Congressman Lud Ashley, one of Bush's closest
friends, believed that if there were a flaw in Bush it was his ability to tolerate compromise. "It's hard to account for his silence
on the issues he cares about," Ashley told the Washington *Post*.
Loyalty, Ashley observed, could be counterproductive. Perhaps
Bush did not learn as much from the Watergate experience as
he should have. But Ashley knew his buddy well. "Emotionally," said the Congressman, "George feels you can't be too loyal."

Though Reagan sometimes had only a tenuous grasp of
facts, he seemed to have little trouble standing firm on conten-
tious issues like abortion, which he opposed. That ability to ig-
nore complexity never failed to astonish Bush. Alone with his
staff, the Vice President was dogged and decisive, especially on
foreign policy subjects. Bush told them he had a coherent view
of the world that Reagan lacked. In public, however, Bush
seemed a different person. He followed the President's lead
slavishly. "I'm for Mr. Reagan, blindly," he often declared.
Without too much discomfort, he adopted many of Reagan's
views. Though he had once denounced supply-side theories as
"voodoo economics," for example, Bush became a cheerleader
for Reagan's supply-side tax cuts.

At the start Reagan had been lukewarm about his Vice
President. He had settled on Bush partly because he posed few
problems. As the years passed Reagan's appreciation for the

Vice President's loyalty and silence grew steadily. Bush never sought advantage for himself. As he had done before with higher-ups, Bush won Reagan over. He took on any number of unpleasant chores, like addressing a hostile N.A.A.C.P. convention that the President had chosen to duck, or paving the way for the delicate removal of an ambassador.

There were moments of high achievement too. Reagan sent the Vice President to Western Europe in February 1983 to press for the installation of cruise and Pershing II intermediate-range missiles. Bush's forceful articulation of the U.S. position helped persuade European leaders to proceed with the deployment despite widespread popular opposition. Later that year Bush went to El Salvador and firmly told right-wing military leaders that the country's death squads were getting out of hand. For whatever reason, officially sanctioned death-squad activity later diminished.

Both Bush and his wife courted the Reagans at every opportunity. Routinely they dispatched approving notes after the President or his wife made public appearances. Sometimes Bush's extraordinary capacity for punishment was sorely tested. During the uproar over the sale of U.S. arms to Iran and the diversion of funds to the *contras,* as the President was drawing considerable criticism, Bush maintained his usual discreet silence. This time it got him into trouble. Nancy Reagan soon began running Bush down in her private conversations, arguing that Bush should be speaking out in her husband's defense. The Vice President's silence, she told friends, was inexcusable. That was a remarkable point of view, considering Bush's long and obsequious service.

The real dilemma of Bush's vice-presidential silence was that it gave rise to suspicions he had nothing to say. Before he could prove otherwise, his admirers argued, Bush needed first to discover himself. The long shadow of his father, and Bush's history of pliability and subordination to others, had created uncertainty in his own mind about what he believed in. For nearly eight years he had faithfully remained at the side of a President, taking pride in Reagan's accomplishments but not bothering to carve out a separate public identity for himself.

Only when Bush stepped before the Republican Convention in New Orleans to accept his party's nomination for President did he seem to shed the heavy burden of servility to Ronald Reagan. At last he was on his own, and the experience was visibly liberating. As the campaign progressed, the vigorous, decisive Bush that close friends had long recognized came to the fore, and the awkward, deferential servant of Reagan began to fade. He waded into Michael Dukakis, his Democratic opponent, with almost unseemly glee. Bush was more aggressive than he had ever been, still lurching out of control at times but clearly more sure of himself. There remained the large, unanswered question of his ability to stand alone and lead. But his oft repeated claim to leadership—"I am that man," he kept telling the country about his new sense of purpose—had a different ring. There was George Bush, speaking in the first person singular. Old family lessons about modesty and teamwork seemed to fall away. The young Greenwich schoolboy who claimed no more than his fair share of time and attention was now ready to claim the presidency.

5

The Democrats

HARRY S TRUMAN WAS ELECTED PRESIDENT OF THE U.S. IN 1948, upsetting Republican Thomas E. Dewey and the applecarts of prognosticators from Las Vegas to Lloyd's of London. As the doughty Truman explained it, the significance of his victory was clear: so visibly and viscerally had the Democrats become the party of the ordinary American that the Republicans might never win another presidential election.

Truman outlived his prophecy by quite a few years. Republican Dwight D. Eisenhower easily toppled Truman's handpicked candidate, Adlai Stevenson, in 1952 and 1956, and the worst was yet to come. In 1968 Truman's least favorite politician, Richard Nixon, won the White House, and he retained it in 1972, sweeping 49 states. The myopic Missourian was not around to witness the muggings administered to his party by former Democrat Ronald Reagan in 1980 and 1984. Were it not for a Republican-engineered constitutional amendment limiting Presidents to two terms, Reagan—at 77—might have managed to inflict a third drubbing in 1988.

Far from obtaining an exclusive franchise on the White House, the Democrats lost four of the five presidential elections from 1968 through 1984, three of them in Republican landslides. The G.O.P. captured all of the once solid South against Democrat Hubert Humphrey in 1968, except for Texas, where Lyndon Johnson and John Connally—then Governor and still a Democrat—were in control. In the West, national Democrats also were becoming personae non gratae. Nixon that year won everything in the region except Hawaii and Washington. Four years later, George McGovern was wiped out in the West, South, North and East, except for Massachusetts. In 1976, in the wake of the Watergate scandals and with Georgian Jimmy Carter at the head of the ticket, Democrats managed to carry twelve Southern and Border States, but blanked in the West, winning no states there. In 1980 not even regional pride could propel Carter in the South. He carried only five states besides his own and was completely shut out in the West. Walter Mondale in 1984 duplicated McGovern's dubious feat of carrying only a single state, in his case his native Minnesota.

The country was not happy with the Democrats. Was this still the party of Truman and Roosevelt? For the most part, the answer was yes. But just as the Democratic Party of Thomas Jefferson and Andrew Jackson bore little resemblance to the party of Roosevelt's New Deal or Truman's Fair Deal, so the party that was led—most often to defeat—by Stevenson, McGovern, Carter and Mondale differed dramatically from that of the Democrats of the 1930s and 1940s. The soufflé of change contained numerous ingredients, the most challenging of which was race. Another element difficult to swallow: the Democrats had somehow allowed themselves to appear unpatriotic.

Thus as Democrats pondered how they could win back the White House in 1988, they faced gigantic obstacles, including, unfortunately, a field of seven candidates who were immediately labeled "the seven dwarfs." The name stuck, even when the

field grew to eight. Should a giant have emerged from this band
of relative nonentities, he would still have faced what had become for Democrats a daunting hurdle: of 270 electoral votes required to win the White House, the Republicans, based on recent elections and barring aberrations (such as Watergate and
Carter), had a near-automatic lock on 202. For a Democrat to
win, he would have to take nearly 90% of the remainder. The
Democrats had to make inroads in the South and the West or
else remain on the outside looking in at 1600 Pennsylvania Avenue. They could not afford to let 1988 slip by. For the first time
since 1968, an incumbent President would not be on the ballot.
Of equal importance: Ronald Reagan would not be around to
batter the party to which he had once belonged.

In the 1960s John F. Kennedy and Lyndon B. Johnson
presided over a Democratic interregnum that both followed and
preceded modern-day Republican dominance in presidential
elections. Kennedy bequeathed two major legacies to his successor: the war in Viet Nam and an uncompleted, in fact, barely
launched, civil rights agenda. Both of those issues sundered the
nation. Kennedy won the presidency in 1960 by a hair, but by
1963—and despite the Bay of Pigs—he had captivated the
country and much of the world. He had not flinched in impos-
ing court-required integration at the University of Alabama
and the University of Mississippi. Even more impressive, he
had forced Nikita Khrushchev to blink first during the 1962 Cu-
ban missile crisis.

These triumphs merely deepened the national anguish
when Kennedy was assassinated. Johnson, proud but painfully
aware that he lacked the effortless charm of his predecessor,
played to his own strength: remarkable legislative skill that enabled him to force through Congress a civil rights revolution
that no non-Southerner, and perhaps no one but Lyndon Baines
Johnson, could have achieved. A side effect grossly underestimated at the time: from the 1960s on, the Democratic Party, in
the eyes of many white Southerners particularly but of many

whites elsewhere as well, was the party of black America and no party of theirs. Franklin Roosevelt was the first Democrat to attract a significant number of votes from blacks, whose Republicanism harked back to the Reconstruction. But the trend toward the Democrats was to accelerate for blacks. Unhappily for the party, whites fled in their wake, at least in presidential balloting.

Under Democratic regimes and auspices, black Americans had broken free of the poll tax. They had gained voting rights. They had been admitted to public accommodations and to public schools and universities. They had been freed from legal restrictions on where they could live. True, it was the Supreme Court that put an end to the doctrine of separate but equal and ruled the poll tax and racial covenants in real estate unconstitutional. But it was Democrat Truman who desegregated the armed forces and Democrat Johnson who bulldozed voting rights and civil rights bills through to enactment. Decades later, 85% to 90% of black voters were still choosing Democratic candidates for President.

But the other spokes in the wheel Roosevelt had forged —the winning coalition of the South, organized labor, the elderly (thanks in part to Social Security), Northern liberals and ethnic blue-collar voters—were weakening, and in the case of the South, crumbling. The perception Roosevelt had managed to avoid attached itself to his successors: the Democratic Party became the party not just of blacks, but of "welfare queens" (Ronald Reagan gets credit for an assist here), of high tax rates to support the swelling public-assistance rolls, of mindless Government spending on programs that did not work, of huge deficits and finally of a frightening underconcern for the nation's security in the face of an ever present Soviet threat.

The Democrats opened their gates wide to accommodate the changed demographics of the nation. They were, they insisted, the party of inclusion. Toward the banner of Roosevelt-Truman-Kennedy-Johnson flowed not just blacks but Hispanics, Asians, feminists, gays, lesbians: the left-outs. But the problem for the Democrats, in political analyst Richard Scammon's memorable phrase of the late 1960s, was that the American electorate was, for the most part, "unyoung, unpoor and unblack." In the 1970s and 1980s, Scammon could have added that it was also un-Hispanic, un-Asian, unfeminist and unhomosexual. Not only did the politics of inclusion offend the majority whites, but some of the newly included turned each other off. Perhaps the most disenchanted of all were blue-collar ethnics—Poles, Irish, Czechs, Italians, most of them Catholics—who saw themselves as victimized by Democratic programs that their tax money paid for and that they believed chiefly benefited people who lived on the dole. Organized labor invariably endorsed the Democratic candidate for President, except for McGovern. But just as invariably, the rank and file voted in large numbers for the Republican.

Kennedy's second bequest to Johnson, the war in Viet Nam, plunged much of the nation into protest and gloom. The long-haired, unwashed masses led marches on the Pentagon, the Capitol and the White House, smoked illegal substances, tossed rocks and torches, and turned the 1968 Democratic National Convention into a funeral pyre for Hubert Humphrey's presidential prospects. Previously, the protesters had driven Lyndon Johnson from the race. They saw the Democratic Party as their only hope for change, but their methods sickened what journalist Joseph Kraft would describe, and Richard Nixon adopt, as Middle America. This was your ordinary, patriotic, hardworking American, bewildered that in time of war all citizens would not rally behind their Government, right or wrong. Civil disturbances, whether for civil rights or against the war, deeply offended white Middle America. The left regarded the Republican Party as sterile and as the preserve of the rich, stodgy and predictable. But to Middle America, Republicans had come to represent stability and patriotism. The Democrats would be made to pay the price for their tolerance of dissent and diversity. The price was the White House in 1968. The price was paid again in 1972, when George McGovern, at best a poor choice for the nomination, could not live down the unfair charge that he was the candidate of amnesty, acid and abortion.

Nixon, whose intelligence was never enough to offset his deficiency of character, gave the Democrats an opportunity to regain respectability and competitiveness in presidential elections when he resigned his high office in 1974 in the wake of the Watergate scandal, just a step ahead of impeachment. In 1976 Jimmy Carter, a Georgian pillar of rectitude, gave the Democrats their only victory in a presidential race since 1964 when he defeated Gerald Ford, the pardoner of Nixon. But by 1980 Carter—bedeviled by record-high inflation, his inability to gain freedom for 52 Americans held hostage in Iran and what he termed a national malaise—was forced by voters to yield the office back to the Republicans after a single unremarkable term. Ronald Reagan, a former movie actor supposedly too far right to be electable, easily turned away Carter's bid for re-election in 1980. With even less effort, Reagan defeated the Georgian's Vice President, Walter Mondale, in the 49-state debacle of 1984.

But despite its .200 batting average in the five previous presidential elections, the Democratic Party was very much alive at the congressional, statehouse, courthouse and city-hall levels as the 1988 election approached. Except for a two-year hiatus in the Eisenhower years of 1952-54, the House of Representatives has been solidly Democratic for nearly four decades. Democrats also controlled the Senate, most of the governorships and a majority of the state legislatures, and had a virtual lock on big-city mayors' offices.

Many Democrats believed they could recapture the presidency in 1988 only if the party's noisy constituencies would mute their "special interest" pleadings, which had been so damaging to Mondale. To that end, a group of middle-of-the-road elected Democrats, including Georgia Senator Sam Nunn and former Virginia Governor Charles Robb, the latter a son-in-law of Lyndon Johnson, made plans to form the Democratic Leadership Council with two avowed aims: 1) to nudge the party back toward the center, where elections are won, and 2) to organize a Southern-states primary to blunt the power of the liberal Democrats. The liberals had dominated the crucial Iowa caucuses and New Hampshire primary for years, and thus had had a disproportionate voice in selection of the Democratic nominees.

The D.L.C. was seen by the party's left as a disruptive influence intent on converting the Democratic Party into a pale offshoot of the Republicans. The council's founders included a dominant number of white Southerners. Among them were Albert Gore, Tennessee's engaging freshman Senator, and Richard Gephardt, the Missouri Representative so popular with his colleagues but hardly known to anyone else. Gephardt made no secret of his presidential ambitions. Nunn and Robb were thought to have been bitten by the same virus. But if this was a power grab by the moderates, the party's left seemed to be in a poor position to resist. Its elements simply did not add up to enough electoral votes to win a national election. Walter Mondale, experienced, intelligent and decent, had not even tried to obscure the fact that he was the candidate of labor, the education lobby, blacks, Hispanics, gays, feminists (he did, after all, comply with the National Organization for Women's demand that he choose a woman as his running mate) and other voter blocs with their own agendas. Even before he got to the general election, Mondale had been challenged during the primaries by Gary Hart, the upstart Senator from Colorado who came within an inch of stealing the nomination from Mondale. Hart dared Mondale to state one issue on which he disagreed with organized labor. When it took Mondale three days to come up with "substantive" but unspecified differences, he was indelibly stamped.

But the D.L.C. alone would not be able to force the Democrats to the center. The party would need the resources and the apparatus of the Democratic National Committee, plus whatever other help it could obtain. To that end, the elected officeholders who would later form the Democratic Leadership Council had tried to elect one of their own as Democratic national chairman. Their choice was Terry Sanford, a former Governor of North Carolina, a former president of Duke University and a John Kennedy Democrat, who gave the party an opportunity to wrest control from its liberal wing. But other moderates thought Sanford too old and insufficiently dynamic in the television era. So a multicandidate field competed hotly for the chairmanship, and the fractured centrists watched with dismay as Paul Kirk, a Boston attorney who was a veteran of the Senate and presidential campaigns of Massachusetts Senator Edward M. Kennedy, was elected to the post.

Kirk had campaigned for the chairmanship as a moderate who knew the Democrats had to shake their "special interests" image in order to win. But he gained few converts from the party's center and none from its right. In fact, Kirk would have been a prohibitive favorite from the start to win the chairmanship save for the Kennedy connection, which was poison with Southern and Western delegations. Kirk's protestations that he would steer the party on a moderate course went unheard. Yet he won the post, largely because of the strength of his liberal backers and the weakness of the fragmented opposition.

After his selection, Kirk met with Nunn, Robb, Gephardt and others, urging that they forget about forming a Democratic Leadership Council and instead join in strengthening the national committee for a victory in the 1988 presidential election. Kirk insisted that he shared their objectives, but they found that difficult to swallow from a Ted Kennedy liberal. Even when Kirk named an advisory committee headed by the moderate former Governor of Utah, Scott Matheson, they were not convinced. The Nunn-Robb group looked upon itself as the party's future. The Democratic Leadership Council was formally organized exactly a month after Kirk's election as D.N.C. chairman.

What the D.L.C. could not sense was that the low-key Kirk was fundamentally of a mind with them. He set about both to convince them and to advance his own agenda. Kirk persuaded the national committeemen and -women that the party's midterm convention, held halfway through a presidential term, had become an albatross, an event at which special interests could showcase their causes and pressure prospective candidates in an unseemly spectacle that turned off voters. The midterm session was abandoned.

Next he took on organized labor, urging leaders of the AFL-CIO not to endorse a presidential candidate until after the primaries and caucuses. In declaring support for Mondale before a single vote had been cast, labor had painted him in its own hues, a minus to much of the electorate and especially deadly in the South. The labor bosses publicly spurned Kirk's plea, but they clearly heard it. In 1988 labor did not endorse a candidate until after the Democrats had chosen their nominee. (Nonetheless, almost half the delegates at the 1988 Democratic National Convention in Atlanta were representatives of organized labor, a fact that went virtually unnoticed by press and politicians alike.)

Next, Kirk turned to the party's special caucuses, which had proliferated over the years of "inclusion." The blacks had their own caucus within the Democratic National Committee. So did women, Hispanics, the elderly, educators, organized labor, gays and lesbians. Kirk succeeded in abolishing nearly all of them. He managed in subtle ways to assure these interest groups that the Democratic Party still had their concerns at heart but that it could not advance them most effectively without winning national elections. Having witnessed the Mondale debacle, leaders of the various caucuses were, for the most part, persuadable.

Kirk's pitch to them boiled down to this: what is important to your group is your issues, not having center stage. Your prominence at the convention and elsewhere is irrelevant; your issues are not. Kirk, a quiet, unassuming sort, would never have uttered a comment attributed to Peter Kostmayer, a Pennsylvania Congressman, which caused a furor but contained at least an element of truth. Kostmayer in an unguarded moment had said, "Just shut up, gays, women, environmentalists. Just shut up. You'll get everything you want after the election. But just for the meantime, shut up so that we can win." The editorial page of the *Wall Street Journal,* not accustomed to praising Democrats, sarcastically gave Kostmayer high marks for his "honesty."

The Eight Dwarfs

And so the Democratic stage was set for 1988, through arduous, behind-the-scenes finagling by party officials who not only sensed the problem (even the man-in-the-street sensed the problem) but were determined to fix it. That repair work well toward completion, the way was cleared for the entrance of the main players. Eight would-be candidates—six fresh, two leftover—presented themselves to America in 1987 and 1988, and were greeted for the most part with derision.

The memory of the electorate is short. In all presidential elections, aspirants seem wretchedly inadequate, except perhaps for an incumbent. Once having reached or nearly reached the White House, politicians are strangely ennobled. Death helps too. Harry Truman is no longer that commonplace Missouri haberdasher and lackey for boss Pendergast, as he was depicted, accurately, in 1944 and 1948. Jack Kennedy is no longer perceived as a misplaced Hollywood glamour boy of limited intellect and flexible convictions, as he was known circa 1958-60. Hubert Humphrey, in his day discounted as a blabbermouth, lives in memory as a compassionate and beloved public servant. Even Richard Nixon, whose presidential potential was scorned in 1960 and again in 1968, is respected today for his foreign-affairs expertise. Ronald Reagan, the Hollywood has-been who, given half a chance, would supposedly lead the world to nuclear holocaust, was in 1988 about to leave office with the threat of human annihilation somewhat more remote than it was when he started. Regrettably, the lessons of history must be relearned.

Thus America looked with disdain at the Democrats who entered the 1988 presidential race and lavished its esteem on those who did not. When a players' strike forced the Washington Redskins to field a football team of castoffs during the fall of 1987, a political dinner speaker observed that the Democrats, like the Redskins, were playing the game but were unable to field their first string. In the minds of many Democrats, the first team consisted of New York Governor Mario Cuomo, he of the golden tonsils and a personality borrowed from Hamlet; Sam Nunn, the answer to every Southern double-dog Democrat's prayers but a nightmare to the party's dominant liberal wing; Bill Bradley, the New Jersey Senator, Rhodes Scholar and former New York Knicks basketball hero who found even Third World debt a fascinating topic for leisure-time chitchat; and Senator Kennedy of Massachusetts, the marred and scarred no-longer-young brother of two martyred national heroes.

Pundits decided that the cream of the Democratic Party had chosen to sit this one out because 1) no Democrat could win, 2) even if one could, he would be fated to preside over a hair-curling recession that would guarantee him a niche in history just below Herbert Hoover's, or 3) after four more years of Republican-mismanaged economic distress, 1992 would look much more promising. In truth, Cuomo vacillated until it was no longer possible for him to make a graceful entry; the pragmatist Nunn realized his Southern-fried voting record would cause a left-leaning Democratic National Convention to gag; Bradley, who kept insisting that his "internal clock" told him it was not the time for adventure, sincerely wanted to get a deeper and more realistic grasp of the country before he made his move; and Kennedy had at last realized that he could not successfully carry into a presidential campaign all the baggage from his past.

That left the dwarfs.

Jesse Jackson

Making his second try for the presidency, Jackson was both a refreshing breeze and an ill wind for the Democrats. In 1984 he had attempted to form a multihued "rainbow coalition" of blacks, Hispanics, Asians, disenchanted whites and whoever else cared to tag along. His coalition never coalesced; but by depriving Mondale of the black vote, essentially all that Jackson attracted that year, the black preacher enabled Gary Hart to survive all the way to the San Francisco convention. Had Jackson not been in the race, Mondale would have received the bulk of the vote from blacks, who knew little about Hart and did not particularly care to learn more. Had Jackson not deprived Mondale of the urban black vote in New York and Pennsylvania and the votes of rural blacks in the South, Mondale would have been swept to the nomination with ridiculous ease.

Jackson had proved himself a burr in the Democratic hide. He constantly complained about the party rules, seeking to change them even after he had played the game. His very presence in the race shouted what Democratic strategists preferred to whisper, that this was the party of non-whites. Alternately, he had pledged fealty to the Democratic organization and threatened to abandon it and lead his followers elsewhere, though it was never clear exactly where. Forced by Jackson into a balancing act, the Democrats wobbled between promising blacks too much, thus alienating more whites, and promising them nothing, thus tempting black voters to stay home on Election Day.

Jesse Jackson was never a credible contender for the 1988 presidential nomination nor a truly serious possibility for Vice President. In the late stages of the campaign, Jackson insisted that "I am qualified—qualified, qualified, qualified," ignoring the dictum that if he were, people would know and he would not have to keep telling them. True, Jackson could be an inspiring speaker, yet has never held nor even run for public office, other than that of President. His administrative experience has been limited to directing Operation PUSH, a Chicago-based self-help organization for blacks, hardly a training ground for a would-be leader of the free world. Jackson refused to seek offices of lower rank than the presidency, nor did he go out of his way to mend his tattered relations with Jews, who were uneasy over his affectionate encounters with Yassir Arafat, his 1984 reference to New York as "Hymietown," and his refusal to repudiate black Muslim Louis Farrakhan for anti-Semitic public bellowing. Jackson in his two races at least took clear and courageous stands on the issues, but those positions were too far left to have wide appeal.

Although not a plausible potential nominee, Jackson would be more formidable in 1988 than he had been four years earlier. He milked the farm belt for votes, even if they were just protest ballots from a segment of society that saw itself as neglected. Jackson's rhetoric was less biting, less radical and more populist in 1988. He talked to janitors, assembly-line workers, secretaries, nurses, the underpaid and the underappreciated of society, of whatever color or origin. No candidate of either party saw, or dared to say that he saw, the plight of the oft-hated and shunned homosexual as clearly and as sympathetically as Jesse Jackson.

His one impressive primary-campaign success came in Michigan, a caucus state. For the first time, he received a significant vote from whites, briefly igniting hope in his followers and fear in his foes. But postcaucus analyses pointed out that only a tiny fraction of Michigan Democrats participated in the caucus. Worse, Jackson's white vote was heavily weighted with support from two groups: 1) young people, who tend to disappear when general elections roll around, and 2) affluent white liberals, who turn pragmatic after a few shouts of "I'm mad as hell, and I'm not going to take it any more!" during primary season. In 1988 as in 1984, it was Jackson's fate to instill pride in millions of blacks, no mean accomplishment, but in the end to wither and die unplucked from the political vine.

Gary Hart

To some students of politics, the Democrats' singular lack of success in presidential politics is not a subject requiring much thought. Among those who believe that the problem is evident are Hale Champion, former dean of the Kennedy School of Government at Harvard University, and former Attorney General Griffin Bell, who so effectively managed John Kennedy's 1960 campaign in Georgia that the young Senator carried the Peach State by a larger percentage than he did his native Massachusetts. When asked, as he often is, how the Democrats can regain their lost luster in the South, Bell replied, "There's no mystery to that. All they have to do is nominate somebody we want to vote for. It's as simple as that." A transplanted Californian, Champion applies somewhat the same yardstick to that other graveyard for Democratic presidential aspirations, the West. Musing about his party's repeated burials in Western landslides, Champion some years back observed, "You can't sell a personality like Carter's or McGovern's west of the Mississippi." He might have added the equally unsalable Mondale to that list, but he did not, and some years later the former Vice President went out and proved there had been an oversight.

In Gary Hart, the Democrats had a 1988 front runner who at least projected the virile, Marlboro Man persona of a Reagan or a Jack Kennedy, who in some ways he resembled. After finishing second in the 1984 Iowa caucuses, Hart had gone on to New Hampshire and emerged as the candidate of the large and amorphous "Anybody-but-Mondale" crowd. Hart was destined to rise—and fall—like a meteor. After winning New Hampshire and several other primaries, he responded poorly to the intense scrutiny that is the lot of any presidential contender. He could not explain satisfactorily why he had changed his name from Hartpence to Hart or why he had lied about his age. Mondale inflicted the mortal wound by borrowing a popular slogan —"Where's the beef?"—from Wendy's TV commercials. The shot was cheap but effective. Hart actually had more substance than he was able to convey. Mostly, however, Hart came across as weird, as someone who could not permit the electorate to know him as he really was. The reason for that became universally clear in late 1987, when Gary Hart's fling with model Donna Rice and revelations of numerous other dalliances knocked him off the front runner pedestal and, eventually, right out of the presidential race. Hart had had a long-standing and well-deserved reputation as a politician with a roving eye. But his closest followers were buoyed when the Coloradan assured them, prior to announcing his candidacy, that he was well aware what it meant to be the front runner: that the scrutiny from the press and rival camps would be intense. He would ensure that it also would be futile, Hart told these people about to give up jobs, home life, opportunities and personal ambitions to advance his candidacy. The New York *Times* Magazine published a cover story on Hart in which he acknowledged the swirl of rumors about his sex life, though without denying them, it seemed. He invited reporters to "put a tail" on him, adding that they would be "very bored."

The Miami *Herald* took up the challenge, and no one was very bored. A *Herald* detail spotted Hart and Rice entering his Washington town house late one night and leaving several hours later. Soon it was discovered that they had been together at least once before, on a boat devastatingly named *Monkey Business* on a cruise to Bimini. For days thereafter, Hart was talking about nothing other than Rice and his views on adultery. When the Washington *Post* questioned him about his relationship with another woman, Hart quit the race, angrily denouncing the press for his woes. Later, his loyal wife Lee at his side, he declared he would rejoin it, saying "the people" had the right to decide. When he finished out of the money in Iowa, Hart realized the people had decided that he was not presidential material. He withdrew a second time, and the Democrats continued their search for a nominee.

Albert Gore

Race is rarely mentioned in political circles, except when the doors are closed. Republicans agree—not all of them gleefully—that race is an issue that works for them. Some will protest that it cuts both ways, since the large black vote is the most monolithic of any bloc's, and it is reliably Democratic in all regions of the country. But only about 15% of the population is black. Spoken or not, there is a reason why the Democrats' formerly solid South is now the Republicans' most reliable base. For decades the South could not forgive the party of Abraham Lincoln and Ulysses S. Grant for the Civil War, the Reconstruction and carpetbagging. Not until the Democrats in 1928 nominated a Catholic, New York Governor Al Smith, could a substantial number of Southern voters bring themselves to vote Republican. They returned to the Democratic fold for F.D.R. and Truman, but clearly the Democratic Party was becoming too liberal (i.e., pro–civil rights) for white Southerners, and for many Northerners as well. Republican Eisenhower carried much of the South against Stevenson, and Kennedy needed Texas' Lyndon Johnson on his ticket to ensure victory. Even Barry Goldwater in 1964 did better in the South than anywhere else. From 1968 on, as far as the Democrats were concerned, the South was gone. The lone exception, Jimmy Carter's 1976 win, could be attributable to regional pride. But even though Carter carried some Southern states that year and in 1980, in neither case did he take a majority of the Southern white vote.

In fact, there was a school of thought that the Democrats should forget about the South and focus on the West in an attempt to break the Republican lock. The notion gained support from a number of state and regional polls indicating a growing sentiment in the usually anti-Washington Rocky Mountain states and the Pacific Northwest for more Federal Government action on social issues, including free health care for the needy, national health insurance and help for the homeless. The trend was later confirmed in a Times-Mirror survey by Gallup that found Democrat Dukakis favored over Republican Bush 51% to 39% in the Rocky Mountain region. For other reasons, such as Dukakis' inept campaign and his position in favor of gun control, the lead proved evanescent. But chairman Kirk and other Democratic leaders would not hear of giving up the South. When, they would ask, had a Democrat been elected President without carrying the South? The answer was never. Thus they chose Atlanta as the site for their 1988 convention, even though the city was only marginally adequate for handling the horde of delegates and journalists sure to attend. But Atlanta was in the South. There the Democrats would look for electoral votes and, in furtherance of that search, for someone to put on their ticket.

Thus in 1988 the Mondale-Geraldine Ferraro pairing of four years earlier (Northerner and Northerner, liberal and liberal) still pained, and the Democratic need was for an un-Carter-like Southerner either as presidential candidate or running mate. (Jackson frequently identified himself as a Southerner since he was born and grew up in South Carolina; but even if he had not become a Chicagoan, he was not what the Democrats had in mind.) Carter had at least proved that for the first time since the Civil War, a candidate from the Deep South could be elected. Alabama's Governor George Wallace, Florida's former Governor Reubin Askew and South Carolina's Senator Ernest Hollings had offered themselves at various times but found few takers. The Democrats were eyeing people like Georgia's Sam Nunn, chairman of the Senate Armed Services Committee, whose expertise and hawkishness on defense matters would defuse that potent Republican issue, and Virginia's Charles Robb, who had molded his state's moribund Democratic Party into a force that twice swept the top three state-wide offices. But Robb was biding his time (at 49 he had plenty of it) before seeking national office, and Nunn decided that remaining one of the Senate's most powerful committee chairmen was preferable to a high-risk bid for a nomination probably beyond his grasp.

Enter Albert Gore, the handsome and able though still moist-behind-the-ears Senator from Tennessee. Little known nationally and late getting into the race, Gore correctly anticipated poor showings in Iowa and New Hampshire and cushioned the adverse fallout by investing little time and money in each. He would demonstrate, Gore said, that these two small and unrepresentative states were not crucial to the nomination. His remarkable showing on Super Tuesday, when he captured five Southern and border states plus Nevada and 26% of all votes cast that day, seemed to vindicate his judgment. Now if Gore could win a Northern primary, talk that he was really after the vice-presidential nomination would dissipate. Gore would be a genuine contender for the brass ring.

"Tonight we said no to the old ways of doing things," he exulted as the Super Tuesday vote was tallied. "Tonight we showed it could be done. Our much maligned strategy turned out to be right all along." Was the handsome Tennessean the Southern savior for whom the Democrats had been searching? Perhaps. But reporters interviewing Gore voters detected a possibly fatal barrier. The Alabama speaker of the state house of representatives, Jimmy Clark, said he had urged people to vote for Gore "because he's very Southern." Said former North Carolina Governor Jim Hunt: "He has tremendous energy and ability." Hunt added, tellingly, "He's a Southerner." Susan Pemberton, another Alabaman, chose Gore "because he's a Southerner and a gentleman." Gore would have to engender support elsewhere in the country, where Southernism alone would not be such a positive force. But few Super Tuesday voters had cited any other reason for voting for him.

The Tennessean, who was then only 39, zeroed in on New York for the desperately needed Northern breakthrough. Not only was its primary election crucial to his plans, but the state's demographics were encouraging. Jackson would win the large black vote and also capture a huge chunk of the left-liberal crowd, which would prefer Massachusetts Governor Michael

Dukakis to Gore if Jackson were not in the race. Now, thought Gore, if only I can appeal to the Jewish vote, which is about 25% of the total in the New York Democratic primary. Conservative Democrats would surely be his in any face-off with Dukakis and Jackson. Unfortunately for Gore, there are not enough Jews or conservative Democrats in New York. Still, the Empire State for a moment looked promising. The two most visible Democrats in the state, Governor Cuomo and Mayor Ed Koch, had not taken sides. That was considered a blow to Dukakis, who had expected Cuomo's endorsement. Koch was a loose cannon, but he had taken Gore under his wing, teaching him such campaign skills as how to talk in broadcast-ready "sound bites," how to eat standing up and how to say all the right things about Israel. After declaring that Jews would have to be "crazy" to vote for Jackson, the mayor bit the bullet and endorsed Gore.

Although it was not considered so at the time, the alliance with Koch was the final nail in the coffin of Gore's presidential hopes. As controversy swirled around the prickly mayor and the question of why he was backing Gore, the candidate could barely be seen, much less heard. He was relegated to the wings while Koch held center stage, fending off verbal attacks from local black leaders and his numerous other opponents. Gore finished a poor third in New York. Although he would go through some more motions, essentially his campaign was over. The experience may have seasoned Gore for a future year. But in 1988 the most he could hope for was that the Democratic nominee would ask him to be his running mate.

Biden, Babbitt, Simon and Gephardt

Four of the Democrats' dwarfs had their brief moments in the campaign of 1988, but none of the four metamorphosed into a truly serious contender. Underfinanced and underknown, each clung to a slender thread of fantasy: if only the electorate could come to know him as he really was and understood his positions on the issues, he would be transformed. It is a common and recurring delusion of the genus *Politicus,* afflicting Vice Presidents, Senators and Governors. They are spurred to greater goals by two factors: susceptibility to the sycophancy in which they dwell, at least until the next election, and a tendency to survey the field of candidates and adjudge themselves superior to it.

Congressmen, by contrast, are typically propelled into presidential politics by memory lapses: they forget that no one outside their home districts has ever heard of them, and that no President has been elected from the House of Representatives since James A. Garfield in 1880. Lionel Van Deerlin, who ably represented a Southern California district in the House during the 1960s and '70s, was startled by a poll indicating that after several years of appearing regularly on a local television program, writing a newspaper column that carried his picture and winning several elections to Congress, his name was familiar to only 38% of his constituents.

Bruce Babbitt, a two-term Governor of Arizona, launched his presidential campaign two years early. That did not give him nearly enough time to make a positive impact on the national Democratic Party. Even if Babbitt had succeeded in creating a favorable impression, he was as doomed as a soldier who runs off to battle without his weapon. Since at least 1960, television has been a crucial tool of the political trade. That is especially true at the national level, where TV is the only means through which a candidate can eventually reach millions of voters. Yet Babbitt, an earnest and effective politician in his home state, seemed blissfully unaware of that dictum. In the first televised debate with his rivals for the nomination, Babbitt looked like the crooked man with the crooked smile. He sounded like an uncontrollable gusher. His views were courageous and nonconformist, and included use of the dreaded "T" word, taxes. In a subsequent debate, Babbitt rose dramatically to his feet, declared that whoever became President would have to raise taxes to cut the deficit, that he would do so if elected, and asked,

Would any of his rivals care to stand up and also acknowledge this truth? None did. After the negative reviews of his performance on television, Babbitt made the endearing concession that he would submit to coaching, on the theory that if Mr. Ed, a horse, could be trained to talk on television, so could Bruce Babbitt. Alas, Mr. Ed received his training *before*, not after, he first went on television. The Babbitt campaign never became airborne.

An even briefer stroll through political fantasyland was that taken by Senator Joseph Biden of Delaware, a garrulous and glib Eastern liberal with a modest reputation for oratorical persuasiveness. Biden was just what the party was not looking for, a candidate more representative of its problems than of its solutions. In the Senate, he had risen to prominence by the only route that body venerates, seniority. As ranking Democrat on the Judiciary Committee, he became chairman when Ted Kennedy, now a certified graybeard with top seniority on two committees, resigned the Judiciary post in order to chair Labor and Human Resources. For a brief moment, Biden took on the appearance of a running back for whom a huge lineman had just opened up some daylight: the Judiciary Committee would be holding hearings on the controversial nomination of Judge Robert Bork to the Supreme Court. What an opportunity for Biden, presiding as television cameras whirred, to appear before a national audience and break out of the pack of dwarfs! It happened, but not the way Biden and his followers had in mind. As the hearings got under way, Biden was caught delivering, without attribution or more than minor alteration, a political speech used effectively by the British Labor Party leader Neil Kinnock. "Why is it that Joe Biden is the first in his family ever to go to a university?" Biden asked in imitation of Kinnock's quote: "Why am I the first Kinnock in a thousand generations to be able to get to university?" Examination of his other speeches indicated that Biden owed a considerable unacknowledged debt to Robert Kennedy, or at least to Kennedy's speech writers. Plagiarism was not a new twist in Biden's life—he had been accused of it years before in law school. The revelations ended Biden's presidential quest. He had committed the political sin for which there is no redemption: confirming a widely held suspicion about him. In Biden's case, it was that he was shallow, with ambitions that far exceeded his qualifications. He was sidelined. Or rather, like Gary Hart, he sidelined himself. Another casualty of this episode was John Sasso, campaign manager for Dukakis, who admitted providing news outlets with videotapes of Biden and Kinnock delivering the same speech. The transgression was minor, but after Hart's demise, squeaky clean became the order of the day. Sasso was fired. But when the Dukakis general election campaign floundered in September 1988, Sasso was restored, primarily because he was the only one who could speak candidly to Dukakis.

Political professionals are repeatedly dumbfounded when confronted by a cold, undeniable fact: a lot of people "out there" know nothing and care less about politics. One new piece of evidence pointing to this truism was a 1988 poll revealing that a lot of Democratic primary voters thought the Paul Simon listed on their ballots was the singer who used to team up with Art Garfunkel. Not so, although a balladeer in the White House is not so unthinkable after two terms of a former Hollywood actor. Candidate Paul Simon in reality was the bow-tied junior Senator from Illinois, a former Congressman, author of eleven books (ten more than Ronald Reagan has read, according to Mrs. Simon) and the possessor of a voice deeper than the Grand Canyon. Campaigning as an old-fashioned, Truman-style Democrat, Simon in his personal platform reached back even further—to Franklin Roosevelt, whose Depression-era Works Progress Administration he proposed to emulate in order to solve the day's pressing unemployment problem. Simon came in first in his home state's primary, second in neighboring Iowa and out of the money in New Hampshire. He bowed out of the race shortly after a dismal finish in Wisconsin.

Richard Gephardt, a red-haired, freckle-faced Congressman from Missouri with a pale pair of eyebrows that tended to disappear in the glare of television lights, seemed to be everyone's favorite but the voters'. A co-founder of the Democratic Leadership Council and one of the most popular members of the House, Gephardt briefly seemed to be the one 1988 sleeper who just might wake up. He was acceptable to the D.L.C., and his border-state origins made him a candidate who could conceivably create a big splash on Super Tuesday, when 14 Southern states would hold primaries. It was not to be. Sooner or later, everything Gephardt tried backfired. Enthusiastic House colleagues volunteered to campaign for him on weekends, but they found themselves flailed as carpetbaggers presuming to tell the locals how to vote. And most of them were too unknown to create any appreciable stir. Gephardt adopted a populist theme pegged to his protectionist amendment to an omnibus trade bill. Spurred by clever television commercials created by veteran image-maker Bob Shrum, Gephardt shocked voters by claiming that a $10,000 Chrysler K-car costs $48,000 in Korea with taxes and tariffs. Gephardt managed to win Iowa, but his treasury depleted and his message by now threadbare, he fared poorly after New Hampshire. On Super Tuesday, given the choice of a border-state Southerner or the real thing, most Southern states went for Tennessee's Gore or, in the cases of electoral-vote-rich Texas and Florida, for a liberal New Englander who would supposedly not "sell" in the South, Michael Dukakis.

Michael Dukakis

Did he want to be Governor of Massachusetts forever? asked David Nyhan, a political columnist for the Boston *Globe*. Dukakis was in his third term. Would he seek a fourth and perhaps even a fifth? Better that he run for President in 1988, Nyhan wrote in 1987. There would never be a bigger opening for him. The state's senior Senator, Edward Kennedy, just might get that old feeling and run in 1992, and the junior Senator, young John Kerry, would jump at his first opportunity, probably in 1996. So unless Dukakis was willing to spend the rest of his political life in the Massachusetts statehouse, he had better sample the presidential waters in 1988. Whether influenced by Nyhan's column or not, Dukakis announced his candidacy for President a short time after it appeared. The thought undoubtedly had crossed his mind before.

Dukakis' plunge did not create a great splash. Beyond New England he was little known. The greatest volume of national publicity he had ever reaped had come when he sought re-election as Governor in 1978—and was dumped in the primary by a party that had found him arrogant, disdainful of his supporters as well as his enemies and in general need of a come-uppance. Having spurned the people whose efforts had helped him win the governorship in the first place, Dukakis—to his utter astonishment—now saw them abandoning him. Defeat shattered the severe, workaholic son of Greek immigrants, who appeared to have reached the end of his political career at the age of 45.

An interlude of humility, however, may have been precisely what Dukakis needed most. The realization overtook him that loss is part of the human experience. In addition; friends were to say later, he also had time during his exile from public life to reassess not just his performance as a Governor but his performance as a human being. It became clear that the world was not Mike Dukakis' personal oyster. Not everything that he did was right, nor was it all done in the right way. After a period of introspection, during which he apparently was unsparing in self-criticism, Dukakis decided that he was not through with public life. Public service was a part of his soul. He could earn more money doing other things. But he was not interested in doing other things or in earning money. He would run again for Governor and he would win. And so in 1982, four years after an ex-football player named Edward J. King had defeated him in the Democratic primary, a somewhat chastened and a more knowing Dukakis returned the favor. He easily won election to a third term in 1986. He loved the job, but as Nyhan would write, did he want to hold it forever?

Even before delivering his first speech or raising his first dollar, presidential candidate Dukakis clearly had a problem. His foreign-sounding name, analysts agreed, might be a handicap in the South and parts of the West and Midwest. But even worse in those military-minded regions was his vulnerability to the charge from which his party had already suffered enough: that he was soft on defense. Dukakis had made clear many times that he opposed the MX and Midgetman missiles (so did George McGovern during his brief 1984 attempt at a comeback). The Massachusetts Governor likewise considered President Reagan's Strategic Defense Initiative, also known as Star Wars, to be a far-out notion on which tax dollars would be wasted. He also opposed sending any more aid, military or humanitarian, to the Nicaraguan *contras*. In that, Dukakis was of a mind with most Americans, according to several polls. But what support the *contras* do enjoy is heavily concentrated in the South.

Even though Dukakis was just one of several Democratic candidates and although he described his bid as a long shot (at the time he entered, many still thought Hart would win or Cuomo would be nominated at a brokered convention), Dukakis obviously had advantages over his rivals. He was from a relatively big state—not Colorado or Arizona or Delaware, but Massachusetts, with 13 electoral votes. He had had more administrative experience than any of his rivals. Moreover, as the three-term Governor of a major state and the pride of the Greek-American community, he would be able to raise money more readily than the rest. (Dukakis' chief fund raiser, Robert Farmer, quickly demonstrated the truth of that assertion. While several of his rivals operated hand-to-mouth, Dukakis was awash in funds. "Money is the first primary," Farmer would later exult. "And we won that.") As host of a public-television talk show, *The Advocates,* during the hiatus between his first and second terms as Governor, Dukakis had developed an ease before the camera. He would be a formidable campaigner, and the other candidates knew it. Moreover, he would be a prohibitive favorite to win the crucial first primary in the neighboring state of New Hampshire, where he was as well known as in Massachusetts because both states are served by Boston television stations and newspapers. In addition, Dukakis' opposition to the Seabrook, N.H., nuclear power plant was a popular stance with Democratic-primary voters.

As might have been expected, it was Tennessean Gore who early on recognized Dukakis' vulnerability in the South. Gore had a well-deserved reputation as an expert on defense, and he knew Dukakis' opposition to new weapons systems, even though rooted in a conviction that Pentagon spending is out of control, could be exploited. And after Dukakis won New Hampshire, he became a favorite target, especially for Gore, whose hopes now depended entirely on a good showing in the South. Thus when Dukakis made his first major foray into that region sometime before Super Tuesday, he was hammered by the press corps on themes first advanced by Gore: Would Dukakis be willing to use military force? Did he approve of the 1986 bombing attack on Libya? How much would his lack of foreign-policy experience hurt him? Finally a questioner got to the point: Was Gore the "toughest" Democrat in the race?

Dukakis exploded. "I don't think he's the toughest. I don't think he's the toughest at all. He wants to spend $50 billion on the Midgetman missile. I think we ought to put some of those resources into conventional defense. I don't yield on toughness to Al Gore in any way, shape or manner." It was good training for Dukakis. Should he be nominated, his weak credentials on defense and foreign policy would be the focus of the Republican campaign against him.

But on Super Tuesday, Southern whites for the most part chose Gore; Jackson took the black vote. Dukakis clearly had not caught the fancy of the Southern voter, but by virtue of his superior organization and funding, he won in delegate-heavy Texas and Florida and even managed to gain a slender plurality in total delegates elected that day in 20 states. So the Northeastern liberal, suspect on defense, had survived the megaprimary. Looming just ahead were primaries in which Dukakis was expected to do well—in industrial states like Massachusetts, where the Governor would feel more at home than he did, for one example, in Iowa. There he unwisely recommended that farmers increase their earnings by planting Belgian endive.

But the Dukakis express was rudely jolted back to reality by poor results in two major industrial states, Michigan and Illinois. Finance director Robert Farmer thought "we had a chance to put away Michigan." The polls also said so. In fact, Farmer received a telephone call from Dukakis' Michigan headquarters, informing him erroneously that Dukakis had won. "I'll never believe the numbers again," Farmer groused. Campaigning for the Illinois primary that followed, the candidate tried valiantly to eat, drink and dance his way into the hearts of ethnic blue-collar Illinoisans. Nothing seemed to work. He nibbled on veal sausages at a Serbian nightclub, rolled dough at an Italian bakery, downed ouzo at a Greektown taverna and waved to half-sloshed marchers in a South Side Chicago St. Patrick's Day parade. He donned a hard hat in a Cicero steel mill, slipped on a white coat in a high-tech lab and fired up a D11N tractor at Peoria's Caterpillar plant. For his efforts, Illinoisans rewarded Dukakis with a weak third-place finish. True, those who came in ahead of him—Simon and Jackson—were both residents of the state, but Dukakis' showing was nonetheless disappointing to the candidate and his supporters. He picked up not a single delegate. More important, his ethnicism failed to attract Reagan Democrats, crucial swing voters who deserted their party for Reagan in 1980 and 1984 and for whom Dukakis' Greek immigrant heritage was supposed to have some appeal. Illinois clearly crippled the front runner. It was a worse blow to him than his setback in the Michigan caucus.

Fortunately for the image of inevitability that the Dukakis forces were trying in vain to project, the next primary was in friendly Connecticut, which borders on Massachusetts and where the Governor is well known and respected. Before panic induced by Illinois and Michigan could run rampant, Dukakis' win in Connecticut restored a measure of sanity. He had ignored Michigan and deserved to lose it, and the lesson was learned: never again would he take a state for granted.

But as Dukakis' troubles were doubling, those of his competition were quadrupling. Several of his rivals were gone, and more were going. Gephardt's flop on Super Tuesday was the end of the trail for him, although he took a while getting around to admitting defeat. In fact, while Dukakis was not looking very good, compared with those around him the Governor resembled a peacock who had wandered onto a turkey farm. The money Robert Farmer raised had won more than the first primary. There had never been a doubt that Dukakis would have enough money to go the distance. No other Democratic candidate enjoyed that luxury. The others would have to win, often and big, or drop out. The only exception was Jackson, who knew how to campaign on the cheap.

Intent on there being no other Michigans, the Dukakis campaign poured money, television commercials, the candidate —and the candidate's wife Kitty—into Wisconsin. In addition, Dukakis sharpened his basic stump speech and seemed more at ease with himself. He even offered a cogent and, for him, emotional rationale for his campaign: "I have no particular interest in going down in history, if I am elected President, as being the Great Communicator. I want to be the Great Builder. I want to be someone who makes a real difference in the lives of real people. That's why I'm in public life."

In Wisconsin, even though Jackson captured 23% of the white vote, his greatest share ever, Dukakis won decisively. Simon's poor showing prompted him to withdraw from the race.

Now only Jackson and Gore stood in Dukakis' way, and barring a surprise somewhere or other, neither had the organization or the resources to match those of the Governor in Pennsylvania, Ohio and most particularly in New York. As Gore well knew, he would have to topple Dukakis in New York or head back to Tennessee. New York was his only remaining chance for a vital win in the North, yet his alliance with the mercurial Mayor Koch ended up demolishing his meager chances. Koch may have convinced New York Jewish voters they would be "crazy" to support Jackson, but they did not support Gore either.

So Dukakis effectively wrapped up the Democratic nomination with his April 19 victory in the New York primary. Jackson vowed to carry on through the last two primaries, the California and New Jersey ballots on June 7, and so he did. Oddly, his continuing presence in primary contests worked to the benefit of Dukakis. Alongside Jackson, Dukakis appeared more conservative than he actually was. And the big nearly-every-Tuesday victories repeatedly presented the Massachusetts Governor to the American people as a winner on the nation's front pages and the network news.

With only a few lapses, Dukakis continued to campaign as if the contest were still in doubt. His victory in New York was an overwhelming 51%, but on a flight to Philadelphia when the dimensions of his triumph were clear, he insisted on doing state business. And when Pennsylvania Democrats greeted him with congratulations, the candidate remained stoically silent. But as he gave a brief speech that night, Dukakis watchers detected a softening, a suggestion that even an iceman can melt a little in the warm glow of arriving at the end of a long trail. Dukakis told supporters at the Philadelphia dinner: "Last week . . . the Vice President said that we Democrats are going to be judged this fall by what he called the economic legacy of the last Democratic Administration. Well, this fall George Bush is going to be judged by a Republican legacy of more red ink than all the Administrations from George Washington to Jimmy Carter, by pink slips for our workers, golden parachutes for high rollers and greenmail for sharp operators on Wall Street."

It was standard campaign rhetoric, but that was not the point. Michael Dukakis was aiming it at George Bush, not at his Democratic opponents. Although he would not be caught whispering it to his closest friend or perhaps even to his wife, Dukakis knew: he would be the Democratic candidate for President. And he had done it his way, without revealing much of himself or what he stood for to the American people. Just about the most specific campaign theme Dukakis sounded on the primary trail was "good jobs at good wages." He never elaborated on where he would find them.

That bland vagueness would have to change. So would Dukakis' relatively passionless, humorless platform demeanor. The candidate may have sensed those exigencies as he returned to New York to savor his newly won primary victory. In any case, he seemed more relaxed, more at ease with himself. In a room filled with BEAT BUSH signs and with an audience chanting "Let's go, Mike," the great stoneface even managed a self-deprecating one-liner: "All it takes is a strong message, lots of hard work and plenty of charisma." He could not have known then how close to the truth his quip had landed.

6

Dukakis: the Loner

LIKABILITY. THE WORD HAS SHADOWED MICHAEL DUKAKIS throughout his political life. He was constantly advised to be more likable, to reveal more of himself, to develop some kind of emotional bond with voters. To a remarkable degree, Dukakis found that difficult. One all too typical voter, Barbara Kummerer, a family counselor in River Forest, Ill., told reporters in October that she had followed Dukakis closely for a year but was frustrated. She still could not picture the real person inside.

Intimacy and self-disclosure have never come easily for Dukakis. He has few friends. Even to them, he carefully measures out his trust. Over the years, Dukakis has invested little emotion in personal relationships. He has been able to discard longtime allies with little discomfort. As Massachusetts Governor, he was a stern, principled leader whose drive and success won him admiration but seldom affection. His campaign for the presidency, at least at the beginning, was virtually a one-man operation. That combination of self-reliance and aloofness raised serious questions about his suitability for the presidency. Could Dukakis ever establish enough rapport with his fellow citizens so that when he led, they would follow?

At the start of his presidential quest, Dukakis declared that personal character more than anything else would determine who was elected. Thus the question in 1988 would not be who had the better road map but who would be the more reliable driver. On that test Dukakis seemed confident. What you saw, the Governor insisted, was what you got. Yet there was another side to Dukakis that few people understood. Even after 18 months of campaign-trail scrutiny, he remained a puzzle.

The candidate was, in fact, not all that different from the earnest young man who had lived most of his life in his home town. Dukakis sprang from a family of remarkable achievement. In 1912 his father Panos, then only 16, migrated to this country from an area of Asia Minor near Troy. With no knowledge of English and only $25 in his pocket, he made his way to the mill town of Lawrence, Mass., where two of his older brothers owned a restaurant. Eager to learn and assimilate, he temporarily assumed the name Peter Duke for quicker acceptance in landing part-time jobs. At trade schools he learned to speak English and at night took enough courses to be accepted at Bates College. Within twelve years after arriving in America, Panos had become the first Greek immigrant to graduate from Harvard Medical School.

A determined, unostentatious man, Dukakis was thrilled by his new country. It was ironic that 75 years later his son Michael would be accused by George Bush of somehow not standing up for patriotism. Panos never stopped telling friends how much he loved America. His Harvard medical degree gave him and his family great standing in Boston's Greek community. For 50 years, until his retirement in 1978, one year before he died, the doctor poured his energy and devotion into medicine, working six days a week. On the seventh day, he kept his Boston office open to treat relatives and Greek friends who sought his care. "My dad was not an intellectual," Michael said later. "His two passions in life were medicine and his family, in reverse order." Michael told people he seldom saw his father. Routinely, Panos worked 80 hours a week. When family members showed up from nearby towns on Sundays, the doctor's face would light up, and immediately he called his wife. Would she whip up a favorite dish, meat pie, for the cousins?

Michael's mother Euterpe Boukis was born in Greece. She was brought to America one year later than her husband, at age nine, on a converted coal freighter. Unable to speak a word of English, she became a diligent student and eventually worked her way to Bates College, where she graduated Phi Beta Kappa, the first immigrant Greek woman ever to do so. Euterpe was a serious and dignified woman who, like many immigrants, kept up her guard. She was also a perfectionist. Said her Bates roommate Alice Esty: "Euterpe was definitely the kind of person who kept everything under control. She wasn't into socializing. She wasn't playing cards. She was totally dedicated to her work." There was never the need to cram for an exam. Euterpe was always well prepared. To pay for her Bates tuition, she worked during the summers at a shoe factory. After graduation in 1925, she became a teacher in a small high school in Ashland, N.H. Later, Euterpe would become the dominant role model for her younger son Michael.

The two Greek immigrants had met briefly when Euterpe was a junior in high school. In 1929 they came together again, and after only two dates, Panos proposed. Wed six months later, they lived across the hall from his doctor's office. In ten months they had their first son Stelian, named after his paternal grandfather. Three years later, in 1933, second son Michael was born. By now the family had moved to Brookline, Mass., a cozy suburb populated by Yankees and increasingly attractive to successful Irish and Jews. The two brothers were close but at the same time developed a strong sibling rivalry. "It was a love-hate relationship," recalled Euterpe. Michael idolized Stelian. When the older brother outgrew a shirt or pair of slacks, Michael was thrilled to inherit the hand-me-down. As the years passed, he began to outshine Stelian. Increasingly, the pattern became familiar. Stelian made the honor society; Michael a few years later was elected its president. Stelian failed to make eagle scout; Michael succeeded. The rivalry intensified and years later became mysteriously ugly.

The Dukakis boys turned out to be quite dissimilar. While Stelian liked to chat and visit and attend dances, Michael was solitary. Stelian was a favorite of many relatives because of his gentle, outgoing nature. Michael was more competitive, less interested in pursuing relationships. "If Stelian asked how you were," recalled one cousin, "he really wanted to know. Michael was always in more of a hurry." The boys loved sports and often tossed a basketball at a backyard hoop until after dark and staged track meets in the driveway. Michael was physically smaller than Stelian. That seemed to make him more dogged about outperforming bigger boys in the neighborhood. One day during a baseball game, Michael remembered, he struck out. Nonetheless, he argued brazenly that he had foul-tipped the ball. He knew he had not, but he liked hanging tough. In an argument, associates learned, he was hard to budge.

Both boys looked up to their successful father, but they did not see much of him. The warmest memories Michael held of his father were the evenings Panos would make it home in time to tuck his son into bed. Once, the family rented a cottage on the Massachusetts shore for a week's vacation. On the first night the senior Dukakis got a call reporting a mother in labor, and the family returned with him. After that, they never planned another long vacation.

The Dukakis family was described by friends as close but not joyful, never relishing success so much as holding on to it. When he was around, Panos Dukakis stressed goals and achievement. Neither boy received an allowance for chores around the house. They were expected to work. Still, Panos was not very demanding. Often he sat quietly at the dinner table in his three-piece suit and listened in amusement as family members argued politics.

Relatives decided the softer Stelian was more like his father. Michael had his mother's drive and smarts. Panos tried to get home each evening for dinner and usually listened to the CBS radio news. He voted Republican in those days, while his wife was the liberal of the family. Later, when campaigning for President, Michael sometimes got carried away reminiscing about his family. From time to time he would tell audiences about the lively Greek dancing that went on at family gatherings. His mother had no memory of any such dancing. "We were living an American life," Euterpe put it plainly. Which is not to say that the family ignored its ethnic heritage. Though Euterpe once was turned down for a teaching job because she was Greek, a painful experience she has never forgotten, Greek was spoken at home. Panos' mother Olympia lived with them, and she spoke no English.

Euterpe was the driving force in the family, eager to set standards and motivate her sons. At one point Panos expressed concern that his younger son was working too hard. "If this boy doesn't slow down," Panos protested to his wife, "he's going to get sick." Euterpe had no patience for such a prognosis. "Does he look sick?" she challenged. Whenever Michael mispronounced a word, Euterpe would carefully correct him. Later, he would stand intently in front of a mirror mouthing the word until it felt right. Sometimes the boy dared to oppose his mother. One morning Michael put on a pair of socks that did not match his outfit. Euterpe told her son to change them, but he refused. Michael was banished to his room, where he remained for an hour before emerging, finally, with the correct socks on. Euterpe was pleased at his stubbornness. "He was persevering," she said. "He never gave up until he finished the task." It was a quality Dukakis the politician later displayed constantly.

Euterpe was a planner, and things around her had to be

correct. Her nephew Stratos Dukakis remembered that in Euterpe's household everything was neatly organized. Thia Euterpe, as he called his aunt, often reminded the children to save rubber bands and paper bags. She condemned waste. At the meal table, plates were eaten clean. In the bathroom, Stratos remembered clearly, his aunt never failed to return the toothpaste tube to the same spot by the sink. She was severe but almost never lost her temper. Recalls another nephew, Stratton Sterghos, in latter-day wonderment: "The more I think about it, I can't really remember Thia Euterpe ever being wrong. Everything was so well thought out." Euterpe, he believed, was determined to show no sign of weakness, a lesson that her younger son learned perfectly. Michael rarely lost control. For years, political associates tried to figure out, after some particular goof, how angry Dukakis really was. There was no way to be sure except that, like Euterpe in such instances, he would fall silent.

At Brookline High, a competitive public school that pushed scholarship, Michael brought home straight A's on his report cards. His parents glowed in approval, and, as recognition, the family went out for a favorite dinner, fresh clams or oysters. Small but aggressive, Michael competed in sports, playing catcher on the varsity baseball team and putting the ball in play as a starting guard on the basketball team. In his senior year, at 17, he faked his age to enter the 26.2-mile Boston Marathon. He trained for weeks and finished 57th in a field of 191, an impressive mark of his stamina. Michael played trumpet in the school band and was elected head of the student council. He was voted at graduation the most brilliant boy in his class, and his yearbook picture carried the caption "Big Chief Brain in Face." Already a streak of primness was beginning to show in Michael. During his last year, the school cafeteria decided to switch from milk bottles to cartons. The immediate result was litter, and Michael chided classmates who scattered containers. "It's not right," he told offenders, "to make other people pick up after you."

Michael was not so successful socially as he was academically. In affluent Brookline, youngsters rarely took jobs and life centered on social activities. There were numerous clubs—the Spartans, the Trojans—and most boys joined. While Michael would have been received cheerfully, he avoided the clubs. Around town he never turned up at Jack and Marian's delicatessen, a favorite hangout, or at the nearby Totem Pole, where students went to hear the traveling big bands and to dance. "We never saw Michael," recalled Beryl Cohen, a year behind Dukakis. "He used to shut down at 5 o'clock in the afternoon and disappeared on weekends." Cohen, who later collided with Dukakis politically, had a theory that Michael embraced public service partly as a way to overcome his lack of social skills. Politics, Cohen believed, forced the withdrawn Dukakis into relationships, however uneasy they were.

Brother Stelian, for once, had an edge on his sibling. Stelian liked to dance and, with not much effort, invited girls to local functions. Michael held back. Not until his senior year did he have his first date. Then he got to know and like Sandy Cohen, an attractive and vivacious blond. Years later, Sandy Cohen Bakalar remembered that her girlfriends used to wonder why a boy as smart and presentable as Michael Dukakis never went out with girls. Before long, Michael had a crush on Sandy. That spring, in her living room, Sandy showed Michael how to dance the fox-trot. A few weeks later, Michael hesitantly told her he had never been to a dance and asked her to the senior prom. She already had a date and tried to break it. When that failed, Dukakis turned up at the dance and checked coats.

About that same time, in May 1951, Stelian, then a junior at Maine's Bates College, called home to tell his parents that his life was coming apart. The older Dukakis boy was experiencing a nervous breakdown. He returned home and, within a month, attempted suicide. The family was shattered. No outsiders were told, not even Dukakis relatives. "We knew that Stelian was sick," remembered cousin Arthur Dukakis, "but never had any idea he was having mental problems." Michael kept his sadness to himself. One day, sitting with Sandy Cohen on a stone wall near the school, he started to talk about his brother. Suddenly, tears filled his eyes, Sandy remembered. She had never witnessed such a rush of emotion from Michael. "He was so unhappy," she recalled, "I just wanted to die." Michael told her he was going off to Swarthmore College that fall. Would she keep an eye on his brother? She said she would.

For the next 22 years Stelian worked at various jobs, driving taxis or teaching school. He was in and out of mental institutions, receiving insulin and electroshock treatment. Relatives avoided the subject. The tragedy tore at the enterprising Dukakis parents, who blamed themselves for Stelian's troubles. For Michael, who tended to internalize his feelings anyway, the episode was especially troubling. "If you shook Michael to see what makes him tick," said a family friend who grew up with the brothers, "the one rusty key to drop out would be Stelian." Not that Michael avoided talking about his brother. One Brookline friend, Don Lipsitt, a psychiatrist, recalled a number of conversations with Michael when Stelian's name would come up. Always, Lipsitt remembered, the talk was clinical rather than emotional. Even to a close friend, Michael withheld his personal feelings.

A dozen years after the nervous breakdown, in 1964, when Dukakis was running for re-election to the state legislature, illness led Stelian to distribute hundreds of leaflets around Brookline urging voters to reject his brother. Dukakis aides quickly fanned out and retrieved most of the leaflets. Michael and his family were horrified. It seemed clearer than ever that Stelian could not cope with his brother's success. Nine years later, in 1973, Stelian was riding a bicycle in Brookline when he was struck by a hit-and-run driver. For four months he lay in a coma. Night after night Panos, Euterpe and Michael sat by his hospital bed. Finally he died. So hard did Michael struggle to put the tragedy out of his mind that years later he told one biographer he had forgotten that Stelian had even attempted suicide. As a presidential candidate, Dukakis mainly turned away questions about his brother.

In 1951, a few months after Stelian dropped out of Bates, Michael was off to Swarthmore, a small, academically rigorous liberal-arts college near Philadelphia. Even though he could easily have won admission to Harvard, he decided against that school. It was Michael's first time away from home. He began a premedical program, intending to go along with his father's wish that he become a doctor. An unexpected D in freshman physics ended that plan. But the rest of his grades were so good that he was elected to Phi Beta Kappa. Classmates were struck by his maturity. No one recalled him as ever sweating over courses. Said Jay Levine, a former fellow student: "He was never the kind of person to stay up all night."

At Swarthmore, Dukakis began to form his political ideas. Michael joined Students for Democratic Action, an affiliate of the liberal Americans for Democratic Action. Already Dukakis was thinking of politics as a career. He told a few classmates that he wanted to return to Massachusetts and become Governor. When reform Democrat Joseph Clark ran successfully for mayor of Philadelphia in 1951, Dukakis threw himself into the campaign. It was his first taste of reform politics.

Dukakis' social life was still inactive, and he continued to spurn fraternities. As a young man and afterward, Dukakis shunned élitism. One day a student asked where he had prepped, meaning where he had gone to prep school. "I didn't prep," Dukakis snapped. "I highed." On campus he earned spending money clipping hair. When some Nigerian students were kicked out of a local barbershop, Dukakis cut their hair. Later, he talked the barbers into accepting them. He also demonstrated occasional daring: in 1952, as a backer of Democratic presidential candidate Adlai Stevenson, he climbed the school water tower and pulled down a Dwight Eisenhower sign. Michael's antilitter streak stayed with him at Swarthmore. As a freshman, he helped organize workdays when students would clean up the campus.

During his college years Dukakis finally got a look at the world. In the summer of 1954 he traveled to the University of San Marcos in Lima. There, at first hand, he witnessed an angry protest against the U.S.-sponsored overthrow of the Guatemalan government. Another summer he hitchhiked, along with a friend, across the U.S. and into Mexico. At graduation in 1955, Dukakis decided to get his military obligation over with and joined the Army. His father was disappointed. Panos Dukakis wanted his son to go right to graduate school. Michael was assigned to Korea and served there for 21 months as a clerk-typist. The fighting had ended two years earlier.

In cold and desolate Korea, the drab routine of Army life depressed him. His mind was on his future. Discharged in 1957, he enrolled at Harvard Law School. By the time he finished, three years later, Dukakis was as involved in Brookline politics as he was in his studies, though his grades were respectable enough. He finished 71st in a class of 468.

If law did not hold his attention, politics did. While in law school, he had run unsuccessfully for a seat on the Brookline redevelopment authority. The next year he ran for one of the 21 seats on the Brookline town meeting, and this time he won. In 1960, attacking cronyism and corruption, Dukakis and other liberals tirelessly knocked on doors and eventually ousted entrenched party leaders. It was a startling upset. He had established himself as the leader of the reformers and was made ward chairman. By graduation in 1960, Dukakis, now 26, knew where he wanted to head. For the next ten years, he immersed himself in state politics, always the insurgent reformer ready to attack rooted interests.

While running for the state legislature, Dukakis had a blind date with Katharine Dickson, 24, daughter of a first violinist in the Boston Symphony Orchestra. Michael liked her immediately. There were problems, however. Kitty was Jewish and divorced, with a three-year-old son. Michael's parents disapproved. But Michael was determined to marry her, more certain even than Kitty.

The two were absolute opposites. She was volatile and had hair-trigger opinions; he concealed his feelings and was careful about everything he said. She had expensive tastes; he was a notorious cheapskate. She slept late; he was up early. "Marrying Kitty," observed cousin Olympia Dukakis, the actress, "was the single most rebellious thing Michael Dukakis ever did." High school friend Sandy Cohen, who had brought the two together, told Dukakis biographers, "Kitty has what he doesn't: she exudes passion. He feels it but doesn't show it. She acts out what he can't." Michael's affection for her son John helped win Kitty over, and they were married in 1963, when Dukakis was 29. Three years later, they had the first of their two daughters, Andrea. The evening Kitty went into labor, Michael, by then in the legislature, tried to rush home on the subway. But it was the night of the great Northeastern blackout of 1965. He ran two miles to his house and got her to the hospital.

Later, when Dukakis was Governor, Kitty took an office down the hall. She created her own agenda, primarily trying to help Asian refugees enter the country. To Dukakis staff members, she could be an unsettling presence, tossing her weight around and even berating secretaries. Unannounced, she would burst into the Governor's office with questions of her own, while visitors sat and looked at each other uncomfortably. Never did Dukakis display annoyance. Recalled one Dukakis aide: "We used to be embarrassed for him. We always wondered whether he told her off later. We learned he never did."

Dukakis cared too deeply about Kitty to criticize her, and he drew strength from her support. Later, she benefited from his support when it was revealed that she had for 26 years suffered an addiction to diet pills. At the statehouse she had a tendency to talk too freely, so her husband withheld sensitive information from her. Staff members remembered conversations in which

Kitty took a position contrary to her husband's. "Don't tell Michael about this," she would begin, and immediately staffers would tense up. When Dukakis seemed unsupportive of homosexual rights, Kitty privately got reassuring messages out to gay leaders. In the presidential race, Kitty basked in the glitter surrounding the campaign. Michael paid little attention to it.

Dukakis in 1962 had run successfully for the state legislature and later won four consecutive two-year terms. He became a skilled debater and dedicated himself to reforming the political process. He pushed to reduce political influence over the selection of judges. He won passage in 1970 of the country's first no-fault insurance legislation, a bill that reduced the number of costly automobile-accident lawsuits. He was the guiding force behind the measure, staving off singlehandedly a last-minute push by opponents that nearly succeeded in killing it. Dukakis biographers Robert Turner and Charles Kenney described the final scene: "In the house, Dukakis took the microphone and for two solid hours answered questions calmly and in detail, drawing from a deep well of knowledge to describe the bill's intricacies and implications." When the last question had been asked of Dukakis, they wrote, "his colleagues rose in applause, an extraordinary tribute rarely seen in the chamber."

By 1970 Dukakis had his eye on higher office. Beryl Cohen, his Brookline High classmate, preceded Dukakis to the legislature, and through the 1960s the two reformers had waged numerous battles together. In 1969 they made a pact: in the next year's election, Cohen would run for Lieutenant Governor, and Dukakis for state attorney general. The two men would support each other. Unexpectedly, a short time later, a top Democrat decided to run for attorney general. Dukakis was crushed. There was no practical way for him to continue. One night around 10 o'clock he showed up at Cohen's front door. Dukakis had decided, he told Cohen, to run for Lieutenant Governor himself.

Cohen listened, shocked. He told Dukakis he would fight

him, and after a few minutes the conversation ended. "There wasn't a bit of remorse," Cohen recalled. "Michael had convinced himself it was correct." Dukakis went on to defeat Cohen for the nomination, but the Democratic gubernatorial ticket lost in the general election. Observed Cohen: "It had nothing to do with our relationship. It had to do with his own single-mindedness. If it was right for Michael, it must be the right thing to do." Said a longtime aide: "Michael needed to be shaken. But he had no one to do it."

After the election, Dukakis returned to the law, which he had practiced intermittently but never seriously. Making money did not stir him. The political loss in no way discouraged Dukakis. Rather he believed that his ultimate goal, to be Governor, had been advanced. Now, in 1973, shortly after Stelian's death, he made his move. His reputation for integrity gave him an edge in the 1974 autumn of the Watergate scandal. Candidate Dukakis pledged that under no circumstances would he raise taxes. His campaign slogan: "Mike Dukakis SHOULD be Governor." He won easily.

Shortly after the election, Dukakis discovered to his surprise that he had inherited a huge budget deficit. As if that were not enough, the state's economy was sinking. He struggled at first to reduce outlays, cutting deeply into several key programs, including welfare. It was not long before the liberal Governor started catching heavy flak from his old colleagues. State legislator Barney Frank, for instance, labeled him an ingrate. Ultimately Dukakis was forced to break his word and raise taxes, a painful act for him. More than most politicians, he had a dread of seeming duplicitous. Thus even routine changes of mind troubled him.

Although voters were resentful, Dukakis' intelligence and energy gradually won him wide respect. The economy improved. He brought reform to the state's court system. Still, his confident, hectoring manner continued to make him an unsympathetic figure. Even legislators in his own party found it hard to pull for him. One columnist wrote of Dukakis: "His attitude too often is 'I'm better than you are, and we both know it.' " Kevin Harrington, the Democratic president of the state senate, dealt constantly with Dukakis and found him rigid and sanctimonious. Some days, the towering Harrington declared, he felt like picking Dukakis up and physically shaking him.

Harrington, however, also remarked that in 40 years of Massachusetts politics, he had never seen a more personally honest politician. The Governor asked no favors and granted none. Soon after Dukakis took office, a longtime Brookline political ally, Sumner Kaplan, was interested in a Brookline district judgeship. Though Kaplan was well qualified, Dukakis refused to push his nomination. He hated cronyism. Later, Harvard Law classmate Fran Meaney, who had dutifully managed several campaigns for his friend, ended the relationship after Dukakis pressured Meaney's law firm not to serve as counsel on a city bond issue, a thoroughly legitimate business agreement.

The Governor showed his worst critics a calmness under fire. One day a legislative leader called on Dukakis and made a fervent plea for support. Dukakis tersely said no. Furious at the decision, the leader lost his temper and began kicking at chairs and even flicking cigarette ashes across the Governor's desk. Dukakis sat unmoved, arms folded across his chest, staring silently until the leader ran out of steam and left.

Eventually politicians learned to live with the Governor's opaque personality. Sometimes he treated opponents better than allies. "If you wanted something," observed one Democratic legislator, "it was better to oppose him." By the end of his first term, Dukakis felt he had mastered his job—and he loved it. Indeed, he had two passions in his life, family and politics, in that order. Each night, just like Panos Dukakis, the Governor was home at 6 o'clock to have dinner with his family, no matter what the press of business.

In 1978, facing a primary challenge by former Baltimore

Colts lineman Edward King, Dukakis was mostly unconcerned. At one point he led King by 50 points in the polls. Not until election night did Dukakis realize the disaster that had befallen him. To the Governor's astonishment, the voters had thrown him out. Dukakis was devastated. Son John told of finding his father days afterward at home, sitting alone and staring out the window. At night Dukakis was unable to sleep. Family friends described him as depressed, although he never required professional help.

Dukakis had badly overestimated himself. Some believed they understood what had happened. Observed Martin Linsky, a fellow Brookline legislator: "Michael never looked for or expected affection from constituents. He never tried to create support on that basis. He always wanted to be judged on what he did." Some supporters even enjoyed seeing the cocky Governor cut down to size. Euterpe Dukakis had an explanation for that. "It comes from his pride, you know," she told a Greek journalist about her son's manner, "and that pride will never change. People who aren't familiar with Greeks often confuse that pride for arrogance. They don't like it. Michael wanted to do what was right and good. But he did not learn to bend."

Dukakis gradually pulled himself together. "I didn't listen," he told political associates. Now his mind was fixed on how to get his job back. For months he systematically reviewed his mistakes, cornering those who knew him and asking blunt questions. Aide Michael Widmer said Dukakis questioned him closely on the subject of his aloofness. Another associate, Ed Lashman, said Dukakis did what few politicians are able to do: instead of externalizing his defeat and blaming others, he internalized it. "To see Michael being reflective and self-analytical," said his psychiatrist friend Lipsitt, "was an unaccustomed experience for those of us who knew him." An inner drive—or perhaps the example of his striving parents—saw him through the crisis. Soon Dukakis took a job at Harvard's Kennedy School as a lecturer in state and local policy. In 1982 he challenged Governor King in a return primary match and beat him. Triumphant in the general election a few months later, Dukakis told voters in gratitude that they had given him something rare in politics, a second chance.

In his second term, Dukakis tried hard to alter his approach. Visitors to his corner office found he did listen better. As the national economy expanded, so did state revenues. Dukakis launched an innovative education and training program to move people off welfare, coaxed labor and business associations to come together, aimed state aid at depressed towns and cities to encourage business investment. He hailed entrepreneurship and promoted high-technology enterprises. He also undertook an innovative tax-collection program, including amnesty for past evaders, that brought in millions of dollars in unpaid levies. Everything seemed to work. But some people were not so sure Dukakis had changed all that much. "Now he listens," said one dubious state senator, "and still does exactly what he wants." Superficially or not, Dukakis seemed to have shed a bit of his certitude.

Something else was new. Dukakis had discovered his first real political confidant. John Sasso, then 35, an unknown but resourceful political operative, had been hired to manage the 1982 campaign. Affable and shrewd, Sasso was a natural politician. He had all the personality tools the Governor still lacked. Dukakis stiffened at plain political talk. If conversations stayed on issues, he was fine. But in a room behind closed doors, he remained uncomfortable at political deal making. "He tries so hard not to be a politician," one state senate leader said in frustration after an unsuccessful meeting.

Now the Governor had found a political bridge. As chief secretary, Sasso became the Governor's alter ego, huddling with political allies and even opponents, accomplishing in the Governor's second term—known colloquially as Duke II—the kinds of things Dukakis had failed to do in his first. No key decisions were made without Sasso. Often observers wondered what the

Governor really knew of the pressure exerted on his behalf by Sasso. There was never a clear answer. The fastidious Dukakis stayed out of the trenches. Staff members recalled his coming to the door of Sasso's office while a delicate undertaking was in discussion. The Governor paused silently, got the drift of the conversation, and quickly turned and left.

Profoundly conservative in his personal life, Dukakis had certain policy prejudices that showed up mostly on social issues. He did not easily take advice on things he opposed, such as state-provided needles for drug users and programs that allowed homosexuals to become foster parents. Alone with his staff, Dukakis was a tight presence. Aides said his mind was like a heat-seeking missile. The Governor immediately identified weak spots in arguments. He interrupted with answers sometimes before questions were even completed. "Next," he would declare, and the discussion moved on.

He also had little inclination to hand out compliments. One day he wondered aloud to his chief financial adviser why people so often needed to be thanked. They must have known they were appreciated, Dukakis went on. Otherwise they would not be there. The aide held his answer to himself.

In his off-hours, Dukakis was indifferent to movies and novels. He preferred sports or the Boston Pops Orchestra. Aides did not smoke around him. Language was mostly cleaned up in deference to the Governor's sense of propriety. Dukakis exhibited little sense of irony, and his jokes were as forced in private as on the stump. Said one cabinet officer: "Don't get the idea we hang around Michael. He's not that interesting."

With Sasso at his side, Dukakis acted more like a politician. He began to reward loyalty, to make appointments that in years past he would have waved off. Gradually Dukakis built a strong political organization. In 1984 he reluctantly let Geraldine Ferraro borrow Sasso to run her vice-presidential campaign. When he returned, Sasso told Dukakis that the Governor was the match of any political leader he had encountered. That impressed Dukakis. Soon Sasso's view was reinforced. The National Governors' Conference made Dukakis its chairman. In an informal poll, the Governors voted Dukakis the ablest of them all.

Now Sasso began urging that Dukakis consider running for President. In his travels with Ferraro, Sasso said, he was struck by how many voters believed Democrats could not be trusted to run the economy. The Massachusetts economic miracle was the perfect argument to counter that. Despite Sasso's urgings, Dukakis was hesitant. He loved the Governor's job. In 1986 he rolled to the largest victory in the state's history, winning 69% of the voters. One week later, Sasso handed him a long memo that mapped the way to the White House. Dukakis, wrote Sasso, had three sizable assets: access to big money, an outstanding executive record and the stamina to endure a long campaign. He warned that the Governor's dovish foreign-policy positions—support for a freeze on nuclear weapons and opposition to American intervention in Grenada and Libya—had to be offset.

After two months of reflection, Dukakis decided to run. One obstacle was whether New York Governor Mario Cuomo would get into the race. If he did, Dukakis would stay out. To feel out Cuomo, he sent the agile Sasso to New York. Dukakis knew Cuomo personally. Yet he was unwilling simply to pick up the phone and ask his friend what he was going to do. Eventually Sasso divined that Cuomo was not going to run. That was all Dukakis had to hear. Months later, Dukakis displayed a similar lack of political deftness. When he announced his candidacy, he knew he could use endorsements from the same Democratic Governors who in the past had spoken so well of him. But Dukakis had not kept up his ties. He rarely called the Governors. Now when he asked for help, they made excuses and backed away. Dukakis, they felt, was a hard man to relate to. Governor Bill Clinton of Arkansas, who had virtually promised to campaign for Dukakis, explained lamely that the Arkansas legislature would take too much of his time.

Once again Dukakis' remoteness and fierce self-reliance were causing him problems. In the end, the candidate had grown only a little. He still fell back on the safe and the obvious. The essence of a politician is a confidence that the voters, once they come to know the candidate, will like what they see. Dukakis, however, seemed to fear that once he showed his true feelings, voters would not like him at all. But now he had to take that risk. To win, he had to convince the great electorate that his clipped and controlled exterior was only a mask that concealed a more expansive, adventurous and caring self. Americans crave that kind of connection with the person of the President. In ways that would haunt him throughout the campaign, Michael Dukakis was still the proud, independent, immensely capable but aloof boy from Brookline.

7
Jackson: the Spoiler

"I don't feel no ways tired . . ."

JESSE JACKSON MOCKED THOSE WHO SAID HE COULD NOT WIN. From the moment he declared his candidacy in September 1987, Jackson criticized reporters, pundits and opponents who maintained that the only sure thing about the 1988 campaign was that the party would not nominate the 46-year-old Chicago civil rights leader. The conventional wisdom sounded like a self-fulfilling prophecy: because he was black, Jackson was unelectable. And because he was unelectable, he could not be taken seriously, no matter how well he did.

He was slowly proving that logic wrong. A steady gain in delegates, particularly in heavily white states, had led some skeptics to reconsider. By the evening of March 26, as reporters relayed early hints of his decisive upset of Michael Dukakis in the Michigan caucuses, Jackson said uncharacteristically little, perhaps doubting his own good fortune. But by the next morning the returns were clear. Helped by a huge turnout of the state's blacks, Jackson had won a stunning 54% of the 200,000-odd votes to Dukakis' 29%. In addition to a lopsided victory in Motown, Jackson won in such predominantly white cities as Flint, Kalamazoo, Lansing and Battle Creek. By Sunday night, even Jackson began to wonder: Could he, in fact, really win this thing?

If the question dawned slowly on the candidate, it came crashing down on a host of horrified others. Jackson's upset threw the Democratic race into disarray. Dukakis, the erstwhile front runner in delegates and cash, had survived a Super Tuesday challenge but was having trouble in Rustbelt states crucial to Democratic chances in the fall. Jackson, the front runner in message and momentum, was everything party leaders dreaded: outspoken, liberal, black, feared by a large number of white Americans and presumed unelectable. Once again, the Democratic Party seemed ready to self-destruct before the primaries were over. "The party is up against an extraordinary end game," said Paul Maslin, a Democratic poll taker, reflecting the apparent dilemma. "If this guy has more convention votes than anyone else, how can we not nominate him? But how can we nominate him?"

By Monday morning, as a veritable tornado of free publicity, public support and sheer frenzy slammed into the Jackson campaign, everything around him was transformed as if by some force of nature. Crowds, which for months had far exceeded those of his rivals, mushroomed. Supporters overran police barriers at every stop, pressing up against his limousine, reaching to touch Jackson, thrusting $20 bills and homemade handicrafts into his hands, crushing his staff and terrifying his Secret Service bodyguards. Hundreds of blacks chased him down a dark street at nightfall on Milwaukee's north side.

The Wisconsin crowds transfixed the candidate, suggesting to him that the Michigan results were no fluke. The situation had the normally calculating Jackson confused, caught between his heart and his head. Jackson knew that Dukakis held the edge in money, organization and history. Yet Jackson's romantic side could not help feeling that perhaps this tide of white support was growing, that perhaps history was somehow working to his advantage. Another victory here and a couple of breaks in New York, and he might just pull off a miracle. Sure, he figured, it was a long shot, but it *was* a shot. As Jackson crisscrossed the state in the first week of April, flush with optimism, he would look out on teeming crowds of whites and whisper to reporters, "Archie Bunker has changed."

So had Jackson. In contrast to his first bid four years before, Jackson was no longer the reluctant candidate, insecure about running, quick to criticize the party and aimless in strategy. His 1984 campaign was based on one issue: black political empowerment. In 1988 he developed a more inclusive weave of populism, self-betterment and anticorporatism, which was defining the Democratic race and serving as a thematic cheat sheet for his rivals. While they specialized in negative campaigning, Jackson adopted an irrepressibly positive bearing, making him the conscience of his party and its spiritual, if not its secular, leader. His advisers, once all blacks, were now mostly whites. Four years after Jackson's campaign had nearly aborted when he described New York City as "Hymietown," his campaign manager, Gerald Austin, was a Bronx-born Jew. Most important, the crusade that had appealed almost exclusively to blacks in 1984 had become a full-blown campaign that was winning support from white Americans.

And now, exactly 20 years after the murder of his mentor, the Rev. Martin Luther King Jr., Jackson was on the verge of testing America's racial tolerance. Jackson was, by his steady gain in delegates, forcing Americans to ponder the prospect not only of a black nominee but also of a black President. Jackson had by his success set off a chain reaction of tiny, almost immeasurably small, recalibrations of assumptions and expectations in the minds of voters. Those reassessments might not be enough to land a black in the Oval Office in 1988, but they dented the invisible Whites-Only barrier at the White House gate. For those of his race, Jackson's success was the long-delayed redemption of one of America's many unfulfilled promises, a dream deferred for more than a century.

And what of the man who 46 years before was born out of wedlock to a Greenville, S.C., hairdresser, the man who recalled tearfully that his third name was Jackson, after Jesse Burns and "bastard"? With bug-eyed political experts talking seriously in Washington about a Jackson nomination, the candidate, for the first time in his life, knew he was caught up in something larger than he was, something beyond his understanding and control. Something even larger than King. "People are listening to me now," he said. "King never had that."

Jackson's ascendancy was measurable not only on the barometer of race relations. His soaring message and powerful personal dynamism also exerted a strong leftward tug on the Democratic Party in the twilight of the Reagan era, even as its likely nominee, Michael Dukakis, resisted liberalism's solutions to the nation's problems. Jackson's rivals had already appropriated his themes: Richard Gephardt was a relative latecomer to Jackson's farms-and-jobs style of populism; Dukakis adopted Jackson's powerful complaint that 37 million Americans lacked health insurance; and nearly all the candidates of both parties joined Jackson's chorus for an all-out war on drugs. He was providing not only the race's excitement but, increasingly, his party's message as well.

As the full light of the moment began to shine on the candidate, questions remained about Jackson himself. Did this man, or any man who had never held elective office, deserve to be President? Had Jackson, who ended his divisive 1984 campaign with the reassurance that "God is not finished with me yet," truly matured as a national figure? And if, as seemed certain, the party ultimately chose another as standard-bearer, would Jackson support the nominee, or would he bolt and bring four more years of Republicans to power?

Those questions were distant problems in 1985, when Jackson began his second bid for the nomination. His first challenge was to recruit the many black elected officials who in 1984 had been resistant not just to a black candidacy or a protest candidacy but to a Jackson candidacy in particular. Jackson was criticized by blacks in 1984 for seeking the top elected office without ever having mounted a campaign for a lower job. "We had to move on the leadership," Frank Watkins, Jackson's longtime confidant, speechwriter and perennial top aide recalled, "so he didn't get run over again."

Jackson assured his colleagues that even if it failed, his candidacy would energize black voters and, in turn, enhance the re-election chances of black officials. But to convince them that he would not lose, Jackson made a mathematical argument: Mondale won the 1984 nomination with 6.8 million primary votes, while eligible black voters alone numbered some 20 million. If blacks turned out in greater numbers, Jackson calculated, the nomination was within reach. Jackson needed black leaders for another reason: the earlier he locked up the black vote, the sooner he could get on to wooing white voters. It was a formidable assignment. In 1984 Jackson had run a largely race-based campaign and made little effort to broaden his appeal to include whites. He received only 5% of the white vote. In 1988 he would need to hold nearly all the black votes and triple his share of white votes in order to secure the nomination.

Fashioning a message that would appeal to whites as well as blacks was not an easy task. Jackson never abandoned his interest in civil rights, but his 1988 message was based squarely on the notion that the divisive racial violence of the 1960s had given way to a Reagan-inspired "economic violence" in the 1980s. Better than any of his rivals, Jackson isolated economic ills at a time when prosperity was generally on the rise. He set out to show that in the Reagan era whites and blacks shared political struggles and economic goals. "Common ground," he called it. Both races suffered under a Government that backed management against la-

or, from a social order under which women were paid only a raction of men's wages for comparable work, in a nation where oo many citizens lacked basic health insurance. "We are a better ation than that," he said. In fact, Jackson noted, many whites were worse off than blacks. "Most poor people aren't black— hey're white, female and young." Jackson's point was that race lid not matter. "I was searching for what would make whites and olacks find common ground," he later recalled. "Just sort of hammering away at what they had in common."

Jackson had kept his campaign message squarely in the vernacular, simple, straightforward and, as George Wallace iked to say, "down where the goats can get it." Blessed with an uncanny ability to alter his message, timing and syntax to each crowd, he molded himself to the setting: irreverent and informal with aging '60s radicals; ponderous and weighty with groups of traditional whites; full of old-time religion when talking in olack Baptist churches (though Jackson was visiting far fewer of hese in 1988 than he did in 1984). Jackson also worked hard to, as he put it, broaden the narrow mainstream of the Democratic Party to include his motley constituents. Soon after he formally leclared his candidacy, Jackson preached to Lutherans at a small church in Winterset, Iowa, spoke to gays and lesbians marching in Washington, and then jetted to New Hampshire to talk to environmentalists. At each stop he urged his audiences to look beyond their own narrow concerns and respect the concerns of his other supporters. "I'm making the mainstream a wide river," he said during his announcement swing. "There's no sense in having a mainstream that's a skinny creek." But voters seemed less interested in Jackson's brave political gymnastics than in the clarity of his message: "Stop drugs from coming in. Stop jobs from going out. Keep America strong. Make America better." And this: "We must choose day care and prenatal care on the front side of life, rather than jail care and welfare on the back side of life."

By keying such themes as drugs, jobs and the benefits of

job security, Jackson blurred his image as an ardent liberal an
at times appeared remarkably moderate. Yet Jackson's pro
gram was unrefined liberalism, not so much in quality as quan
tity. The policies he favored all came from the standard Demo
cratic playbook, and Jackson wanted *all* of them: he favored a
increase in the minimum wage from $3.35; comparable pay fo
comparable work done by women; and massive infusions o
funds for housing, education and welfare.

More directly, Jackson set out in 1986 to earn the trust o
farmers in Iowa and workers in states across the North an
South. Unable to offer—as Representative Richard Gephard
did—millions of dollars in legislated farm or trade benefit
Jackson used his negotiating skills on behalf of family farmer
in Minnesota, when local banks threatened foreclosure. H
walked the picket lines at countless factories, assiduously court
ing the Teamsters and, in particular, the paperworkers, wh
during the 1980s were victims of industry-wide restructuring
But if he pandered, he did not grovel. In early debates throug
the fall of 1987 and 1988, Jackson won high marks for his clarit
of vision. While his rivals quoted from position papers and legis
lation, Jackson played bold cards. At a December debate i
Edinburg, Texas, where Gephardt and Babbitt rambled o
vaguely about trade and economic development in the Ri
Grande Valley, Jackson drew the biggest applause when h
called for construction of a law school, a medical school and a
engineering school in the region, as well as housing and th
training needed to build the houses.

Yet when whites at first turned out to vote as well as hear
Jackson, few observers noticed the increase in interest. Dis
tracted by the muddled Iowa caucus results, pundits paid little
attention when on caucus night Jackson nabbed nearly 9% o
the turnout, 9,773 votes, in a state just 1% black and where he
was outspent by as much as 5 to 1 by his opponents. Jackson re
peated the stunt a week later in New Hampshire, where he net
ted 7.8% of the vote. Jackson scored in the Minnesota caucus a

week later, on Feb. 23, placing third with 20%. He finished second to Dukakis in both of Maine's tiny caucuses on Feb. 28 and in Vermont's low-key March 1 primary, where he won 26% of the vote.

While most of his rivals flitted from Iowa to New Hampshire and back through much of 1987, Jackson toiled in the South, site of nearly half the 21 primaries and caucuses to be held on a single "Super Tuesday" in March. Jackson made repeated trips to Texas, Florida, the Deep South states of Mississippi, Alabama and Georgia, as well as two states he regarded as home: South Carolina, where he was born, and North Carolina, where he went to college. With blacks making up an ever increasing portion of registered Democrats in Dixie, Jackson's aides counted on winning up to six Super Tuesday states outright and scoring well in nearly all the rest. Campaign manager Austin calculated that if white Democratic senatorial candidates such as Wyche Fowler and Richard Shelby had won seats in 1986 with 90% of the black vote and 30% to 40% of the white vote, Jackson could take most of the Deep South with nearly 100% of the black vote and just 10% of the white vote. Jackson combined his home-field advantage with a more sophisticated state-by-state organization than any he had mounted in 1984. Aided by top delegate hunter Steve Cobble, Austin targeted nearly 100 House districts across the region, 75 of which were winnable, and 20 more that were expected to produce Jackson delegates.

With Dukakis largely skipping the Deep South states, Jackson solidified his base in predictable fashion: visiting black colleges, recruiting black clergy to organize Sunday-morning get-out-the-vote efforts, staging high-profile rallies at such key battlegrounds of the civil rights movement as Birmingham, Selma, Ala., and Atlanta. Recalling his days of service to King, Jackson told blacks, "I stood with you. Now you must stand with me." The candidate's appeals to white voters were growing more sophisticated as well. Partly to deflect conservative criticism about his policies, he asked voters to consider his candidacy symbolically, not so much by itself but in the context of a generation of deepening racial harmony in what he called the "New South." Southerners once divided by history, fear and race, Jackson argued, must stand together for common economic rights and justice. "We'd learned to live together these last 25 years. Go to school together, pay taxes together, go to war together, get shot at together, die together. Now we got to figure out how to eat together." At a stop in the Texas refinery town of Beaumont in February, Jackson was onstage shaking hands when local pipe fitters' union official Bruce Hill approached the civil rights leader and recalled how in 1965 both men were at the Edmund Pettus Bridge in Selma. "So this is a reunion," said Jackson. Replied Hill: "I was on the other side." The former Klansman had become a Jackson supporter.

Four years after Jackson ran his first campaign out of his hip pocket, he recruited Austin, the smart, savvy and outspoken Ohio political consultant, to manage his operation. Austin inherited a hollow, bankrupt organization in Chicago—it lacked telephones and wastebaskets—modernized it, computerized it and began experimenting with direct-mail solicitation. Four years after Jackson self-financed a national campaign with pass-the-bucket church appeals for $20 bills ("Jacksons for Jackson," the candidate would beg), his manager was erecting a fund-raising network of 180,000 contributors that would eventually net more than $16 million before it was all over, nearly half of that through direct mail. The aggressive fund raising allowed Jackson to charter a DC-9 jet the day after the Iowa caucuses, enabling him to crisscross the country in brutal, 20-hour days.

While Dukakis and Gore could place their well-produced ads in big media markets, Austin by necessity wielded a scalpel, buying time in such cheaper, middle-size markets as Richmond, Roanoke, Va., and Midland, Texas, on the weekend before the vote. (Austin's paltry $100,000 Super Tuesday media purchase was nonetheless more than Jackson's television buy for the en-

tire 1984 campaign.) But most of the publicity was of the free variety. Austin calculated that the best media draw was flying
Jackson around to ten different cities each day with film crews
in tow. There was no money, moreover, for polling. As Jackson
said, "We have the poorest campaign but the richest message."

The combination worked better than almost anyone had
expected. On March 8 Jackson outpolled Dukakis overall, won
five states—Virginia, Georgia, Mississippi, Alabama and Louisiana—and was second in nearly all the rest, including Massachusetts, where he won 19% of the vote. Jackson swept his base
of support, taking 95% of the black vote and 10% of the white
vote. He picked up 368 delegates, second by only 14 to Dukakis,
and was the sole candidate to take delegates in each primary
state. Though outspent by rivals Dukakis and Gore by 20 to 1
and 30 to 1, respectively, Jackson in one night netted nearly as
many delegates as he had won in his entire 1984 campaign.

Exit polls suggested that Jackson had successfully stitched
together the crazy quilt of various special interests of which he
so often spoke. He did well among factory workers, trade union-
ists, environmentalists, feminists, young professionals and the
unemployed. Some patches did not find a place in Jackson's
homespun design: according to ABC News exit polls of the
Southern region, he fared less well among Jews, independent
voters and, not surprisingly, Reagan Democrats. Jackson's dogged courtship of Hispanics also fell flat; voters in South Texas
and South Florida were more attracted to Dukakis, who had
wooed them relentlessly in the Spanish language and found an
even stronger bond in the common language of the immigrant.

The results proved the law of unintended consequences.
Conceived to boost the chances of a moderate Democrat with
Southern roots, the megaprimary had underscored a black liberal's appeal. Rather than creating a clear front runner, as expected, the balkanized results instead created more confusion.
Dukakis, who scored a "four corners" victory with wins in Florida, Maryland, Washington and Texas, and Gore, who won

across Border States with the help of the white vote, emerged along with Jackson to fight another day.

Jackson was not well poised to capitalize on his surge. Though he followed Super Tuesday with easy victories in Alaska and South Carolina, he faced formidable odds in the next big state, Illinois. While he was beloved by many of the state's urban blacks, Jackson had few fans in the white wards, where voters had been watching his headline-grabbing antics for decades. At a cold, drizzly St. Patrick's Day parade two days before the primary, Irish Americans chanted "Get Jesse, get Jesse" as local pols, swathed in Kelly green, strolled by.

Meanwhile, party bigwigs forced another Illinois favorite son, Senator Paul Simon, who was running out of money, to remain in the race through the March 15 primary so that they—and not Jackson's people—would be credentialed as delegates to the Democratic National Convention. Jackson pulled to within a few points of Simon the weekend before the vote, but that news may only have driven people to vote against him. In any event, Simon prevailed, taking 43% of a million and a half votes, to Jackson's 32%. While Jackson won more than 90% of the black vote, he took only 1 in 12 white votes.

Illinois' lessons were bittersweet for Jackson. After campaigning in 1984 to abolish such disenfranchising party procedures as runoff elections in Southern states, Jackson now felt the pinch of an even better dodge in Northern industrial states: winner-take-all primaries. Though Jackson captured nearly a third of the popular vote in Illinois, the state's rules allocated convention delegates on a winner-take-all basis in each congressional district. Thus Jackson was awarded only 22% of the delegates; the soon-to-exit Simon received all the rest. And Jackson faced similar rules in other key states: Pennsylvania, New Jersey and West Virginia.

But Jackson, as ever, saw good omens elsewhere. The fragmented nature of the race was working to his advantage. With four white candidates—Gore, Simon, Gephardt and Dukakis—

splitting the white vote, Jackson could amass 30-point pluralities and walk into second place. He could even win a few states. He had won both the Alaska and South Carolina caucuses with little effort or money. (In Alaska, Austin authorized only $15.50 for shipping charges to send a box of campaign buttons to supporters. Dukakis all but conceded South Carolina outright.) Several days after Illinois, Jackson took 31% of the vote for a second-place finish in the Kansas caucus after spending only five hours in the state.

Meanwhile, in Michigan, Jackson's top organizer, Joel Ferguson, wagered that his state, still suffering in many places from the recession, was ideally suited for an upset. Ferguson, a real estate developer, knew that the state's screwball "firehouse caucus"—not really a deliberative caucus but a mere four-hour opening of the polls on a Saturday afternoon—was forbidding enough to dampen turnout among all but the truly committed. Plus, with Gephardt making a desperate last stand with the aid of the United Auto Workers, Ferguson knew Dukakis faced another three-way white-vote split.

For six days Jackson campaigned as he never had, giving six, seven, sometimes ten speeches a day. He attracted unexpectedly large crowds, ten times that of Dukakis' draws: 2,000 in Muskegon, 4,000 in Kalamazoo. On March 17 Jackson announced in Detroit a sophisticated and controversial plan to funnel $60 billion of public pension funds into bonds for the purpose of rebuilding roads, bridges and schools. He stepped up his attacks on George Bush but refrained from attacking his Democratic rivals. Ferguson capitalized on confusing last-minute changes in polling places and set up a toll-free hotline through which voters could learn where to vote. Austin purchased $70,000 in television airtime—the Jackson campaign's first paid advertising in major TV markets—as part of a $120,000 advertising budget. By the end of the week, even as the New York *Times* gave Dukakis "an edge" in the contest, Ferguson privately expected to win with a 40% plurality.

The margin proved even larger, 53% to Dukakis' 29%. Jackson increased by fivefold his take of the popular vote in 1984, winning more than 100,000 votes in Michigan. He swamped Dukakis by more than 9 to 1 in the predominantly black districts. He gained half again as many delegates as the Duke, who suddenly was in a dead heat for delegates, with 605.55 to Jackson's 606.55, according to the Associated Press. Experts estimated that Jackson's share of the white vote was about 20%.

Almost instantly, the campaign was transformed into chaos. Crowds, which for months had always easily exceeded those drawn by Jackson's rivals, tripled in size. A near frenzy overtook the campaign. Dukakis' lead in the next contest, Wisconsin, fell to nine points virtually overnight. Jackson's own advisers, who by March knew that their man was a shoo-in for second place, had not expected the real gains to come until later. "We were really thinking about New York for this kind of surge," said Willie Brown, speaker of the California assembly and cochairman of Jackson's campaign. "But this thing has just turned us around." Commented Bert Lance, former Carter Administration budget director, who was emerging as Jackson's closest adviser: "It's something akin to a volcano exploding."

Suddenly, everyone wanted to see, and be seen with, Jesse Jackson. The campaign invited 40-odd white and black Democratic pols for a high-profile power breakfast four days later at Washington's Jefferson Hotel, partly to underscore Jackson's role as party insider and reassure nervous pooh-bahs that he was no longer a disruptive force. After 25 years of scratching his way to the top, Jackson had finally bagged his quarry: he had the party's élite—Clark Clifford and Edward Bennett Williams among them—eating, if briefly, out of his hand. Money began to pour in at the Dukakis-size rate of $60,000 a day.

Fretting in private over the "What does Jesse want?" question, party leaders and rivals began to sing Jackson's praises in public. Hundreds of news organizations requested interviews;

Jackson's picture appeared on the cover of TIME, *Newsweek* and *U.S. News and World Report*. He drew intoxicatingly large, mostly white crowds throughout Wisconsin. When more than 2,000 showed up late one night in La Crosse, where no event was planned, Jackson kidded his audience: "Don't you people never sleep?" The crowds astounded Jackson's staff and impressed the candidate. "There is a growing affection taking place between the people and me," he explained.

But "Big Mo" could be a centrifugal force too, and Jackson's campaign began to spin out of control. Inside Jackson Central, excitement edged toward the level of fantasy. Less than a week after advisers had been divided over whether to abandon a district-by-district delegate strategy for direct appeal to popular votes, victory now seemed not only possible but, to some, inevitable. After months of sticking closely to his schedule, Jackson reverted to making unscheduled stops, leaving reporters and staff stranded at events scratched by the candidate, thus missing the evening news reports.

Rather than pouring some of the money into polling (which would have shown Dukakis back up by 20 points four days after Michigan), Jackson coasted. Buoyed by the crowds, he left Wisconsin for 48 hours just two days before the vote to devote time to the comparatively insignificant Colorado caucuses. A world-class extemporaneous orator, Jackson began to give boring speeches from prepared texts. "I'm trying to be presidential," he said. After all, as the candidate whispered to a TIME reporter as Jackson's DC-9 carried his swollen press entourage to Wisconsin for the final push in that state, "I am the party leader now."

But if that was to be Jackson's new position, it was also to be the standard against which he would be measured. In Wisconsin he entangled himself in a foreign policy faux pas from which he would never recover. Late in March, liberals and conservatives were pressuring the White House to do something about Panamanian leader Manuel Antonio Noriega in light of reports that the dictator had for years been on the CIA payroll even while being involved in drug-running activities. Jackson announced in Wisconsin that he had dispatched a courier to Panama City to deliver to Noriega a letter asking him to step down voluntarily. Jackson called his letter a "moral appeal," but the State Department criticized the action as an annoying interference in delicate U.S. diplomacy. "Proliferation of channels is a tactic Noriega likes to use to buy time," said State Department spokeswoman Phyllis Oakley. Dukakis, Gore and countless editorial writers also criticized the maneuver, questioning the wisdom of a presidential candidate's trying to wrestle a thug from power with moral suasion, and raising many of the old doubts about Jackson's foreign policy credentials.

The flap might have died quickly, but Jackson grew defensive and raised the issue at nearly every stop in Wisconsin, obscuring the economic and social-justice issues that had carried him to victory in Michigan. (After Dukakis won the nomination, Jackson would criticize the party standard-bearer for talking about Noriega at all.) Worse, the heady rush of momentum seemed at times to deprive the candidate of his balance and cause him to slip into unalloyed demagoguery. During an Easter Sunday sermon at the First Baptist Church in Denver, where he had jetted for a 48-hour swing, Jackson likened the late Martin Luther King Jr. to Christ and compared his own campaign— and by extension himself—to the Resurrection and the Life. "Twenty years later, the stone has been rolled away," he said. At a statehouse rally the next day in Madison, Wis., Jackson recalled, as he often did, his grandmother's love of F.D.R. Then, omitting his normal reference to Roosevelt's belief in public welfare programs, Jackson instead said, "I want to be that close to you! I want to love you that much, and I want you to love me that much!"

It was not to be. The following day Wisconsin voters handed Dukakis his most important campaign victory so far, turning out for the Governor by a tally of more than 47% to Jackson's 28%. Jackson ran poorly outside the big-city black wards, making little dent in either farm districts or college towns. He fared worst in the heavily ethnic blue-collar wards of south Milwaukee. While Jackson netted an estimated 23% of the white vote, many of the late-deciding voters, most of whom were whites born before World War II, swung en bloc in the final days not to Jackson (or even Dukakis) but to Gore.

Jackson reacted to the defeat in Wisconsin, and to a similar bruising at the Duke's hands in the Colorado caucuses, with a mixture of hope and disappointment. On one hand, Jackson claimed victory after Wisconsin, genuinely pleased that he could win such a high percentage of the vote in a state that was only 3% black, confident that he was being listened to and taken seriously as a presidential contender. On the other hand, there was no mistaking the flight of many whites to Gore and Dukakis. Nor could Jackson miss the fear of a black nominee that seemed to emerge after Michigan. Just days before the Wisconsin contest, Jeanne Simon, the Illinois Senator's wife, likened Jackson's powerful speaking style to that of Adolf Hitler. Though she later issued a retraction, the comment cut Jackson deeply. Gore, a former divinity-school student, signaled that the race was about to get ugly when he commented that voters needed to elect Presidents, not preachers. (Austin labeled Gore a "chickenshit" for that barb.) Jackson was also privately furious when Democratic Party chairman Paul Kirk declared after Wisconsin that the race was "finally straightening itself out." It was as if Jackson had come too close to the prize.

But Jackson hardly had time to weigh the Wisconsin results before he was engulfed in the racial and religious tinderbox of the New York primary. Though Dukakis led in every major New York poll by nearly 20 points, Jackson had taken 26% of the vote in the state in 1984 against Walter Mondale, and experts figured he would win a minimum of 35 percentage points this time around. Working against Dukakis from the right was Gore, whose desperate last-stand effort was based almost exclusively on a courtship of the state's Jewish community. Gore had won the endorsement of Mayor Ed Koch, who said Jews would be "crazy" to vote for Jackson. Though Austin branded Koch a lunatic and an idiot, the dirt-ball tactics kept Jackson off guard and on the defensive for two weeks. Gore's seconds also began an erroneous whispering campaign that Jackson was still in touch with Black Muslim leader Louis Farrakhan, reviving the memory of Jackson's Hymietown comment and angering Jews, blacks and Hispanic leaders simultaneously.

Jackson calmly denied any association with Farrakhan, but privately he was boiling. He felt that he had atoned for his sins by pleading for freedom for Jewish *refuseniks* while visiting with Mikhail Gorbachev in Geneva in 1985. Jackson at first refused to meet with Jewish leaders, at one point asking, "If someone wants my head, why should I hand them a hatchet?"

But the issue dogged him across the state. At the State University of New York at Binghamton, hostile students chanted, "If Jesse can't, Farrakhan." Jackson only made matters worse when he consistently brushed aside questions from Jewish Americans, complaining that candidates need not pander to African, Haitian or Panamanian immigrants though they live in New York in proportions similar to that of Jews. After two weeks of nonstop questions, Jackson aides assembled a group of 50 conspicuously moderate Jews for a private Sunday brunch in New York City. Even that was a dismal failure. One Reform rabbi accused Jackson of being too thin-skinned for a politician; another grilled Jackson on his failure to repudiate Farrakhan: "It is not enough to say one 'disagrees' with Farrakhan any more than it is enough to say one 'disagrees' with the Ku Klux Klan . . . Please don't slough this off again with talk of redemption." But the candidate did not get the message. "I don't believe," he said, "in repudiating human beings."

Meanwhile, Jackson's New York campaign suffered from a diffuseness of purpose that undermined the strategy laid out for him by aides. Jackson walked across the Williamsburg Bridge, which had been closed as unsafe, arguing that he was

the only candidate with a plan to rebuild the nation's fraying infrastructure—an issue strangely lacking in the dynamism that
was once his specialty. Jackson's black New York organizers,
pursuing personal political agendas, confined Jackson to five
predominantly black congressional districts in New York City.
Nursing a cold and drained by the hurly-burly, Jackson retreated regularly to the safe harbors of black churches for major
speeches and to Harlem soul-food restaurants for unplanned
meal stops. As one top New York organizer said, "It was a very,
very black campaign."

By primary day, Jackson was openly bitter. He accused
Koch of prompting the increase in death threats received by the
campaign and blamed the press for allowing Koch and Gore to
get away with the race baiting. At a cold, rainy Harlem rally on
the eve of the primary, Jackson's bitterness and frustration
came tumbling out in a torrent. "Can't get a headline about
health care, can't get a headline about welfare hotels, can't get a
headline about drugs, or affording AIDS, or a falling bridge. It's
all about diversion, it's all about bright lights, and show time
and deflection. It's all about jive."

Two days later, a New York *Daily News* headline told the
story: THE DUKE DOES IT. Dukakis took 51% of the statewide
vote to Jackson's 37%. Jackson narrowly won New York City.
But Dukakis thoroughly trounced him elsewhere, sweeping upstate by more than 2 to 1. Jackson won 97% of the black vote but
only 16% of the white vote.

The result was also part of a clear but discomfiting pattern
that indicated he fared better with whites in states where there
are fewer blacks. Indeed, the New York defeat was replicated
by a bigger defeat a week later in Pennsylvania, where Jackson
was hopelessly unorganized and deprived of a proportional
share of delegates due to winner-take-all rules. Dukakis defeated him 67% to 27%. Poor organization plagued Jackson again
in Ohio, where Dukakis smashed him 63% to 27%, as well as in
Indiana, the same day, where the vote was 70% to 22%. In each

case, Jackson's share of the white vote dwindled further. He got 12% in the Keystone state, 17% in Ohio and 11% in Indiana. Conversely, in later states such as Oregon, where blacks constitute a much smaller percentage of the population, Jackson did better with whites, winning 38% overall and 35% of the white vote. In the final contests, much as in the preceding primaries, familiarity seemed to breed contempt: whites appeared more inclined to a Jackson candidacy where the fewest blacks lived.

The defeats took their toll on the Jackson campaign. The candidate began to spar in public with his caustic campaign manager, who told reporters on the morning after the New York defeat that Jackson should set his sights on the vice presidency. Jackson began to isolate Austin as punishment for his candor, though within five weeks the candidate would make the same argument even more forcefully.

Though he had for months artfully kept internal factions harnessed in common cause, Jackson watched as the fragile unity between longtime supporters and newer, more moderate operatives unraveled after the New York primary. The factions split chiefly over strategy. With the nomination no longer a realistic option, many of the more militant supporters began agitating for a full-blown bid for the vice-presidential spot. Members of the Congressional Black Caucus, playing a card sure to be popular with their constituents, called for a Dukakis-Jackson ticket in order to send a positive message to young blacks. Moderate aides, confident that Dukakis would inevitably turn to a white running mate, thought this strategy dangerous, sure only to sow disappointment. Under tremendous pressure from blacks to emerge from the primary race with something more tangible than the few moments of prime-time glory he wrenched from Walter Mondale in 1984, Jackson at first took a middle course, giving lip service to the notion that he was uninterested in the No. 2 job but allowing his seconds in the Black Caucus to push the idea. But he refused the pleas of aides who, impatient with the Massachusetts Governor's vague prescriptions for domestic spending, argued for direct attacks on Dukakis during the last half a dozen primaries. Anxious to preserve his fledgling status as party leader, Jackson feared the appearance of what he called the "big black man beating up on the little white guy."

Dukakis made this conciliatory approach difficult. The Massachusetts Governor confounded Jackson by keeping his distance even after the primaries ended. Dukakis knew that Jackson wanted to be taken seriously. What he did not seem to understand is how that translated in Jackson's mind to being consulted, to having regular conversations, to having a place at the table. Politicos and reporters tried to explain this to Dukakis' aides, but the message was not sinking in. Party leaders were clearly relieved when the two rivals began having regular phone conversations after Jackson's Michigan upset, but these chats only served to highlight the differences in style between the two men. In one exchange, Jackson asked his rival if he thought it was fair to take nearly all the delegates in Puerto Rico when Jackson had won the popular vote in a nonbinding "beauty contest" that had no bearing on actual delegate appropriation. When Dukakis replied that it was, Jackson was astounded.

Jackson began to worry not so much that Dukakis thought ill of him, but that he did not think about him at all. On the eve of the June 7 California primary, the two men had a 90-minute session that was grimly businesslike. While piano-playing Dukakis spokesman Mark Gearan serenaded reporters waiting in the lobby with *Getting To Know You*, Jackson and Dukakis spent most of the session avoiding their differences. "We were not making progress on a relationship," Jackson later admitted.

Two days later, after Dukakis had locked up the nomination by winning California, Jackson lunged for the vice-presidential nomination. For weeks Jackson had said that he, as second-best vote getter, had "earned consideration" for the second spot on the ticket, a carefully hedged position designed to keep options open. But after losing California to Dukakis (as well as

New Jersey, New Mexico and Montana all on the same day and by solid margins), Jackson appeared before reporters the morning after and announced that the office was now worth fighting for. The disclosure came after a reporter asked whether Jackson would be "comfortable" playing second fiddle. "Do you understand my background?" he replied, noting that while other men who have been groomed for high-level positions might regard the No. 2 job as a "step down," he did not. "The Vice President is not quite the top, but it's a long ways from where I started."

Aides were stunned, unable to interpret the gambit because they did not understand it themselves. Bert Lance called the candidate within hours and said, "I know you want to keep everybody confused, but now you've confused me." Jackson did not even seem to know what he was up to, suggesting that afternoon it was something of a holding action. "As long as I'm dribbling the ball, no one else can shoot it," he told an intimate.

Jackson's own remarks provided some clues. Several days after staking his claim to the vice presidency, the candidate had calmed down a bit, acknowledging that the second spot was a "consideration" in his negotiations with Dukakis, adding, "but it will be one of many considerations." The South Chicago negotiator in him figured that the sideshow would, at minimum, keep him in the news during the critical post-primary stage. In addition, the imagined threat of a potentially unhappy black constituency might, with luck, force Dukakis to make concessions on a variety of obscure rule and platform matters key to Jackson's future and to his ability to point to accomplishments at the Atlanta convention. Indeed, within several weeks, Jackson had won from Dukakis' agents a sweeping reform of party rules that included abolition of winner-take-all primaries and reduction by nearly half in the number of super-delegates that would be permitted at the 1992 convention. Those changes would have boosted his delegate take in 1988 from under 1,300 to more than 1,500.

Jackson was less successful during June in fashioning a

Democratic platform to his liking. Having tapped former Kennedy speechwriter Theodore Sorensen to craft a document that was long on rhetoric and short on specifics, Dukakis' platform managers allowed Jackson's aides to insert in the platform numerous passages drawn directly from Jackson speeches. But the platform committee balked at including specific Jackson proposals on the budget, taxes, housing and education. Whether Jackson might have won these concessions without his Veep maneuver is unknowable, but the extra pressure probably did not hurt. A banker, Lance explained it in terms he understood: "When folks want to borrow something, they ask for twice as much."

The vice-presidential gambit was not merely a tactical move. Once again, at a critical moment in the campaign, the two locomotives of Jackson's character were on a collision course. The realistic side of Jackson knew instinctively that he would not get the nod, but the romantic side of him wanted it anyway. Jackson believed he had unified liberal special-interest groups that for years pursued separate agendas and deprived the party of victory. He further believed that a place on the ticket would signal to the world that America had finally overcome a heritage of racial prejudice. The nomination would also be an invaluable message for the millions of dispossessed who needed encouragement to, as Jackson liked to say, "keep hope alive." Jackson may also have calculated that a reach for the No. 2 spot in 1988 would smooth the way to a place on the ticket in 1992, just as his 1984 run had readied America for his second try.

But most of all, he simply wanted it. Emerging from his three days of rest at San Diego's La Costa spa on June 10, Jackson told a handful of reporters that the best qualified man in the running was—who else?—Jesse Jackson. "You have Congressmen who have said we should have someone from the South—I meet that qualification. That you have to have someone from that region where Dukakis is weak—I carried the South in a strong way. Someone says someone who has hero stature—I have hero stature."

Jackson spent the weeks before Atlanta wavering between reason and emotion, between threats of disunity and pledges of conciliation. On one hand, he seemed to sense the end, talking nostalgically of the campaign in private, retreating to the backyard of his Chicago home in an endless string of interviews. He remarked to a reporter that his 6.5 million votes had "delighted, but not surprised" him. But his relations with Dukakis were not improving. Jackson bridled when Dukakis came through Chicago in late June without at least telephoning him. He learned from a reporter that party chief Kirk had chosen Ann Richards, Texas' ebullient state treasurer, and not Jackson or an anointed substitute, as convention keynote speaker.

When Dukakis invited Jackson and his wife to Brookline, Mass., for dinner and fireworks on July 4, Jackson presumed that Dukakis was finally ready to talk ticket. But over a meal of poached salmon and clam chowder—a menu suited more to the Dukakis palate than that of a man who has been known to have fried chicken for breakfast—Jackson quickly realized that nothing of the kind was in the offing. Politesse, not politics, was the real fare. While Dukakis sat impassively nearby, Jackson had but 15 minutes to make his case after dinner before the Dukakis children returned with a request for dessert. Then it was off to the Esplanade and, after the fireworks and a concert, Dukakis pleaded for sleep. Frustrated, Jackson never got to make his pitch. "He felt he'd been treated like a nigger," said one top adviser.

Jackson and his aides knew what was coming. Through intermediaries such as Lance, aides began to suggest ways that Dukakis could sell Jackson on someone like Al Gore, Bob Graham or Lloyd Bentsen as running mate. If Dukakis informed Jackson of his choice while asking the candidate to help sell the liberal wing of the party to the conservative Southerner, they said, the candidate would respond positively. But a week after the Boston soirée, the game ended abruptly. A reporter approached Jackson at a Washington airline terminal and asked for his comment on Dukakis' choice that morning of Bentsen. An uncharacteristically flummoxed Jackson demurred, uttering a faint "No comment" while cameras rolled and aides looked on uncomfortably. Somehow, the Dukakis campaign, for all its vaunted efficiency, had failed to reach Jackson by phone earlier that morning in his Cincinnati hotel.

Jackson had supplied Paul Brountas, Dukakis' campaign chairman, with his telephone number the night before, after the two men and their various aides had a 90-minute vice-presidential discussion in Washington. Jackson told reporters what by then many had guessed: he would take the job if it was offered. Brountas, who insisted then that Jackson was still under "serious consideration" (though it would become obvious that he was not), then returned to Boston while Jackson flew to Ohio for a fund raiser for his new "Keep Hope Alive" political-action committee. Brountas preferred to postpone the Veep decision until the next day, but Dukakis insisted on resolving the matter late that night at his Brookline home. After Dukakis chose Bentsen, it fell to campaign manager Susan Estrich to ensure that her boss made the courtesy call to Jackson the next morning. Incredibly, Estrich did not insist that Dukakis make the early-morning phone call to his rejected suitor. By the time the call was placed from the Governor's Beacon Hill office, Jackson was already airborne for Washington.

The oversight, adding insult to injury, turned out to be a major misstep for Dukakis. Jackson immediately seized on his treatment at the Duke's hands as an issue, energizing his listless campaign just as Dukakis should have been enjoying nomination by acclamation. "I'm too controlled, too mature to be angry," Jackson said to reporters that afternoon, leaving little doubt that he was angry. He publicly withheld his endorsement of the ticket and threatened worse. As Jackson's "Rainbow Express" caravan of seven buses left Chicago for Atlanta several days later, Jackson talked obliquely of contesting Dukakis' choice of Bentsen and putting his own name in nomination at the convention.

The maneuver deftly created Jackson's favorite results: panic and uncertainty. House Speaker Jim Wright called him and volunteered to make peace. Jackson also announced that he had asked former President Jimmy Carter to mediate. This was quintessential "Jackson action," working both sides of the conflict, posing simultaneously as peacemaker and the melodrama's chief agent provocateur. For the final five days of the campaign, Jackson by turns spent the mornings fanning the fire storm between himself and Dukakis and passed the afternoons pouring cold water on it. Behind the scenes, Jackson convention manager Ron Brown, who had replaced the deposed Austin as top adviser, worked with Estrich to patch up differences, setting the stage for a final tête-à-tête between the two candidates. Meanwhile, Jackson kept beating the war drum: "I cannot be asked to go out into the field and pick up voters, bale them up, and deliver them to the big house where policy is made and priorities are set around the table and not be a part of the equation."

But in his way, Jackson was finally naming his price. If "what Jesse wanted" was, like the sun, always changing and never changing, it finally was getting more visible: he wanted Dukakis to recognize him as a venerable party leader, to pay homage to his high-minded campaign; he wanted Dukakis to spell out Jackson's role in the fall campaign, provide a greater say in Democratic Party matters and fork over the resources to register voters across the nation in the fall. "I do not seek a job, a title or a position," said Jackson. "I seek partnership, equity and shared responsibility." Thus in the twilight of his second presidential campaign, Jackson played both to his old constituency and to his newer, whiter one. Though he had fallen short of his goal, he vowed continued vigilance to the cause, echoing the emotionally charged rhetoric of Martin Luther King Jr. in Memphis 20 years before: "I may not get there with you, but just know that you and I are qualified." All the while he preached a politics of inclusion that made it clear that the party mattered most. His performance in Atlanta would underscore that.

The final days of Jackson's 1988 campaign proved that the odyssey was not ending at all. It was just taking a short break. Jackson had his eyes on a distant prize. He referred to the "end-less campaign," saying at an Atlanta church service hours be-fore the convention opened that "it ain't over till it's over, and even then, it's not over."

Shortly after that, he reassured a closed gathering of mem-bers of the Southern Christian Leadership Conference that he was ready to "learn the lessons of this campaign and build upon it for victory in the next campaign." With meager resources and many strikes against him, he had built a political coalition from scratch and entered the pantheon of his party's leading figures. He had accomplished most of his goals: he had broadened his base, run a positive campaign, controlled much of the agenda, reformed the rules that had limited his delegate take. Experts could debate whether Jackson had peaked, whether he had bumped against an impassable ceiling at about 30% of the vote, whether he would ever win a greater share of the white elector-ate in his lifetime. But Jackson had won more in terms of votes, delegates and respect than most Americans had ever expected. To continue underestimating him seemed foolish. Indeed, he was, as he often said, "winning every day."

Jackson certainly looked like a winner as his "buscapade" wound its way through the country's midsection toward Atlan-ta, where the leaders of the Democratic Party waited in quiet terror that he was going to spoil their party. Aboard the candi-date's bus, spirits were soaring. Vindication, or at least a mo-ment in the sun, seemed to be at hand. Reflecting that mood, Jackson asked his fellow passengers to sing the stirring spiritual heard at each of his Baptist church appearances. It was the bat-tle hymn of his campaign this time, and the next:

> *I don't feel no ways tired*
> *I've come too far from where I've started from.*
> *Nobody told me that the road would be easy.*
> *I don't believe He brought me this far to turn back now.*

8

Atlanta: In Search of Unity

ATLANTA. A CITY TORCHED AND SACKED BY SHERMAN. Seared into national and international consciousness by Margaret Mitchell and Metro-Goldwyn-Mayer. Derided by author John Gunther for its "rococola" architecture. Known as "the city too busy to hate" by, as British journalist Simon Winchester added, "a people too shortsighted to notice." A bustling Southern metropolis that its mayor, Andrew Young, wants "to look like heaven."

If heaven looks like Atlanta, some people might prefer the alternative. Downtown is a jumble of buildings unrelieved by more than a single patch of grass, which residents grandly refer to as a park. Luckless Jimmy Carter, whom the Republicans gleefully remember and will not let the Democrats forget, built his presidential library in the city, but Atlantans resisted construction of a highway leading to it. In July, 8,000 politicians and 13,500 journalists descended on Atlanta for the Democratic National Convention. The city earned that honor largely because the Republicans had tied up New Orleans and its magnificent 80,000-seat Superdome for six long weeks, during most of which time they did not need it except to keep the Democrats out. Would this ominous early setback establish a pattern, the G.O.P. always a step ahead of the Democrats?

In July that did not seem likely. The Democratic leadership professed satisfaction with Atlanta and its 15,500-seat Omni, a basketball arena—intimate, yes, but more to the point, inadequate. The city's skyscraper hotels, most of them new and glitzy, seemed overwhelmed by the ravenous invaders. Too few telephone lines, too many messages lost, too much luggage misdelivered, too many room-service meals left to grow cold. Many of the city's taxi drivers seemed unfamiliar not only with the English language but also with the local geography.

But the week's main deficiency was the Omni. The Democrats, ever solicitous of the press, issued more credentials than there were seats or floor space. Thus the police and fire marshals, citing safety considerations, shut all the gates early on several evenings when capacity was reached. Some delegates, who had worked for years to attend a national convention, were locked out, their pleas and protestations falling on deaf constabulary ears.

Apart from the glitter of downtown existed another Atlanta. The local poverty rate was second highest among the largest U.S. cities, just behind Newark. And although the delegates and the visiting journalists generally did not see Atlanta's 10,000 homeless, the city shared that growing problem with other American metropolises. Democrats could and did say the problem had been exacerbated by the blackhearted policies of the Reagan Administration, but that, of course, did nothing to relieve the misery.

As usual in recent years, the Democratic Convention delegates bore little resemblance to their Republican counterparts, who would gather the following month in New Orleans. The "party of inclusion" had a delegate-selection policy that ensured a diverse and representative assemblage: 2,056 women, 2,156 men. Of the total 4,212 delegates, there were 2,823 whites, 963 blacks, 285 Hispanics, 87 of Asian-Pacific origins and 44 Native Americans. The demographics of ten delegates were simply not known. Among the total were the 645 super-delegates, who were given seats at the convention by virtue of their political offices: 250 members of Congress; 363 members of the Democratic National Committee, many of whom were also mayors or state legislators; 27 Governors (including Michael Dukakis of Massachusetts, listed as an "unpledged" delegate) and five former elected officials. Taken as a group, the delegates were much more liberal and slightly more affluent than Democrats generally.

Whatever distinguished them from the party faithful, the Democrats in Atlanta shared a goal that could be summed up in one word: win. Thus all present were on guard against the mistakes that had led to bitter defeats in four of the past five presidential elections. Instead of the chaotic, chronically late, disputatious conventions of the past, this one was designed to proceed like clockwork. There would not be a 3 a.m. acceptance speech by the presidential nominee, as there had been in 1972. There would be no pandering, at least not on national television, to special-interest groups, as there had been in 1984. The Democrats in the past had been offering a product that would not sell. This time they were determined to avoid that mistake. Let the liberals complain that this looked like a Republican Convention. Remind them that when their conventions looked like Democratic Conventions, they lost.

One potential problem was the chairman of the convention, Speaker of the House Jim Wright of Texas, who had been chosen for the job six months earlier. By the time the convention opened, Wright was under investigation by the House Ethics Committee, accused of improperly influencing a Government agency on behalf of a Texas savings and loan, and reaping improper royalties from the sale of a book. Wright's presence on the podium might neutralize Democratic efforts to paint the Republicans as the party of sleaze. But if Wright were bumped, that might signal the old disarray among the Democrats and draw even more attention to Wright's difficulties. The problem was solved by allowing Wright to remain as chairman but arranging for him to spend as little time on-camera as possible.

Over everything loomed the ominous shadow of Jesse Jackson. This was a year when the Democrats thought they could win the White House for a change. Ronald Reagan was not running. Alongside this political Gulliver, all prospective Republican candidates appeared Lilliputian, including George Bush, who had sewn up his party's nomination months before the delegates began arriving in Atlanta. The Democrats too had all but chosen their man. Michael Dukakis would carry the Democratic banner to victory, they dared to hope, if only Jackson did not gum everything up. "Unity" was the buzz word. In more ways than one, Jackson was a threat to it. Not only could he refuse to energize blacks to vote for Dukakis—with whom they were not especially familiar—but also Jackson's ability to turn off Jews was the equal of his talent to turn out blacks. His fight for a platform plank calling for creation of a Palestinian state simply reminded Jewish voters of his failure to rebuke Black Muslim leader Louis Farrakhan for anti-Semitic oratory. With good reason, Jewish voters believed Jackson had done too little to alleviate their concerns about where he stood on matters of overriding importance to them.

In truth, no one knew what Jackson would do. The Democrats had been down this road with him before, in 1984, when he blew hot and cold, vowing to support the ticket, threatening to walk out, demanding a new set of rules. He was an angry hornet one day, a benign butterfly the next. Whatever his mood, he seemed oblivious to the fact that 85% of the electorate is not black and that a distressingly large chunk of that 85% resented Jackson and his demands.

The Democrats wanted to be, if not euphoric, at least upbeat. Jackson threatened to make that impossible. He arrived in Atlanta with maximum visibility. The Jackson caravan originated in Chicago, and, with the now twice-rebuffed aspirant looking and acting as if he were the nominee, wended its way to Atlanta. Television camera crews traveled along with the caravan, and others swarmed over it at every stop. A variety of luminaries or would-be luminaries, such as Bert Lance and actress Margot Kidder, clambered aboard along the way. Jackson knew what made television news. While Michael Dukakis dutifully attended to his duties as Governor and Lloyd Bentsen stayed close to the Senate, there was no place for media heavies like Dan Rather to go but to the picture-perfect caravan. Where there is a photo opportunity, there is television.

After the disastrous July 4 outing in Boston, Dukakis had remained ham-handed in his dealings with Jackson. Just days before leaving for the convention, Jackson had stressed in a meeting with Paul Brountas that if he were not to be the choice for the vice-presidential nominee, he at least wanted to be informed in advance of Dukakis' selection. Brountas gave him that assurance. When, a few days later, Jackson learned from a reporter that Dukakis had picked Senator Lloyd Bentsen of Texas, the also-ran was furious.

Jackson had not intended to make things easy for Dukakis. After saying for weeks that he was unsure whether he would accept the vice-presidential nomination if it were offered, Jackson suddenly declared, at a time when he knew the decision was near, that he would accept the No. 2 spot on the ticket, and that he deserved it as well. What other vice-presidential possibility, he asked, had received more than 6.5 million votes for the presidential nomination? The answer, of course, was no one. A more fundamental question was when in history had the runner-up in number of primary votes been chosen as the vice-presidential nominee? The answer: only twice, when Adlai Stevenson named Estes Kefauver in 1956 and when Ronald Reagan picked George Bush in 1980. In fact, several times in this century, the leading vote getter in the primaries was not even the party's eventual nominee for President.

In any event, Jackson was not going to be the choice, and he must have known it. If Dukakis were to have any chance of winning the election, picking Jackson as his running mate would have obliterated it. By the time the black preacher was letting the public, and especially his following, know that he would accept, the Dukakis camp had already narrowed its choices, and Jackson was not among the contenders who remained. The argument within the inner circle was whether to "go South" or whether to, in effect, write off the South and choose someone who could put a hotly contested large state in the Dukakis column.

New Jersey Senator Bill Bradley was, like Dukakis, a Northeasterner, and thus not an ideal choice. But Bradley was articulate, intelligent and immensely popular in his home state, which had been tough for the Democrats to capture in recent years. Some were concerned that Bradley's height, 6 ft. 5 in., would provide too much of a contrast to Dukakis' height of 5 ft. 8 in. But Bradley solved that worry: he informed Brountas emphatically that he was not interested. Another possibility was Georgia's Sam Nunn, who could shore up the ticket throughout the South and help counter Dukakis' weakness in the defense area. But Nunn followed Bradley's example and eliminated himself from contention. As the campaign's self-imposed deadline for making a decision neared, five men were still in the running: two Democrats defeated in the primaries, Missouri's Richard Gephardt and Tennessee's Albert Gore; Ohio Senator John Glenn, the former astronaut; and a long shot, Texas Senator Lloyd Bentsen. Lee Hamilton, the respected Indiana Congressman, was considered briefly but didn't make the final cut.

Gore appeared to be the favorite. He could help not only in Tennessee but also in Kentucky, Missouri, Arkansas and other Southern and Border States. "They're going South," said a former executive of the Democratic National Committee after returning to Washington from a round of discussions in Boston. "And they're very high on Gore." Reporters following Dukakis believed the choice had narrowed to either Glenn or Gore, with Gephardt and Bentsen the odd men out.

On the morning Jackson's plane flew to Washington, John Glenn flipped on his car radio and heard the news. Like Jackson, Glenn was stunned. But he was not furious, just disappointed. Dukakis had telephoned Bentsen twice the night before but had been unable to reach him: the Texan, tiring of press inquiries, had unplugged his telephone and gone to bed. Dukakis caught him while he was shaving the following morning, and Bentsen eagerly agreed to run.

The Dukakis camp wanted Bentsen to help give the ticket some allure in the South and to bring Texas into the Democratic fold. (That latter order was a tall one, given Dukakis' positions on handgun control—he favored a waiting period so a buyer's background could be checked—and his opposition to the death penalty.) Thus the die was cast. The party, as Democratic National Chairman Paul Kirk had urged, would not write off the South. The Democrats would force the G.O.P. to pour resources into the region. But there was a haunting question: Would the Democrats' own resources be wasted in the region? Would they be better employed in Ohio, Illinois, Michigan, New Jersey, Pennsylvania, Wisconsin, states in which the odds were not so daunting?

After the candidate-to-be and his running mate arrived quietly, almost surreptitiously, in Atlanta, Democrats did not know if Jackson would lead a floor demonstration, permit himself to be nominated for Vice President, repudiate the nonspecific platform that Paul Kirk had engineered, or simply fall in line behind the generally acclaimed Dukakis-Bentsen ticket. That last event seemed too much for the Democrats to expect.

What Jackson wanted most, his aides suggested, was a seat at the table. He would not get it. The victory-starved Democrats had long since decided they could not win without the South.

Why else were they in Atlanta? Why else the choice of Bentsen? True, Bentsen and Dukakis were miles apart on many important issues. Still, too much prominence for Jackson at the Dukakis table and the South would be gone, if indeed it was not already gone anyway. Dukakis could not afford to offend Jackson, although he had done just that, and he could not chance too warm and open an embrace. So he had awkwardly kept him at arm's length. "He won't sit down with me," Jackson repeatedly complained to his close advisers. "He won't talk to me."

Perhaps it was because the two men did not speak the same language. As Jackson liked to tell audiences, Dukakis' parents had come to America on an immigrant ship, and his own ancestors had come on a slave ship, "but we're in the same boat now." True enough. But the cool technocrat from Brookline and the hot preacher from South Carolina by way of Chicago did not know how to communicate with each other, and Dukakis apparently did not even realize that inability existed. He was fully aware, however, that he held the better hole card. Jackson would not be walking out in disgust; he had no place to go. He could be—had been—obstreperous. But one of two men would be elected President of the U.S. in November, George Bush or Michael Dukakis. It would not be in the best interest of Jackson or his followers to contribute to the defeat of Dukakis. In the view of Thomas P. ("Tip") O'Neill, the belatedly beloved former Speaker of the House of Representatives and one of the party's grand old men, "Jesse Jackson wants a place in history. There will be a place in history for Jesse Jackson if he helps Dukakis get elected."

Just before the gavel fell, calling the convention to order, the two skirmishing camps made the inevitable accommodations. Lloyd Bentsen, much more at ease than Dukakis was with blacks—and with people generally—served as a sort of translator between the two men at an early-morning summit held in Dukakis' hotel on the first day of the convention. Communication at last established, Jackson became sweetly reasonable. He would take a couple of minority platform planks to the floor for inevitable defeat. He would not allow his name to be placed in nomination for Vice President. But for President, yes—he and his supporters felt they had earned that. He wanted some of his followers to have key roles in the campaign and on the Democratic National Committee. He would like to have the money and an airplane with which to conduct a voter-registration drive. It was little enough. Dukakis had no trouble with any of it. The "peace" was announced to jubilant Democrats. Jackson eventually received $1.8 million from the Dukakis campaign for his registration drive.

The shadow had been lifted. Now a unified party could go out and win back the White House. A few Democrats were bothered that Jackson, whose bulk contrasted with Dukakis' unprepossessing physique and who seemed to dominate news conferences, was coming on so strong. But most simply hailed the newfound "unity" and looked ahead to what now would be a successful, harmonious convention. After the Chicago riots of 1968, the ouster of Chicago mayor Richard Daley and other party bosses in 1972, the bitter Carter-Kennedy feuding of 1980 and the Mondale-Hart mutual destruction of 1984, the Democrats were ready for a little harmony.

Atlanta was Paul Kirk's show. The chairman had succeeded in achieving at least a surface unity. The party platform was too unexceptionable for anyone to take serious exception to it, although for that very reason, liberals grumbled. What was this? Another Republican Party? Who needs that? But Kirk was too busy and too determined to be bothered by grumbling. He had deflected from the 1988 campaign and convention the factors that had foreordained the disaster of 1984. No one could say Dukakis was the captive of Big Labor, as was said of Mondale. The AFL-CIO had not yet endorsed him. There were no stories about this being a labor-dominated convention. Special-interest groups had not scratched and clawed to get their own planks in the platform. Kirk had convinced them it would be useless. In

1984 the platform totaled 40,000 largely unread words. In 1988 the document contained only 3,500 words, also probably unread, but at least easier to carry around. During the primaries, candidates had been critical of one another, but not to the paralyzing extent of four years earlier. And now the Democrats had even remembered the American flag. There may have been more flags than people in the Omni.

All of this was no accident. Kirk had sent a clear signal to the Democratic constituencies: they should cool it. He did not know if they would. Could he get them to see how self-defeating they were, brawling in public over this issue and that, forcing candidates to bow to each group's agenda? The special interests combined might give a candidate 40% of the vote, but it takes more than 50% to win, as Kirk had subtly emphasized. He offered no promises, but the message to the interest groups was implicit: you people will be better off under a Democratic Administration, but there will not be a Democratic Administration unless the party broadens its appeal.

Mary Hatwood Futrell, president of the powerful National Education Association, could sense the wisdom of the new approach. "We are concerned with the issues and not with visibility," she said in her Westin Hotel suite. "And on the issues we are doing well. Both in the party platform and in the convention speeches. Every speaker has talked about education and child care. Our issues have been addressed." She had never discussed convention strategy with Kirk, or been "warned" by him to keep a low profile, she said. But Kirk's subliminal message had been heard and heeded.

Crusty Lane Kirkland, president of the AFL-CIO and a man generally reluctant to entertain the notion that organized labor is a special interest, remained that way. The federation did not endorse a candidate before the primaries, as it had in 1984, because the unions could not agree on one, Kirkland rumbled. That was at least part of the story. The other part was that the AFL-CIO got burned when its executive council backed Mondale and millions of its members voted for Reagan. So did untold numbers of nonmembers turned off by the sight of Mondale wearing labor's cloak. Not until weeks after his nomination did the AFL-CIO endorse Michael Dukakis.

Political oratory, particularly at national conventions, is largely predictable, pedantic, dull and deservedly unlistened to. But there are exceptions. William Jennings Bryan electrified the Democratic Convention of 1896 with his historic "Cross of Gold" speech, won the nomination that year and twice more, though never the presidency. Today, of course, no one wins the nomination by mesmerizing the crowd in the convention hall. In this era of seemingly endless primaries, the candidate is picked before, not after, the gavel falls. Under the old rules, Edward Kennedy in 1980 with his "Dream Shall Never Die" speech and Mario Cuomo with his eloquent 1984 evocation of principles the party holds dear might have walked away with the prize. But in 1988 the Democrats' most cherished hope was that Michael Dukakis—a "word processor" rather than a poet, as Richard Nixon had called him, implying absence of heart and soul—would be able to avoid embarrassment. Dukakis' clipped cadence carried with it a disdain, a smugness. He understood what he was talking about, his manner suggested, and he was not going to go into a lot of detail to get you, his mental inferior, to comprehend. Millions of Americans who had paid scant attention to the primaries would be seeing and hearing this strange, diminutive New Englander for the first time. He was quite capable of bombing out.

Comparisons could be odious as well. Jesse Jackson had a supply of passion sufficient for himself and Dukakis and perhaps many others. He had outshone all his rivals for the nomination both in 1984 and 1988, on occasion working audiences to a frenzy. Ann Richards, the Texas state treasurer who was chosen to be this convention's keynoter, had a reputation for down-to-earth, no-holds-barred oratory, sprinkled with humor and easy-to-grasp imagery. Kennedy was also going to address the convention, and he had proved at the 1980 gathering that he could rise to the occasion. Could Michael Dukakis, short on charisma, long on mechanistics, possibly compete?

Ann Richards, white-haired, red-lipped, with dark arched eyebrows, less a grandmotherly type than like a headmistress whose insistence on stern discipline was leavened by a delightful sense of humor, spoke first and hit hard. In little more than 100 days, she said in her slow Texas drawl, "the Reagan-Meese-Deaver-Nofziger-Poindexter-North-Weinberger-Watt-Gorsuch-Lavelle-Stockman-Haig-Bork-Noriega–George Bush Administration will be over." But hers—and perhaps the convention's—most memorable line was, "Poor George. [Pause] He can't help it. [Long pause] He was born with a silver foot in his mouth." The convention roared.

Ted Kennedy's speech was similarly partisan and slashing. The Senator reeled off alleged Administration failures and, after each one, asked, "Where was George?" After a while, the audience was chanting that refrain along with him. Thus, midway through the convention, Richards and Kennedy had set a hot oratorical pace. Dukakis would have a hard time matching it. Moreover, he had to follow Jesse Jackson.

Jackson, tall, intense, proud, did not disappoint. Skilled as he is in oratory, Jackson is just as strong on symbolism. Although he had ably addressed the 1984 convention in San Francisco, he did not have anything close to top billing at that gathering. This time his appearance would be a historic occasion. He was a black man, descended from slaves. Yet here he was, the second-place finisher in the race for nomination by a major party as President of the U.S. Now he was going to address millions of Americans. After the decades of slavery, all the lynchings, the Ku Klux Klan, the poll taxes, the "whites only" drinking fountains and rest rooms, the segregation in education, housing, transportation, public accommodations, the discrimination in employment, Jesse Jackson was not in the back of the bus. He was in the midst of the red, white and blue bunting in the front of the convention hall. It was his triumph, of course, but mostly it was a victory for his people. Jackson wanted to remind blacks—and whites—how far he and his people had come and in how short a time. Jackson's special guest that night was Rosa Parks, the black woman whose refusal to sit in the back of a Montgomery bus helped trigger the civil rights movement of the late 1950s and '60s. Now 75 and frail looking, Parks was a living symbol of the anguished decades during which her people had moved into a place in the forefront of national life.

Rosa Parks did not speak, but her mere presence was evocative of a struggle long past. Jackson's five children, on the podium to introduce their famous father, each spoke briefly to underscore what they were most concerned about: the future. The Omni was a sea of red signs with JESSE! in large white letters.

Jackson told the delegates, "My right and my privilege to stand here before you has been won, in my lifetime, by the blood and the sweat of the innocent." And who were they? Jackson ticked off several: Fannie Lou Hamer and Aaron Henry, Mississippi Freedom Democratic Party delegates locked out of the 1964 Democratic National Convention in Atlantic City; Jimmie Lee Jackson, killed in the struggle over blacks' right to vote; Viola Liuzzo, a white civil rights worker, murdered; "Schwerner, Goodman and Chaney—two Jews and a black— found in a common grave, bodies riddled with bullets, in Mississippi. The four darling little girls blown up in the church in Birmingham, Alabama. They died that we might have a right to live."

He noted that "Dr. Martin Luther King Jr. lies only a few miles from us. Tonight he must feel good as he looks down upon us. We sit here together, a 'rainbow coalition'—the sons and daughters of slave masters and the sons and daughters of slaves sitting together around a common table to decide the direction of our party and our country. His heart would be full tonight." Jackson shouted, to wild applause, "When my name goes into nomination, your name goes into nomination!"

He wound up in typical, stirring fashion: "Hold your head high. Stick your chest out. You can make it. I know it gets dark sometimes, but the morning comes . . . Don't you surrender. Suffering breeds character. Character breeds faith. In the end faith will not disappoint. Keep hope alive. Keep hope alive. Keep hope alive!"

Now the spotlight turned to Dukakis, and his address would have to be a winner. Yet as late as Tuesday of convention week, the most important speech of Dukakis' life was in dreadful shape. Ira Jackson, a former aide to the Massachusetts Governor, had provided a draft that the candidate decided was unusable. Then Dukakis' chief speechwriter, Bill Woodward, wrote a new version. But the candidate, by then caught up in a whirlwind of convention activity, had no time to focus on it. Jesse Jackson's speech, stemwinder though it was, had so heavy a liberal emphasis that Dukakis felt obliged to offer some balance—to reach out to moderate and mainstream Democrats, the kind who had voted for Ronald Reagan. One top Democrat advised Dukakis: "Get Joe Sixpack into this convention. You've got to talk to him and include him." Dukakis also felt that he could be statesmanlike in his speech, since Richards and Kennedy had done all the Bush bashing that would be needed. Any more would be overkill. Still, the pressure was on Dukakis to thrill the largest audience he had ever faced. To that point, it had been Jesse Jackson's convention. Now Dukakis had to make it his.

By late Tuesday night, Dukakis still had not focused completely on the task. Woodward's draft was not far off the mark, but it needed work. Ira Jackson flew down from Boston and helped with Woodward's second draft. Mario Cuomo offered some advice.

All day Wednesday and into the night, Woodward wrote and revised, edited and polished, with Ira Jackson at his side. Dukakis was not easy to write for, uncomfortable with emotional or sentimental touches. A late version of the speech was rushed to Theodore Sorensen, John Kennedy's wordsmith, in the wee hours of Thursday morning for some last-minute advice. At last the candidate received Woodward's final draft, deemed it essentially suitable but made inserts and revisions of his own. One of those was uncharacteristically sentimental and at the same time a gesture to Jackson: Dukakis scribbled in a passage weaving his theme of America's dream around Jesse Jackson's youngest daughter. Finally candidate and staff agreed that the speech was good. The question remained: Could Dukakis bring it off?

The mood was electric when he made his entry. Instead of simply walking onstage from the rear of the podium, as had all the other speakers, the Governor made his way through the Omni, greeting and being greeted warmly by the startled—but pleased—delegates. This seemingly minor departure from custom fired up the audience, and their enthusiasm seemed to pump up Dukakis as well. While the cheering went on and on, preventing him from beginning his speech, the candidate looked sharp and supremely confident.

The expectations game had been played well by the Democrats. Kitty Dukakis had even been quoted a few days earlier as saying she had fallen asleep as her husband practiced his speech. Dukakis aides had assured reporters that the speech itself would break no new ground. The campaign, in fact, passed out some very middling excerpts a few hours before delivery. Reading them, journalists were not surprised. They had been conditioned to expect little.

After the obligatory paean to "the American dream," Dukakis cited his credentials for speaking to it: "I am a product of that dream." His father had brought it to this country 76 years ago, and a year later, his mother had arrived. They were, of course, penniless "but with a deep and abiding faith in the promise of America . . . tonight, as a son of immigrants with a wonderful wife and four terrific children, as a proud public servant who has cherished every minute of the last 16 months on the campaign trail, I accept your nomination for the presidency of the United States."

But it was less Dukakis' words than his manner that buoyed Democratic spirits. Tears welled in his eyes when he mentioned his deceased father and how proud he would have been on this occasion. His voice was filled with emotion. His cadence was superb—the best it had ever been, said some who had heard him speak a thousand times. He punctuated his lines in the proper places. He smiled broadly. He was not, he seemed to be demonstrating, just a "word processor." He was flesh and blood, heart and soul, capable of love, wit, hope, understanding and, yes, tears.

He continued, "My friends, if anyone tells you that the American dream belongs to the privileged few and not to all of us, you tell them that the Reagan era is over and a new era is about to begin." It was time, he said, to meet the challenge of "the next American frontier," a phrase he had used early in the campaign then dropped. He promised "good jobs at good wages," perhaps the most worn-out phrase of his campaign. He spoke of young Jackie Jackson's "eyes filled with the sparkle of life and pride and optimism" when she and her siblings had introduced their father. The candidate concluded on a note that invoked his Greek heritage and at the same time underscored his present and future Americanism. Dukakis cited a covenant taken on important occasions in ancient Greece: "We will never bring disgrace to this, our country, by any act of dishonesty or cowardice. We will fight for the ideals of this, our country. We will revere and obey the law. We will strive to quicken our sense of civic duty. Thus, in all these ways, we will transmit this country greater, better, stronger, prouder and more beautiful than it was transmitted to us."

This, said Michael Dukakis, "is my pledge to you, my fellow Democrats. And that is my pledge to you, the American people."

The roars of approval wafted over the candidate. Hardly anyone in the Omni had the least doubt: Michael Dukakis had faced a critical test, and he had passed it. Among those who were certain of that was the candidate. Soon the pollsters would confirm for him what he already knew. In the first surveys taken after his speech, Dukakis led George Bush in virtually all the polls, in some by as much as 18 points.

But there would be many more tests ahead. Yes, Dukakis had been splendid, and yes, the party was more unified than it had been in years. Democrats from John F. Kennedy Jr. and Barbara Jordan to Tip O'Neill and Sam Nunn vowed to the press that this time they would get the job done. In Atlanta that week it was easy to be optimistic. But the Democrats in Atlanta numbered only a few thousand. Millions of Americans formed their impressions of the party and its candidates from watching television. Former party chairman Charles Manatt, asked for his observations, touched on an undercurrent of unease that afflicted many party regulars. "Well," said Manatt, "we had three and a half days of Jesse Jackson and an hour and 45 minutes of Michael Dukakis. Now I agree that it was a hell of an hour and 45 minutes. But was it enough?" A lesser-known Democrat put it this way: "If you're watching your TV set in Peoria, even if you're not a bigot, maybe you're a little unsettled, maybe even subconsciously, at all those blacks who seemed to be running the show."

After the Republicans had held their convention in New Orleans and Bush assumed a lead in the polls, columnist William Safire, writing in the New York *Times,* wondered about the impact of the two conventions and their effect on the candidates' standing. Did the largely white audience watching the Democrats think, "That's not us," and then conclude, when watching the Republicans, "That's us"? But such doubts did not trouble Michael Dukakis as he left Atlanta to hit the campaign trail in Texas with Lloyd Bentsen. Jesse Jackson had been tamed. The party had been given more unity and enthusiasm than it had enjoyed in years. Their candidate was suffused with the serene confidence that, barring any major mishaps between Atlanta and Nov. 8, he was just about certain to be elected President.

9

New Orleans: "A Kinder, Gentler Nation"

THE NIGHT OF WEDNESDAY, AUG. 17, SHOULD HAVE BEEN A
time of cheerful anticipation and convivial gluttony for the officers of the Bush high command. Only an hour earlier on that
third day of the Republican National Convention in New Orleans, their man had been nominated by acclamation. The next
evening's schedule called for anointment of the vice-presidential candidate and for the acceptance speeches. Bush's carefully
honed, well-rehearsed address was planned as the week's rhetorical acme, his symbolic passage from Vice President to the
party's standard-bearer.

But for Bush's most senior advisers there would be no languid late suppers at Galatoire's, K-Paul's or one of the city's other famous restaurants. Instead of Creole seafood, jambalaya and
other regional specialties, the crowded 38th-floor suite in the
Marriott Hotel was stocked with pretzels, coffee, diet cola—and
more tension than the occupants, most of them veterans of numerous election and White House crises, found palatable. Like

scores of journalists in New Orleans and Indiana, these political pros were spending their evening hurriedly examining the young life and easy times of James Danforth Quayle.

Jim Baker, newly resigned from the Treasury and officially installed as campaign chairman that very evening, presided over a series of meetings that would run to 4 a.m. Thursday. The sessions took place in his staff office at the Marriott, a cramped room containing typewriters, TV sets and a makeshift desk. A Bush intimate for a quarter-century, Baker would have the grim responsibility, if events made it necessary, of telling the Vice President that Quayle should be dropped from the ticket. Pollster Robert Teeter and media consultant Roger Ailes were also present in Bush's room. Quayle had been a client of both these political professionals in his Senate campaigns; they had spoken well of him while Bush was vetting the list of possible running mates. Craig Fuller, the Vice President's chief of staff and a likely power in a Bush White House, lent his cautious presence to the proceedings. Campaign Manager Lee Atwater had initially taken some credit for the selection of Quayle. Now he talked about the need to protect Bush from embarrassment. Margaret Tutwiler, Baker's assistant for a decade, fielded endless calls from reporters who were testing ever larger, ever uglier tales about Quayle.

Rounding out the red-eyed crew on that long Wednesday night were Robert Kimmitt and Richard Darman. Kimmitt, an attorney who had served as counsel for the National Security Council and the Treasury, was responsible for scrutinizing the records of all the serious prospects for Vice President. Darman, once a senior official in Reagan's White House, then Deputy Treasury Secretary, was working as an investment banker while advising Bush on economic policy. He, like Baker, would be in line for an important post in a Bush Administration. Just 36 hours earlier, when Bush announced his choice of Quayle, Darman had been as astonished as most other insiders. But he knew Quayle socially, as a neighbor in McLean, Va., and was more upbeat about the selection than some other Republican leaders. Now, with the press in an investigatory frenzy, Baker deputized Darman and Kimmitt to investigate the rumors.

Rumor, in fact, was too bland a term for the disclosures and conjectures that had surfaced about Quayle's past. Responsible reporters were calling in with a variety of accusatory questions, telling long-standing sources in the Bush entourage that they had information about Quayle's having been jumped over other applicants for a coveted place in the Indiana National Guard, that he had bought his way into law school (purported price: $50,000), that his brief acquaintanceship with Paula Parkinson, a glamorous lobbyist, had been gamier than originally reported. Each item, and others, came in lurid variations. Kimmitt weeks earlier had reviewed Quayle's record; and the strategists at Bush Central were well aware of the nature of his military service. They did not mind that Quayle, a Senate superhawk on defense and foreign policy matters, had served in the Guard rather than in Viet Nam. Nor did they doubt, at least initially, Quayle's assurances that he had no skeletons in other closets of his personal history. Now, however, at least one or two of the allegations began to take on a smell of credibility. "We knew," one participant said later, "that Dan Quayle could not survive if he was telling one big lie."

Kimmitt and Darman started their Wednesday-night exercise with the assumption that there had been a line of applicants for scarce openings in the Guard. At midnight Quayle was interviewed on this and other points. Did he have personal knowledge of a waiting list 19 years earlier? If so, had he been inserted in a favorable place, ahead of other applicants? Quayle could not answer either question. All he knew was that he had been directed to a particular unit, had applied and been admitted. This prompted a series of late-night phone calls to former Indiana Guard officials, as well as to Quayle contemporaries who had known him in law school. At 1 a.m. the brevet investigators also interviewed Quayle's father James. Wife Marilyn's turn came after daybreak. When going to Quayle's hotel nearby, Kimmitt and Darman walked separately, in order not to attract reporters' attention. They also walked quickly; their time was short. If anything drastic was to be done, it would best be done before the Republicans left New Orleans. Memories of 1972, when a damaged Tom Eagleton lingered for agonizing weeks, haunted Bush's advisers. On three items there was virtually no argument:

▶ To sever Quayle would be "almost certain death" for the ticket, as one participant put it, because his selection had been so personal a decision by Bush. It was Bush, after all, who had urged reporters to scrutinize his choice of a running mate because that decision would "tell all" about his judgment.

▶ Thus only if retaining him meant "certain death," as distinct from *almost* certain death, should he be jettisoned. Otherwise Quayle might be able to tough it out.

▶ If he had to go, the only viable alternative would be Kansas Senator Bob Dole, whom the convention and the press would accept with minimal fuss.

Bush, confused and slightly hurt by the downpour of acid rain on his parade, would have hated to turn to Dole. After all, he had passed over the Senate minority leader because of residual tension from the primaries and because he wanted a younger partner with no personal following. Quayle, moreover, had been deftly stroking Bush's ego for nearly two years. Though the two had no close personal relationship—in fact, had never had a serious private conversation about running together—Quayle had worked hard to put himself in Bush's line of political sight. Just after the Reagan-Bush ticket was re-elected in 1984, Quayle rang Bush and asked the Vice President to help him raise campaign funds for his 1986 Senate campaign. Bush, while acquiescing, noted with a laugh that Quayle was a fast worker.

Later, Quayle contrived to drop in at Bush's office from time to time, and got himself included in a small group that briefed Bush on national security affairs at the Vice President's residence.

Once his name was on the pre-convention short list of vice presidential prospects, Quayle made a point of calling the Bush office to ask permission before acknowledging to reporters that he knew he was being screened. Quayle was the only one of the prospects to display such well-mannered deference. That quality was hardly lost on Bush, who had spent much of his career politely deferring to powerful elders.

So the Vice President was greatly relieved when he learned from Kimmitt and Darman that none of the lurid allegations against Quayle checked out. There had been more than one opening in the Guard unit when Quayle applied. True, an editor at the Indianapolis *News,* which was owned by his family, was a retired officer in the Guard and had intervened on Quayle's behalf, but there was no proof that Quayle had been jumped ahead of other applicants. Nor was there any corroboration or even circumstantial evidence to support rumors about law school bribery. Instead, there was the unedifying reality that Quayle had been a marginal student who often received the benefit of a doubt.

The Paula Parkinson episode remained as petty as when first aired many years before. Parkinson had spent a weekend with Quayle and two other Congressmen at a Florida condominium in 1980. The escapade and other of Parkinson's adventures were investigated by the FBI. Press disclosures were blamed for the defeat of two other Republican Congressmen with whom Parkinson was closely linked. From the beginning, Quayle insisted that he had spent the weekend playing golf, and no one had ever tried to contradict him. After the convention, however, a new wrinkle developed. Parkinson, according to her lawyer's notes, told FBI agents that Quayle had propositioned her and been rebuffed. Quayle promptly denied the story, and it soon died.

Quayle's performance at New Orleans strengthened the perception that he was a .22-cal. man pressed into a .38-cal. assignment. Aside from his cosponsorship of a moderately successful job-training bill, colleagues in the Senate were hard put to describe Quayle's legislative accomplishments. Though a member of the prestigious Senate Armed Services Committee, he was not generally recognized to be among the panel's leading lights, and he had at one time criticized the Reagan Administration for reaching arms-control deals with the Soviets.

Bush announced his choice in an odd venue, at dockside in New Orleans, after a photo-op cruise on the Mississippi. Quayle had received the good news only an hour before. His mood as he joined his patron on a makeshift podium resembled that of a high school football cheerleader. "Let's go get 'em!" he shouted. At his first formal press conference after being designated Bush's running mate, Quayle displayed almost touching candor when discussing his decision to seek a safe spot in the Guard rather than face regular military service that might have sent him to Viet Nam. "I did not know in 1969," he observed, "that I would be in this room today."

Nor could he have anticipated the invidious comparison that would be made between that decision and his family's hawkish position on the war. His father's newspaper, the Huntington *Herald-Press*, where young Dan worked for a time in various jobs, harangued peace activists and draft dodgers. In a 1969 editorial, published after Quayle's Guard enlistment, the paper attacked those who "enjoy all the comforts and pleasures and extravagances of the good, prosperous life with no more than a passing thought of our soldiers who are fighting so well . . . under such harsh conditions [in Viet Nam]."

Such inconsistencies, along with Quayle's modest record of accomplishment, were not politically fatal. Proof of outright deception or chicanery would have been. As soon as Baker & Co. felt comfortable in announcing that there was no fire found behind the smoke—the glowing embers of Quayle's mediocrity seemed trivial by comparison—the convention presumably could return to its appointed rounds. At least that was the hope. In fact, even with Quayle vindicated of the more serious and salacious charges aimed at him, trauma had been inflicted on the G.O.P. convention and the Bush campaign. Why? Because in choosing an undistinguished junior Senator whom neither he nor the country knew well, Bush had flashed a large signal of weakness. Certainly the flinty, brooding Dole would have posed his own problems. He was capable of upstaging Bush with his sharp wit and furthering his own interests with his considerable following in Congress and the press corps. Soon after Quayle's selection, Dole showed that rough side when, on a network TV show, he said of the Indianan's military career: "No doubt about it. You didn't go to the Guard to go to Viet Nam; you went to the Guard to avoid going to Viet Nam."

Bush would also have had difficulty with Jack Kemp as his running mate. Though Kemp came to New Orleans chattering about his having been a dutiful second-string quarterback before achieving star status in pro football, his standing as a leader of the party's right wing gave him a constituency of his own. That explained why some of the "wingers" were disappointed with Quayle despite his staunch conservative credentials: he would not have the clout in office that Kemp would. Richard Viguerie, one of the godfathers of the New Right, complained in New Orleans that "Quayle is all right on the issues, but choosing him is like kissing your sister."

There were several other stalwarts who would have aroused little if any serious criticism—Indiana's senior Senator, Richard Lugar, for one, and Senator Pete Domenici of New Mexico for another. Bush would also have been supremely comfortable with Alan Simpson of Wyoming, but the towering Westerner had begged off, pleading his preference for the Senate and contending that his proclivity for brutal candor would have caused problems for the ticket. Still, he would have answered a firm summons to duty, just as Lugar, Domenici or a number of others would.

But Bush was determined to go his own way, and in a manner almost guaranteed to cause problems. By keeping his choice a secret even from his closest aides until Tuesday morning of convention week, he gave his staff no time at all to prepare a story line with which to ward off attack. Baker, whose associates let it be known later was unenthusiastic about the selection, might have dissuaded Bush if given some warning.

The crew of handlers selected in advance to serve the vice-presidential candidate on the campaign trail was highly skilled. Its chief, Stuart Spencer, had few peers among campaign strategists. But Spencer had no notion who his new client would be; in fact he expected either Dole or Domenici. The element of surprise, while guaranteeing wall-to-wall news coverage, proved a terrible handicap as Bush's team struggled to get ahead of the story.

A week later they could claim some progress. The press—as often happens in such cases—began to be criticized for exercising excessive zeal. The Bush camp managed to steer the argument away from Quayle and toward the legitimacy of the National Guard in the abstract, thus distracting attention from the central question of Quayle's suitability to be a "heartbeat away," as the ubiquitous cliché had it. But all that would come later, along with new indications of Quayle's frailties as a national candidate. In New Orleans, it became painfully clear, the selection was a huge and negative diversion. The four-day coronation had been designed primarily as a tableau for Bush and secondarily as a launching pad for rhetorical rockets aimed at the Democrats. Yet when the bimonthly magazine *Public Opinion* analyzed network coverage of the event, it counted 92 examples of commentary and reportage devoted to Bush, vs. 197 segments dealing with Quayle or his selection.

That disparity would prove an accurate harbinger. For the rest of the campaign, phrases like "the Quayle factor" and "the Quayle problem" became commonplace in the chatter of insiders. There was no real argument with the proposition that Quayle was a detriment to the ticket. Instead, the debate centered on how many points he was costing Bush. In early October, with Bush enjoying a modest lead of between three and seven points, one of the G.O.P.'s best numbers analysts studied all the available data. He confided, in a tone of relief, that the Quayle drag was "only two or three points, probably closer to two." If that estimate was accurate, it was the presence of Dan Quayle that allowed Michael Dukakis to remain competitive as long as he did.

None of this anxiety had been anticipated when the vanguard of the 2,277 Republican delegates and some 14,000 journalists began arriving in New Orleans a week ahead of the convention. Early birds had flown in to finish the platform, update party rules and adjudicate minor factional disputes. They would also explore the languid delights of one of America's least American cities. The Republicans' choice of venue was amusing. Both parties had looked south for 1988 because the region's electoral votes were critical. The Democrats attempted to recapture at least a few parcels of their old turf, while the G.O.P. sought to protect what had become in recent elections its most loyal real estate. The Democrats selected bustling, business-minded, humorless Atlanta. The Republicans settled on a fading port city with a reputation for sin and permissiveness, and a laid-back humor that seemed impervious to the municipality's endless economic woes.

G.O.P. delegates were reasonably cheerful too, considering that Dukakis had been ahead in the polls for nearly four months. But there was a strong sense that the Democrat's advantage was ephemeral, that a good show in New Orleans could, at minimum, make the contest essentially even by Labor Day. One reason for confidence was a renewed sense of unity. The nomination had been settled early enough in the primary process to allow ample time to heal the relatively superficial wounds inflicted by it. Philosophical disputes had been muted even at the height of the primary season. There would be no Republican equivalent of the Jesse Jackson phenomenon in Atlanta. In New Orleans no competing name would be placed in nomination, even for symbolic purposes; no platform dispute would require resolution on the convention floor.

One highly visible aspect of the Reagan legacy was the conservative homogeneity of the party regulars. Surveys by the New York *Times* and the Washington *Post* found that the delegates were considerably to the right of the party's mainstream. For instance, 61% of Republicans in the country favored a Government-sponsored health-care program, while only 15% of the delegates supported that idea. Two-thirds of ordinary G.O.P. citizens agreed with the statement that large corporations "have too much power for the good of the country." Just 14% of the delegates concurred. Such attitudes were hardly surprising, considering the convention's demographics. According to the *Times* survey, 83% of the delegates were middle-aged or elderly; 66% had family incomes above $50,000; only 3% were black and 2% Jewish.

The old progressive wing of the party was barely visible. Senator Mark Hatfield of Oregon preferred to stay home, explaining that New Orleans was no place for even a moderate liberal like him. Richard Rosenbaum, national committeeman from New York and once a protégé of Nelson Rockefeller's, introduced in the rules committee yet again a measure aimed at increasing black representation in party councils. The proposal was quickly defeated by voice vote. In the platform committee, Senator Lowell Weicker of Connecticut won a tiny victory when he succeeded in adding language acknowledging "the plight of thousands of Americans with catastrophically ill children." But the provision was mute on specific solutions, and Weicker, along with a handful of allies, lost on nearly all their other proposals concerning social policy. Asked why the remnant of progressives did not wage a more spirited contest, Weicker told reporters, "Nobody likes to ram his head into a stone wall."

It was hardly surprising that the 107-page platform became a testament to the Reagan years. Titled *An American Vision: For Our Children and Our Future,* the '88 manifesto was an only slightly updated version of the 1984 edition. To be sure, the new model incorporated a few Bush proposals acknowledging contemporary realities, such as the ubiquity of working mothers. Thus the platform supported the idea of tax breaks to underwrite child-care costs for low-income families. But for the most part, the document was a reiteration of Reaganomics and tough national security proposals. Throughout the lengthy drafting sessions, Bush's representatives, led by New Hampshire Governor John Sununu, dominated virtually every decision to insert a clause or delete a sentence.

The unsurprising result was noteworthy not so much for its densely detailed contents but for the stark contrast it offered to the short, vague Democratic platform. That was the real political point of the exercise: to flaunt the Republicans' zealous conservatism as opposed to the Democrats' refusal to get specific about liberalism. Sununu crowed to reporters, "What we have done is put forth a challenge to the dishonest, deceitful campaign Governor Dukakis and the Democrats have chosen to run." Even discounting for hyperbole, Sununu's formulation was politically apt. A combination of the Reagan legacy and the country's serene mood had placed the Democrats in a dreadful position. The term liberal had become suspect for at least a majority of those expected to vote. So, for the Democrats to attempt to rally their traditional constituencies with old-fashioned class warfare was to risk further losses in the middle. Yet bland centrist positions could not lure to the polls tens of millions of sometime voters, most of them black or brown and close to the bottom of the ladder.

The platform, like the convention that was soon to adopt it without argument, was astonishingly free of contention. It was as if the Republicans in New Orleans had come to renominate a popular incumbent instead of blessing a candidate only lately considered a weakling. At one of the week's innumerable social events, former Mississippi G.O.P. chairman Clarke Reed, a conservative veteran of a score of ideological conflicts, said with a sense of satisfaction, "This is the first time at a convention I'm able to really enjoy a party like this. Usually I'm at the rules committee or someplace heading off liberal mischief."

The one source of anxiety—that is, before the selection of Quayle exploded on New Orleans—sprouted from the polls of spring and early summer. Dukakis stubbornly retained a lead of between five and 18 points over Bush. This caused some Republican strategists to rethink the "G.O.P. lock" theory, which held that any Republican since the late 1960s could start a presidential contest with a lock on many potential electoral votes. That was because the South and the West had become virtual Republican preserves in presidential balloting, though the Democrats still did well there in congressional and local elections. That edge usually allowed the Republican candidate far more flexibility than his rival in competing for political real estate.

This time, however, the G.O.P. was not so confident of its base. Bush, it appeared in August, would have to shoot for something just above the 270 electoral votes needed to win the White House and abandon hope of rolling up the same kind of majorities Nixon and Reagan did. Texas state chairman Fred Meyer spoke for many of the local leaders when he said, "My advice is to go for 270 and forget 400." A TIME correspondent putting together the magazine's initial electoral-vote map got no argument from most of the Republican experts when the survey showed Bush and Dukakis starting with almost identical numbers.

The ground was beginning to shift, however, just before Republican chairman Frank Fahrenkopf tapped his gavel in the Superdome. Bush's incessant attacks on Dukakis, raising doubts about the Democrat's fealty to basic American values, had not been answered effectively. In pollsters' jargon, Dukakis had failed to "define" himself vividly enough. So Bush was able to draw an image of him as a feckless, woolly-minded liberal with an affection for high taxes, short prison terms and a watery defense policy. That depiction would now be reinforced in pur-

ple by a parade of prime-time speakers in New Orleans. Bob
Dole called the Massachusetts Governor "one of those liberals
with strange ideas, Dukak-eyed ideas, about the way the world
works." Pat Robertson, at his defamatory best, declared that in
the Democratic Party "the liberal mind-set reigns supreme.
Criminals are turned loose and the innocent are made victims.
Disease carriers are protected and the healthy are placed at
great risk . . . I submit to you tonight that Michael Dukakis is
the most liberal candidate for the presidency ever put forward
by any major party in the history of the United States of America."

Even Governor Tom Kean of New Jersey, that most civi-
lized, genteel and pragmatic of public servants, had to earn his
favored time slot at the podium with some invective. "The Dukakis Democrats will try to talk tough [on defense issues],"
Kean said. "But don't be fooled. They may try to talk like Dirty
Harry. But they will still act like Pee-wee Herman." Bush had
chosen Kean as keynote speaker, the only moderate given much
prominence, and he responded in tune with the convention's
master script. His Tuesday-night speech received little attention, however, because by then Quayle's selection was the major
news story.

Quayle was still the focus of attention 48 hours later, when
it was Bush's turn, finally, at the podium. The Vice President
faced a daunting challenge. Conventional wisdom had reached
a consensus about Dukakis' acceptance speech a month earlier.
It had been judged a clear success, an example of the Democrat's ability to exceed his normal pedestrian performance as a
speaker. Further, when Dukakis rose to speak in Atlanta, he did
so after being perceived as having dealt effectively with Jesse
Jackson. Bush had two standards to meet. Would his address be
seen as well above par for him? Would it overshadow the tur-
moil caused by his choice of Dan Quayle? The answers turned
out to be a firm yes on the first question and an ambiguous sort-
of on the second.

Drafted by Peggy Noonan, one of the best ghosts in the Republican writers' closet, the text was a good fit for the candidate. It was bold enough to serve as Bush's declaration of independence as the party's new leader. Yet it was adorned with sufficient modesty and enough rounded corners to sound credible coming from this unprepossessing figure. For a Ronald Reagan, the text would have been thin, devoid of overarching themes. For a Bob Dole, it would have been too sweetly sincere to be credible. For George Bush, it was just right, a pleasing blend of biography, self-description and intention.

He answered the why-I-want-to-be-President question with utter simplicity. ". . . To build a better America," he said. "It is that simple—and that big. I am a man who sees life in terms of missions, missions defined and missions completed. When I was a torpedo bomber pilot they defined the mission for us . . . We all understood that no matter what, you try to reach the target. There have been other missions for me—Congress, China, the CIA. But I am here tonight—and I am your candidate—because the most important work of my life is to complete the mission we started in 1980. How do we complete it? We build on it."

Though heir to an Administration that had been myopic about the sensitivities of minorities, Darwinian about the plight of the poor and shockingly permissive about the ethics of its members, Bush tactfully made clear his own sterner standards. He called for "a kinder, gentler nation" than the current one. In perhaps the most moving passage of his long speech, he said:

"I hope to stand for a new harmony, a greater tolerance. We've come far, but I think we need a new harmony among the races in our country. We're on a journey to a new century, and we've got to leave the tired old baggage of bigotry behind. Some people who are enjoying our prosperity have forgotten what it's for. But they diminish our triumph when they act as if wealth is an end in itself. There are those who have dropped their standards along

the way, as if ethics were too heavy and slowed their rise
to the top. There's graft in city hall, greed on Wall Street;
there's influence peddling in Washington, and the small
corruptions of everyday ambition ... And every time I
hear that someone has breached the public trust, it breaks
my heart."

With that last observation, Bush put his hand to his chest,
managing to convey the patrician's distaste for the grimy standards he had lived with, though uncomplainingly, since 1981. In
such moments, sprinkled through the speech judiciously, Bush
hinted at some of the differences between his values and his
mentor's. For the rest, of course, Bush pledged fealty to the major tenets of Reaganism in domestic and foreign policy. And, of
course, he deftly dropped loads of derision on his opponent. But
even the inevitable boiler plate came painted in ways that stuck
in the mind (Dukakis "sees America as another pleasant country on the U.N. roll call, somewhere between Albania and Zim-
babwe. I see America as the leader, a unique nation with a special role in the world").

Close examination of the text would disclose the usual
amount of illogic, inconsistency and hyperbole common in such
rhetorical exercises. For all his talk about wanting "a kinder,
gentler nation," for all the sympathy expressed for the dispossessed, Bush did not attempt to justify the Reagan policies that
had ignored the poor. Nor did he attempt, in any serious way, to
rationalize his no-new-taxes pledge with his stated intentions to
improve the lot of the illiterate and successfully combat the drug
traffic. He promised to create 30 million new jobs in eight years,
a goal so grandiose that his own advisers quickly backed away
from it.

Commentators would pick at those loose threads, as is
their habit, but they could not rend the fabric. Acceptance
speeches, like Inaugural Addresses, succeed or fail on the basis
of the overall impression they create. In New Orleans, Bush

conveyed the image of a leader suddenly liberated from the chains binding a loyal lieutenant. He came across as a man at once more forceful, more thoughtful and more sensitive than generally regarded. Once again Bush had bested that old political trickster, expectations. Network pundits in their sky booths and ordinary delegates on the floor sensed a new level of confidence in him. Bush, the spare, durable jogger, radiated satisfaction like a man on a runner's high. Soon pollsters would discover that voters were responding accordingly. Had Bush not inflicted the Quayle brouhaha upon himself, his triumph at New Orleans would have been nearly total. As it was, the man who arrived talking about himself as the fighting underdog in a difficult contest left town with momentum—the Big Mo, in Bush's 1980 coinage—clearly on his side.

10

The Reckoning

IN THE LATE SUMMER AND FALL OF 1988, THE NATION WAS AT peace. American troops were not firing shots in anger anywhere in the world. Ronald Reagan, the saber-rattling, "evil empire"– flogging President, had, to global astonishment, made it possible for Americans to retire at night less fearful of World War III than at any time since the Eisenhower years. Relations with the Soviet Union were improving, the INF treaty had been signed only months earlier, and public displays of understanding and even warmth by Reagan and Mikhail Gorbachev were still fresh in public memory. The peace issue clearly belonged to Bush.

The economy was also a Bush asset. Descriptions by Michael Dukakis of a "Swiss cheese" economy had been well received in such problem spots as the depressed energy industry, the farm sector and the rust belt. But most Americans thought of themselves and their country as reasonably prosperous. Inflation had been tamed. Lloyd Bentsen's repeated warnings that the illusion of good times was fueled by "hot checks" drawn on a $2.6 trillion national debt went largely unheard. Americans can "see" inflation in the diminishing amount of change returned at the supermarket checkout counter. Higher taxes are similarly visible, especially around April 15. But the national debt is something for economists and politicians to worry about, not average citizens. The pain it causes cannot be felt immediately, so there is always the hope and suspicion that it may not be felt at all.

Thus the two factors that have always been the most persuasive arguments for continuation of a party in power, peace and prosperity, augured a Republican victory. They forced Michael Dukakis to come up with compelling reasons why he should be elected. In the end, he did not.

Only twice in modern history had an incumbent party been rejected at the polls during a period of economic expansion. Once was in 1912, when Theodore Roosevelt split the Republican vote by running on a third-party ticket against incumbent President William Howard Taft. The Democrats were thus able to sneak Woodrow Wilson into the White House through the back door. The second time was in 1976, when unhappy voters decided to throw out the Republican rascals responsible for Watergate, replacing Gerald Ford, who had pardoned Richard Nixon, with Democrat Jimmy Carter.

So 1988 looked like the year for George Bush. But his ad men and pollsters, with the agreement of Jim Baker, were not going to take anything for granted. Their research showed that peace and prosperity, contrary to conventional wisdom, were not foremost in the minds of the voters. Those blessings were, in fact, largely taken for granted. Everyday concerns—crime, education, drugs—were more urgent. They also found evidence that eight years of denigration of the word liberal, by Reagan and other conservatives, had paid off. Once the term had evoked Social Security, Medicare, civil rights, voting rights, a dedication to making society fair and just for all; now it conjured images of tolerance for crime, sexual freedom, homosexuality, high taxes, welfare cheats, weak national defense and a tendency, spawned in the Viet Nam era, to criticize rather than defend America's role in the world. Yes, the Bush campaign would claim credit for peace and prosperity. But it would focus on what liberalism had come to mean in the minds of many voters. Weeks before Labor Day, the traditional start of the formal campaign for the presidency, Bush's advisers came up with a tough, minutely detailed and occasionally vicious media program aimed at painting Michael Dukakis as a liberal.

At the same time, there were three major reasons for the Democrats to hold out hope of victory. One was the tendency of American voters to value both continuity and change and thus, Democrats hoped, to want peace and prosperity to continue with a different team in the White House. A second reason was George Bush. The third one was Dan Quayle.

The polls immediately following the Democratic National Convention sustained the notion that the voters might be ready for change. Dukakis led Bush by 18 points. But in their delirium, the Democrats overlooked two factors. First, the Dukakis lead was too large to sustain. Second, the American people knew next to nothing about Michael Dukakis.

The Dukakis camp was not worried. The voters knew plenty about George Bush, who had become something of a national joke, parodied in cartoons and comic strips. Establishment Democrats, weary of losing, surveyed the two candidates and came up optimistic. Robert Strauss, the former party chairman who reveled in the title "Mr. Democrat," took the luxury of suggesting a role for himself in the transition to a Dukakis Administration. Strauss, early in the campaign, also delivered these observations:

▶ The Republicans will "try to tag Michael Dukakis as George McGovern. But they can't do it, just as they can't make George Bush a Ronald Reagan. George Bush is not a very good candidate. We don't have that problem."

▶ The Vice President "will get better as a candidate. He will do better than expected in debates because he will have such a low hurdle [expectations] to surmount." Strauss admitted his concern over Dukakis' lack of foreign policy experience and even foreign travel. Still, he predicted that the Massachusetts Governor, a quick study, "will do better than people expect. But I do wish he had been in London, had been in Paris."

▶ The Democrats are more unified now than in years. Strauss thought the "Jesse Jackson problem" had been handled well by Dukakis. "He's a tough little bastard. He'll say, 'If we have to screw 'em, we will.' Dukakis doesn't give ground. Jackson intimidated Mondale. He doesn't intimidate Dukakis."

▶ The choice of Bentsen was "very bold. George Bush has got to worry. New England is gone. The Midwest is a battleground. California looks tough. Texas looks tough." But the most salutary development in Strauss's view was that Southern Governors and other elected Democrats in the region, "once they get their fingerprints on the campaign, they have to win it [i.e., carry their states for Dukakis]."

Early on, the Dukakis campaign agreed that George Bush was a disaster for the Republicans. The Governor and his strategists believed Bush was simply not very smart, he projected a flighty, even silly image on television, and—as Bob Dole had taunted the Vice President in primaries—he was a candidate with a résumé but not a record. What more need Dukakis do than remain studiedly vague, so as to avoid the mistakes of past Democratic campaigns, and not dignify Bush's attacks by responding?

The Bush campaign was dogged by the continuing presence in office of Attorney General Edwin Meese, over whom dark clouds of unethical conduct had hovered from the early days of the Reagan Administration. An independent counsel was examining Meese's ties to a scandal-plagued New York City defense contractor, Wedtech Corp., and his relationship with an old friend, E. Robert Wallach, who had involved Meese both in Wedtech and in a scheme to build a billion-dollar pipeline in the Middle East. Other leading lights of the Reagan Administration, such as Michael Deaver and Lyn Nofziger, either had been or were about to be convicted on criminal charges. The "sleaze" factor, as it came to be known, included dozens of Reagan appointees who either had faced charges or had been forced to resign, chiefly for conflicts of interest. Although his own former Massachusetts education adviser was in prison, Governor Dukakis clearly had the advantage as far as integrity in government was concerned.

Dukakis, who tended to trust his instincts, had no shortage of paid and volunteer advisers telling him how to conduct his campaign. He was playing it too cool, they said. He was stiff-arming traditional Democratic constituencies, they warned. Everyone agreed that blacks were a special problem for any Democrat, and Jesse Jackson simply acerbated it, so Dukakis was wise to limit his overtures to blacks. Had not the Republicans already sneered about the "three-headed monster": Jackson, Dukakis and Bentsen? But there were the trade unions, the Hispanics, the Jews and, yes, the huge bloc of Catholics who had been virtually ignored in New York and other primaries where candidate pitches all seemed aimed at the less numerous Jews and blacks.

Dukakis reasoned that his ethnic background, in contrast to Bush's Waspish élitism, would assure the Democrat his share of the crucial Catholic vote. As to the black vote, of course, that would be his, overwhelmingly. So there was no need to alienate whites by making too many joint appearances with Jesse Jackson. Labor? Why risk a repeat of 1984 and become, as Walter Mondale had, the candidate of special interests? So people thought Michael Dukakis was cold? No. Perhaps just cool, and that was how to play the game in 1988. Say little. Do just enough. Don't rock the boat. Let George Bush self-destruct.

The adviser best able to get through to Dukakis was John Sasso, but his contribution had been limited to occasional phone calls since the episode involving the Biden-Kinnock tapes had forced the candidate to fire him. Veterans of presidential campaigns were concerned that Susan Estrich was in over her head as campaign manager and that campaign chairman Paul Brountas, though a decent and well-meaning man, knew little about running a national campaign. Still, suggestions that Democratic national chairman Paul Kirk be brought in to run the campaign received a chilly reception, particularly from Brountas. Kirk did have national-campaign experience, and he was very high on Dukakis. It did not hurt that he was also a Bostonian. Brountas, Estrich and Kirk all could have kept their titles, with Kirk directing the campaign and coordinating it with the national party. Yet such a step seemed unnecessary. The polls and most analysts agreed that Bush was the underdog.

Nonetheless, some Democrats were uneasy with Dukakis' strategy of standing aside and waiting for Bush to fall, a violation of one cardinal rule of politics: always run as if you are ten points behind. Dukakis also seemed oblivious to a second rule of politics: make your opponent the issue. Bush was very much aware of that dictum. Had he not been, two well-known political managers with key roles in the Republican campaign would have made him so. Roger Ailes, a New Yorker of unlimited and not entirely unwarranted ego, and Lee Atwater, a South Carolinian with a sure instinct for the jugular, were handling Bush's advertising campaign and coping with his substantial image problems. Ailes' experience dated back to the Nixon campaigns. Atwater, though only 37, had been battle tested, and proved worthy, in the Reagan years. Both of these Bush advisers were expert in what they termed comparative—and others called negative—advertising. It was Ailes who persuaded Bush to lash out at Dan Rather during a celebrated television interview several months before the New Orleans convention as part of an effort to erase the Vice President's "wimp" image.

Memorial Day weekend was scheduled to be the Bush campaign's holy synod, a meeting of all the chosen at Kennebunkport. Things were not going well; Dukakis had a ten- to twelve-point lead. Dukakis was gaining stature by beating Jackson week after week. Bush seemed like a gawky figure on the sidelines. Bush was still campaigning on the Reagan agenda. He felt an inability to assert himself until the convention, when the torch would pass to him from Reagan.

The day before the weekend meetings began, Bush pollster Robert Teeter arranged for a marketing company in Paramus, N.J., to put together two focus groups made up of people who described themselves as Democrats who had voted for Reagan but were leaning toward Dukakis. Ailes, Atwater, Teeter and longtime Bush friend Nick Brady peered through a two-way mirror at people who had been paid $25 each to discuss the candidates.

The participants, it turned out, knew almost nothing about either candidate. Most thought Dukakis was a Governor, but only three of twelve in one group were aware that he was from Massachusetts. Everyone knew Bush was Vice President, but that was about all.

The moderator began asking rhetorical questions. What if I told you that Dukakis vetoed a bill requiring schoolchildren to say the Pledge of Allegiance? Or that he was against the death penalty? Or that he gave weekend furloughs to first-degree murderers? "He's a liberal!" exclaimed one man at the table. "If those are really his positions," a woman added, "I'd have a hard time supporting him."

The aides were galvanized by the results of the Paramus focus group. While no single issue swayed voters, the cumulative effect was devastating. Dukakis was a blank slate in voters' minds, and Bush had to be the first to write on it.

At Kennebunkport that weekend, the strategy took shape. New Hampshire's Governor John Sununu held forth on Dukakis' weaknesses: the furlough program, Boston harbor, overcrowded prisons. Bush adviser Richard Darman dubbed the "Massachusetts Miracle" the "Massachusetts Mirage." The message was clear: Dukakis should be tarred with the "L" word.

But Bush was uncomfortable with that advice. Conventional wisdom, he knew, suggested that a candidate's own positive qualities should be established before he attacked his opponent. On the final day of the long weekend, aide Craig Fuller sketched two scenarios on a yellow legal pad. One outlined how Dukakis would be ahead by 20 points if the Vice President waited until after the Republican Convention to attack him. The other showed how Bush could reduce Dukakis to a single-digit lead by the Republican Convention. Said Bush: "Let's get started."

Had Dukakis known what Ailes and Atwater had in store for him, he would not have so calmly puttered August away in Massachusetts. While the Governor tended to state business, the Bush camp plotted ways to make the prime campaign issue not foreign policy, not the deficit, not homelessness, not crime, not drugs, not the environment, not education, not health, not defense, not trade—no, none of these. The No. 1 issue of Campaign '88 would be Michael Dukakis, the "liberal" Governor of Massachusetts.

Dukakis should have seen it coming. Not long after the Governor had clinched the nomination, columnist Robert Healy, who has covered presidential campaigns since 1960, wrote a remarkably prescient article for the Op Ed page of the Boston *Globe,* which presumably Dukakis and his entourage read regularly. The Healy message: Define yourself, Mike. If you don't do it, they will.

He didn't. And they did.

One pleasant afternoon in early September, Michael Dukakis, whose lead in the polls was dropping fast, fraternized with some reporters as he "campaigned" back and forth across Massachusetts. The candidate had not yet learned how treacherous it is to meet daily with the press ("They stomp out your message," in the view of Ailes and Atwater). Why, he was asked, was he not responding to implications by Bush that the

Democrat was unpatriotic because of his stand on the Pledge of Allegiance issue? Why, the reporters also demanded, was Dukakis letting Bush make an issue out of the Massachusetts prisoner-furlough program? Bush's alarming speeches about Willie Horton were supplemented by television spots showing prisoners moving in and out of a revolving door, with misleading—in fact, entirely false—information about the Massachusetts furlough program highlighted in the graphics.

Calmly, Dukakis pointed to Bush's unfavorabilty rating in the polls. Nearly 40% of Americans had a low opinion of Bush before his impressive performance at the Republican National Convention, and in the early weeks of the campaign his negatives were still high. The American people did not like negative campaigning, Dukakis believed, and Bush would pay the price some day.

To those familiar with the candidate's way of thinking, there was an additional explanation for Dukakis' unwillingness to mix it up with Bush. Dukakis knew that he, the son of Greek immigrants who had taught him about America's essential greatness, was not unpatriotic. He knew he was not soft on crime, which had declined 13% in Massachusetts while he was Governor. He knew Bush was lying about him, and he could not imagine that the attacks would be believed.

Nick Mitropoulos was an adviser closer to Dukakis than anyone except his wife Kitty and the exiled Sasso. When reporters asked Mitropoulos about the candidate's unwillingness to defend himself, the adviser explained, "You people still don't get it. This is how it's going to be, now and after Labor Day and until November. You're going to keep hearing 'good jobs at good wages.' His message has worked this far, and he's going to stick with it and not get distracted. You people must have forgotten about the months and months of primaries when Gephardt and the others were taking shots at him for not being specific, and he just stayed positive and stuck to his message."

It was an astonishing revelation. Mitropoulos—and pre-

sumably Dukakis—seemed to think there was no difference between winning a nomination and winning a general election.
There was no hint in Mitropoulos' statement that he understood
that in primaries, members of the same party may skirmish
against one another, but almost never do they move in for the
kill. They do not want to risk being accused later of having damaged the party's prospects of winning the big prize. Nor do they
wish to alienate themselves permanently from a member of
their party who might be President some day. For example,
Gore had brought up the prison-furlough matter in the primaries, but he had not belabored it the way Bush was doing. In addition, primaries win the attention chiefly of activists and true
believers, who are not exacting in their demands for specifics.
But when the great mass of voters at last tunes in to what the
candidates are saying, they want to hear more than "good jobs
at good wages."

That fact escaped the candidate. In an interview with
TIME correspondent Michael Riley in August 1988, Dukakis explained his reluctance to counterattack: "It's a judgment you
have to make. I've been through campaigns where you've got to
strike a balance. You know, these are pretty wild charges. And
it's been going on now for weeks and weeks and weeks. This
isn't new. This is the same kind of rhetoric we heard six or eight
weeks ago. Personally, I don't think it's going to work." It
seemed not to have occurred to Dukakis that the reason the
rhetoric was continuing was that it was working.

Since campaigning by television had long since become
standard procedure for presidential contests, a third cardinal
rule of politics had developed: allow no charge to go unanswered. Otherwise, listeners will assume it is true. Thus, Dukakis was violating all three of the cardinal rules of politics: run
scared, make your opponent the issue, respond to all charges.

To one false allegation—not from Bush, though his aides
strongly suggested to reporters that they "look into it"—Dukakis simply had to respond. According to rumors, after the 1973

death of his brother in a hit-and-run accident and after his defeat for re-election as Governor in 1978, Dukakis had consulted a psychiatrist. The rumor was first circulated at the Democratic Convention in Atlanta by followers of political extremist Lyndon LaRouche. Coming from so disreputable a source, it was given little credence. After Missouri Senator Thomas Eagleton was forced to resign as George McGovern's running mate in 1972 because of disclosures that he had twice received shock treatment for depression, both parties were sensitive to the question of psychiatric care.

When asked to comment on the Dukakis rumor, Ronald Reagan said he would not pick on "an invalid." The President could hardly have made a more insensitive remark. But when he explained that he thought he was being "funny," the press and the nation seemed to accept that as an apology. It turned out that Dukakis had never undergone psychiatric treatment. He was at least partially to blame for the fuss. A very private man, he had refused to produce his medical records for publication. Such reticence would inspire rumors even without an Ailes or an Atwater around. The candidate did produce the man who was his doctor for the previous 17 years. When the physician declared emphatically that the reports were unfounded, they died. But Ailes, though always denying Bush campaign involvement in the slander, gave Dukakis fair warning of what lay ahead. Ailes told *Newsweek:* "That little computer heart from Massachusetts isn't going to know what hit him." Atwater, not to be outdone, chirped that when the campaign was over, people would think that "Willie Horton was Michael Dukakis' running mate."

By Labor Day a sense of unease began to permeate the Democratic ranks. Dukakis was still leading in some polls, though his margin was shrinking. There was a gender gap, with women much more inclined to support Dukakis and men favoring Bush. Since 10 million more women than men were expected to vote in 1988, the Dukakis camp was pleased. But there had been a gender gap in 1984 as well, and by Election Day it had largely disappeared. Democratic Party pros feared that it would fade again. Men were put off by Dukakis' support of mild controls on the sale of handguns and by his opposition to the death penalty (as well as, it was said, by his lack of height and his perceived arrogance). Women were swayed by his pro-choice position on abortion and his evident sympathy with proposals for government assistance in establishing day-care programs for children of working parents.

But Dukakis was taking a beating from Bush daily. When would he start fighting back? In Bush speeches and more graphically in Ailes' TV spots, Michael Dukakis, the man who would not define himself, was being defined by his enemies as a big spender, a taxer, a neophyte in defense and foreign policy matters and a soft-headed champion of criminals' rights over those of their victims. He was, as Bush often noted, "a card-carrying member" of the American Civil Liberties Union. That organization had once been referred to by Attorney General Meese as a "criminals' lobby," though in reality it is a defender of the constitutional rights of all sorts of unpopular people, left and right. Bush's allegation that Dukakis' Massachusetts Miracle was in reality a Massachusetts Mirage began to take on credibility; the Governor was struggling during the summer to overcome a 1988 shortfall in state revenues. In addition, Bush claimed that Boston harbor was one of the most polluted bodies of water in the nation because of Dukakis' inaction (Dukakis blamed federal obstructionism). The Republican candidate even took a boat ride across the harbor as TV cameras whirred, declaring himself "an environmentalist," an irony lost on voters unfamiliar with the dismal Reagan-Bush record on the environment.

The Republican attack was effective, if only because it went unanswered. By mid-September the two candidates were running about even in the polls. In the words of a senior campaign aide, "It took a while for Michael and the staff to realize that the negative campaigning by Bush was taking a toll and keeping us from getting our message out, and that a more assertive response was needed." Said another: "Sometimes we seemed to think it was cheating if we didn't repeat the message exactly the same way every day, and then we acted surprised that nobody treated it like news. Or else we would send three messages a day and then wonder why the networks couldn't sort them out."

Even Estrich conceded that Bush had taken the campaign by surprise. He had not been a fool or a wimp. Beginning with the Republican Convention, he appeared to be his own man, out at last from the towering shadow of Ronald Reagan. Even Bush's voice seemed deeper now, as opposed to the high-pitched whine of his 1984 debate with Geraldine Ferraro and some of his appearances in the 1988 primaries. He had also learned to speak more slowly and gesticulate less wildly.

For the Democrats, things were getting worse. At a reception in the Rayburn House Office Building in Washington, Massachusetts Congressman Joseph P. Kennedy II, who was said to have his eye on the governorship if Dukakis were elected President, sought the opinions of journalists and politicians. "Has he bottomed out?" Kennedy asked.

Brountas, no doubt with the candidate's approval, telephoned Ted Van Dyk, a shrewd and outspoken veteran of Democratic campaigns beginning with Hubert Humphrey's 1968 near miss against Nixon. Brountas asked Van Dyk, who was now a consultant, to assess the Dukakis campaign and to write a confidential memo, which Brountas assured Van Dyk that Dukakis would read. Van Dyk's memo, dated Sept. 9 and titled "How to Win the Election," made the following points:

"1. Know the Map and Act on It." By then it was clear, Van Dyk wrote, that Dukakis had little hope of winning any state south of the Mason-Dixon line except possibly Arkansas and Texas, which is "uphill." He urged "decisive allocations" to crucial states that could still be won, mainly in the Midwest and the Northeast.

"2. Send Out Clear and Unequivocal Messages. Reclaim the Initiative." Van Dyk warned that Democrats in Washington and the 50 states "will soon start walking away unless there is a quick demonstration that Mike is strong, in charge and knows where he's going." Dukakis should stop meeting with the press so often, and the staff should be threatened with dismissal for talking negatively with reporters about the campaign or the candidate. Keep Noriega and Iran-*contra* out of the media campaign. "The fact is that George Bush comes across as a nice guy and charges of corruption/lying/deception just are not going to stick to him."

"3. The Central Issues." Dukakis could no longer be vague. He should focus on domestic issues on voters' minds—drugs, public education, acid rain, pollution, health, jobs instead of welfare, providing for the nation's energy future.

Van Dyk also urged the candidate to stop campaigning alone, to get the Democratic Party involved. "Create the impression," he wrote, "that the Dukakis campaign does not consist of Mike and a small group of ambitious young aides but rather of a committed group of Democrats of every conceivable stripe, all of whom are rallying enthusiastically to Mike's flag." The memo contained other recommendations, some of which were implemented, most of which were not. The candidate appeared a few days later with prominent Democrats such as Georgia Senator Sam Nunn and Indiana Congressman Lee Hamilton, a helpful development. But not enough to negate Van Dyk's warning that "if nothing changes, we'll slip a couple of points in the polls each week and lose decisively in the electoral vote." Van Dyk also offered his services to the campaign. He never heard anything.

At last Dukakis did what many Democrats thought he should have done immediately after the convention. He brought John Sasso back. One of Sasso's first acts was to fly to New York to meet Jesse Jackson, who until then had been virtually ignored by the campaign and, as a consequence, restrained in his efforts to mobilize the black vote for Dukakis. For the first time in weeks, Jackson felt that someone understood and appreciated his role. Sasso also intended to fire up both the campaign and the candidate. Sasso, a poker player, thought, as did Dukakis and most of his top advisers, that the Democrats had a great hole card: the debates.

There would be only two. Brountas had wanted four and fought vainly for three. But Jim Baker, the Bush team's debate negotiator, evidently feared that his man would be at a disadvantage. Dukakis, after all, was less prone to slips of the tongue, and his experience as moderator of *The Advocates,* a public-television discussion program, had given him an easy on-camera manner. There would be only one vice-presidential debate. The seasoned and solid Lloyd Bentsen could be counted upon to triumph over Dan Quayle, whose nomination continued to dismay everyone, it seemed, except Bush.

Before the debates Dukakis, in an attempt to counter attacks on his suspect credentials on national defense, took an ill-advised ride in a 60-ton, M1 Abrams tank at a General Dynamics test and design facility in Sterling Heights, Mich. This was one "photo opportunity" where it would have been better for Dukakis if there had been no film in the cameras. In an outsize military helmet and a jumpsuit, the candidate evoked comparisons with the *Peanuts* comic strip's Snoopy, who dons a pilot's headgear, sits atop his doghouse and fantasizes that he is a World War I pilot tracking the notorious German ace, the Red Baron. The Bush campaign appropriated film of Dukakis' ride and used it in derisive commercials to reinforce the claim that the Democrat was a novice in defense matters.

As the candidates prepared for their first debate, Bush had pulled ahead slightly in the polls. The Dukakis camp was concerned, but the situation hardly called for panic. The first encounter, in Winston-Salem, N.C., would give its man a "bump" in the polls. Their confidence seemed to be warranted. Days earlier Bush had mistakenly referred to Sept. 7 as the anniversary of the 1941 Japanese attack on Pearl Harbor, which actually occurred on Dec. 7. Unfortunately for Bush, the debate was scheduled for Sept. 25, triggering an outpouring of derisive jokes (sample: Bush had tried to wiggle out of the debate because he wanted to be home for Christmas). As millions watched that night, the two candidates sparred cautiously, but it seemed to many that the old George Bush had re-emerged. The Vice President was frenetic, disjointed. Dukakis was cool, confident, in command of himself and the facts. Bush made an insipid declaration that in pressing the pledge issue, he was not questioning Dukakis' patriotism, leaving an opening that even someone as slow on the uptake as Dukakis could not resist: "Of course the Vice President is questioning my patriotism," he declared with rare feeling. "I don't think there's any question about that, and I resent it. I resent it."

Most of the media and insiders of both campaigns saw Dukakis as the clear winner, but instant polls and special focus groups returned a different verdict. As to the debate itself, few thought Bush had won, but most judged it a wash or awarded a narrow edge to Dukakis. What was more significant was that viewers *liked* Bush better. His sunny personality contrasted with Dukakis' more controlled performance. There was something endearing about Bush's clumsiness and occasionally tangled syntax. He had alluded during the debate to his tendency to err and referred to his opponent as the "iceman," an apt description of how Dukakis was coming across in millions of living rooms across the country. So in winning, Dukakis had lost. America had not fully decided whom it wanted for President, but if the contest had been about which man to invite to dinner, Bush would have been the clear favorite.

The Bush camp discerned that fact within hours of the debate. But the Dukakis forces, convinced their man had won on substance, regained the cockiness of the post-convention era. "We kept looking for a thousand points of light, but we never found them," said Estrich, attempting to make fun of a Bush line in the debate about volunteerism. Other Democrats referred derisively to "a thousand pints of Lite," wondering aloud if Bush was talking about beer. What such critics missed was that many voters did not care if the line made little sense; they liked the sincerity of the guy who muffed it.

In the vice-presidential debate ten days later, Bentsen was widely expected to shine. He did. Looking more presidential than his running mate as he took the stage in Omaha, the Texan was in the lead even before he and Quayle opened their mouths. Bentsen provided the most memorable line of the evening after Quayle suggested that in age and experience, he was comparable to "Jack Kennedy when he ran for President." Quayle had used the comparison before, so Bentsen was ready with his retort: "Senator," he said, "I served with Jack Kennedy. I knew Jack Kennedy. Jack Kennedy was a friend of mine. Senator, you're no Jack Kennedy." Stung by the remark and the derisive outburst from the audience, Quayle looked like a freshly spanked little boy. "Senator," he pouted, "that was uncalled for." Bentsen coldly reminded him of who had made the comparison.

Ever since he made his embarrassing choice in August, Bush had defended Quayle when asked, rarely even mentioning him otherwise. A true measure of the Bush handlers' feeling about Quayle could be derived from reading his schedule: Quayle appeared nowhere except in small, solidly Republican ports of call. He went unmentioned in campaign commercials. Despite complaints from the Bush campaign that Bentsen's zinger was a "cheap shot," Democrats were delighted. Now it was time for Dukakis to manhandle Bush in their second, and last, encounter.

In a strategy session the day before the debate, Dukakis' managers unanimously advocated aggressiveness. "I don't see it that way," said the candidate. "I'm going to try to be positive." He did, however, agree to attack the Vice President on six subjects: Quayle, Iran-*contra*, abortion, patriotism, drugs and Boston harbor. He was also supposed to dare Bush to look directly into the camera and tell the American people that J. Danforth Quayle was best qualified to be President.

Whether from nervousness or a realization of his plight, Dukakis was ill the day of the debate after a near sleepless night. At 6 a.m. two doctors were summoned. The three-hour morning debate practice was canceled. Dukakis napped fitfully during the day and awoke only an hour before the debate. In the holding room offstage, half an hour before the debate, Dukakis was boning up on his answers and rehearsing prepared lines when Mario Cuomo called. Dukakis spoke to him for 20 minutes. Aides say it kept him from gathering his thoughts and focusing his strategy.

Almost from the opening question in the encounter, held in Los Angeles, it was clear that he was not going to hit any home runs. When Cable News Network's Bernard Shaw, the moderator, asked whether Dukakis would soften his opposition to the death penalty if Kitty Dukakis were raped and murdered, the audience gasped. But not the iceman. He reacted, David Broder wrote in the Washington *Post,* as if he had been asked the time of day. Why did he not attack Shaw for even suggesting so tasteless and bizarre a question? Why did he not at least wince or otherwise indicate that he could not bear to contemplate such a horror? Instead, he launched into a standard Dukakis proposal to call an international drug summit if he were elected. It was a bloodless, heartless response.

Dukakis did complain about the Vice President's frequent references to him as a liberal. But instead of reciting the litany of liberal achievements—Social Security, Medicare, voting rights, civil rights, fair housing, unemployment insurance—and demanding that Bush tell him which ones he opposed, Dukakis seemed offended. The candidate of the historically liberal Democratic Party was not proud but defensive about his heritage. When the debate was over, Bush lingered in the hall shaking hands. Dukakis quickly left the stage. He had raised only one of the six planned issues. He knew he had blown it.

The debate effectively ended the campaign. As the election drew near, and Bush continued to lead in the polls by double-digit percentages, Dukakis finally began to heed the advice of Sasso and such party wise men as Strauss. He became a populist, the champion of the "little guy" and the enemy of the greedy and the privileged. "I'm on your side," he declared over and over. His crowds grew in size and enthusiasm, and there were reminders from his handlers and in the press that Truman had come from behind to win in 1948.

Even the Bush campaign, probably hoping to keep the Vice President's supporters from becoming too complacent, behaved as if the new, fighting Dukakis was closing in. Polls showed the race tightening in several large states, and Dukakis aides renewed their predictions of a close election. To play along, Bush even changed his plans to take a day off on the campaign's penultimate Sunday, and instead visited Pennsylvania, a state where Dukakis was still competitive. Declared Bush, without a hint of irony: "We are in a horse race."

As the campaign neared the finish line, Dukakis at last acknowledged that yes, he was a liberal, "in the tradition of Franklin D. Roosevelt, Truman and Kennedy." Everyone agreed that the candidate had a message, that he looked better, sounded tougher, that his body language had improved. The born-again Dukakis began to exude hope that he could pull within three or four points of Bush by Election Day and rely on the Democrats' powerful field organization in several large states to carry him over the top. In California, for instance, the Democrats had 10,500 volunteer leaders in the state's 23,627 precincts, and they were making a total of 70,000 get-out-the-vote calls a day in the campaign's final week. Critics derided the notion of a grassroots effort of such magnitude in California, of all states. The only way to reach the Golden State's 13 million voters, they argued, is through television. (The outcome in California, 52% for Bush to 48% for Dukakis, suggests the critics were right.)

Dukakis' speeches suddenly seemed to have more punch.

Of Bush's proposal to reduce the capital gains tax, Dukakis yelled, "He wants to play Santa Claus to the rich and Ebenezer Scrooge to the rest of us!" Dukakis even suggested that he and Bush cancel their election-eve television advertising and meet in another debate, a challenge Bush ignored. Yet the Governor's last-minute burst of energy had failed to move the numbers. Less than a week before the vote, the ABC/Washington *Post* poll showed Bush ahead by 13 points, his largest margin ever in that respected survey. But the voters were not happy. The low-road Bush campaign disgusted millions, as they made clear to pollsters and journalists. Toward the end, a few were so turned off they said they would vote for Dukakis, or more likely, not bother to vote at all. For the majority of voters, the Democrat had not made a case for himself. In most minds, he was not an acceptable alternative.

The election of 1988 was closer—or at least less one-sided —in the electoral college than those of 1980 and 1984, scant comfort for a Democratic Party losing its fifth of the past six presidential ballots. The Republican "lock" on the South and the Rocky Mountain West took on a look of permanence, holding as fast for George Bush as it had twice for Ronald Reagan. In fact, aside from the aberrant 1976 election, when a Southerner headed the ticket, the lock dated back to the 1968 and 1972 victories of Richard Nixon—with the exception of a single state (Hubert Humphrey carried Texas in 1968). In the five Republican victories, Democrats had been faced with the dismal necessity of making up for the 234 electoral votes that the Republicans apparently had salted away before the polling places even opened. It was too daunting a task.

Dukakis finished with 112 electoral votes, winning ten states and the District of Columbia, in contrast to 40 states with 426 electoral votes for Bush. It was a Democratic drubbing of monumental proportions, except when viewed from the perspective of the McGovern, Carter (1980) and Mondale wipeouts. In the popular vote, Bush won an eight-point edge, close to what the polls indicated as the campaign came to its frenetic end.

And the close was frenetic. As if to compensate for his belated awakening, Dukakis careened from coast to coast and back again, then back again, always with stops in crucial battleground states like Pennsylvania, Illinois, Ohio, Iowa, Michigan, Missouri, Texas. The jewels, of course, were California and New York, with their rich lodes of electoral votes, 47 and 36, respectively. In 53 grueling hours, Dukakis traveled 8,500 miles, napping occasionally on a lumpy couch on his campaign plane, growing increasingly hoarse as he told the largest and most enthusiastic audiences of his 20-month quest for the presidency that "I'm on your side." The hour, the bleary-eyed candidate knew, was late, perhaps too late. The cards were stacked against him. True, Truman had come from far back to win, but that was against a Dukakis-like opponent, Tom Dewey, who assumed, as Dukakis had early on, that he was clearly the superior candidate and that the voters inevitably would share that perception. To Dewey and the early Dukakis, campaigning hard seemed almost an insult to voters' intelligence. It was akin to pointing out the obvious. Memories of another late blitz that almost succeeded—Hubert Humphrey's against Nixon in 1968—also helped kindle hope aboard the Dukakis jet "Sky Pig" (so called because of its singular lack of amenities). But Humphrey's surge began five weeks before the election. The "real" Dukakis, unprogrammed, fighting mad, proudly populist, made his appearance barely two weeks before ballots were to be cast.

Bush and his handlers knew that voters who had been undecided were moving toward Dukakis. Pollsters for both campaigns picked up a mild but clear trend toward the Democrat in heavily black, strongly unionized Michigan. Could this mean that the historic Democratic base in northern and midwestern industrial states was returning "home"? If so, then Illinois, Pennsylvania and Ohio were within striking distance, in addition to Michigan. Could this closing sprint bring Dukakis across the finish line a winner?

Not likely, but Bush had been running for President for
nine years. He was not about to take chances. If states where the
race was considered still competitive were to be seeing and
hearing a lot of Michael Dukakis, then soon after the "Sky Pig"
lumbered off, Bush's comparatively sleek Air Force Two would
taxi in for some last-minute exhortations. Two Democrats
—Michael Dukakis and Lloyd Bentsen—performed in almost
superhuman fashion through election eve. A sleepless but somehow energized Dukakis was still beaming his message via satel-
lite on the day of the election. The Republicans also fielded two
seemingly tireless campaigners, George Bush and Ronald Reagan. The septuagenarian President had undertaken a 25,000-
mile, 16-state, 35-speech odyssey in behalf of his Vice President.
Dan Quayle, meanwhile, had become an almost invisible man.
His fall from grace was underscored in a 30-minute, $30 million
election-eve commercial message, broadcast over three networks, in which Quayle's handsome face did not appear. The
only admission that Bush had a running mate was inadvertent
and unavoidable: in some of the film clips used in the message,
Bush-Quayle signs were visible.

Dukakis matched the Bush telecast network for network,
and of course showcased Bentsen. But once again, the Republican handlers proved themselves superior to their opposite numbers in understanding what makes effective television. The
Bush telecast was long on family—wife, children, grandchildren, in-laws. The message: values, just like your own. Perhaps
out of necessity, Dukakis took a high-risk tack, featuring ordinary voters expressing misgivings about the candidate, addressing his negatives as repeatedly propounded by George Bush.
Dukakis was on-camera ably defending himself against these
complaints, but that was part of his problem: it was election eve,
and he was still on the defensive. There was time only for cameo
appearances by the Dukakis kin.

Bush and Bentsen repaired to Texas on election eve to
await the returns. Bush, aware that his negative campaign had

left a sour taste, sounded unusually churlish for a supposed "nice guy" about to achieve his goal. He criticized Dukakis for "whining" and, again borrowing from Harry Truman, suggested that if he could not stand the heat, he should get out of the kitchen. Besides, Bush protested, the Democrats had given the campaign its first negative tone at their "idiotic" convention in Atlanta. This was not the language of a gracious winner eager to heal wounds. President Reagan, after an emotional farewell campaign appearance during which he pleaded with supporters to win one more "for the Gipper," flew back to the White House. Quayle was in Indiana, to spend the night at the home of his parents in Roanoke and to visit his dentist in Huntington, an Election Day tradition of Quayle's supposed to bring him good luck.

But Michael Dukakis could not stop campaigning. After a final pitch in California, he began the long flight home to Boston, with a predawn stopover in Iowa and a simultaneous appearance with the sun in Michigan. Iowa was thought to be shakily his and pollsters still thought Michigan, a state vital to a Democratic victory, was winnable. Telling supporters he had taken the red-eye to be with them (his own eyes affirmed the veracity of his statement), the obviously weary Governor made a morning arrival in Boston, but instead of collapsing, he launched his by-satellite interviews to several so-called competitive states.

If forlorn help dwelt with Dukakis, unwarranted jitters took up residence in the Bush camp. The malady is a common Election Day affliction in winning campaigns. Pollster Robert Teeter, whose soundings had played such an important part in shaping Bush's electoral strategy, raised the alarm. Overnight, Bush's lead had shrunk to four percentage points in some surveys. And early exit polls showed that the two candidates were neck-and-neck in several key states. In fact, Dukakis had a solid early lead in Michigan, and indications were that he would carry New York by ten or more percentage points. New Jersey and Ohio appeared weaker for Bush than they had been the day before. And two small states, New Mexico and Colorado, appeared to be in the toss-up category. The significance of these last two states was far greater than the electoral votes involved: both states were part of the Republican lock. If they drifted away, the lock could be history. There could be no doubt that there was some substance to these indications of a late Dukakis surge. Exit polls later showed that 12% of voters had made their choice since the weekend before Election Day. Of that total, 60% backed the Democrat. Dukakis also led among the 7% of voters who said they had made up their minds just before the weekend. Bush's majority came from the 78% who had reached a decision two weeks or more before Nov. 8.

Ironically, all of the worrisome soundings proved to be wrong. Bush won Michigan by eight points, and the Dukakis margin in New York was four points. New Mexico and Colorado stayed in line, and the lock proved impregnable. New Jersey and Ohio did the expected, supporting Bush. But the anxious moments clearly suggested that if Dukakis had come out swinging earlier, he could have won. George Bush had dwelt too long on his essentially vacuous "values" message, and even the seemingly endless patience of the electorate was near exhaustion with Bush's yammering over the pledge and prison furloughs. By Election Day, according to one exit poll, only 12% of voters said these hot-button issues had relevance to them. Another presumed Dukakis negative, his opposition to the death penalty, concerned 26% of those polled, a significant number but lower than had been generally believed. Of far greater concern to average citizens was the federal budget deficit, which went all but unmentioned during the long campaign. Forty percent of those questioned by NBC/ *Wall Street Journal* pollsters gave the deficit their highest priority among problems facing the nation, and of that number, 57% voted for George Bush, who has vowed repeatedly ("read my lips") not to raise taxes and whose campaign-trail solution to the problem was a facile "We can grow out of it." That was about as convincing as Dukakis' approach: improved tax collection, which he said would reap "billions and billions of dollars."

The exit polls did offer some evidence that Bush's attacks were effective in some areas. Although his own record and that of the Reagan-Bush Administration on the environment is nothing short of abysmal, Bush's boat ride across Boston harbor apparently paid off: of 72% of voters who believe that more money should be spent to clean up the environment, 48% voted for Bush, the man who supported two presidential vetoes of the Clean Water Act and assisted in the partial dismantling of the Environmental Protection Agency.

The exit polls made abundantly clear that Reagan-Bush "feel good" politics had worked strongly to Bush's advantage. Sixty-four percent of those polled felt that the economy would either improve or remain about the same, and this group strongly favored the Vice President. Dukakis was the overwhelming choice (73%) of those who felt that the economy would worsen, but they constituted only 16% of the voters. Bush, shown in campaign commercials shaking hands with Mikhail Gorbachev or engaged in conversation with Margaret Thatcher, also won strong support for his foreign-affairs experience. Michael Dukakis had nothing with which to counter. While Bush was visiting 75 countries in the past eight years, Dukakis largely confined himself to the insular world of Brookline-Boston-Cambridge. All of this insularity may be laudable for a conscientious Governor, but it did not strike the electorate as proper training for the presidency. Of voters who valued experience most, 94% voted for Bush. To virtually no one's surprise, Ronald Reagan's chosen heir won 86% of the voters who approve of the President's performance in office.

Negativism exacted its price. More than a quarter of the voters said they did not care for the available options. Of these, 19% chose Dukakis because they could not stand Bush; 13% of this group chose Bush because they were turned off by Dukakis.

Meanwhile, the nastiness of the campaign undoubtedly was a factor in the low voter turnout. About 50 percent of registered voters bothered to go to the polls, the lowest percentage since 1924.

Other voting patterns, according to NBC/ *Wall Street Journal* exit polling: so-called Reagan Democrats were less enamored of Bush than they were of Ronald Reagan. Only 41% of the Democrats who voted for Reagan in 1984 supported Bush. Dukakis won the backing of 52% of Catholic voters to Bush's 48%, whereas Reagan had captured 56% of the Catholic vote four years earlier. Blacks, supposedly disenchanted with Dukakis for his treatment of Jesse Jackson, voted 9 to 1 for the Democrat, about the same partisan split as in 1984. A surprising and heartening development for Democrats looking to the future was the 51-to-49 edge given the Dukakis-Bentsen ticket by voters between the ages of 18 and 24. The vaunted gender gap did not disappear: men favored Bush by ten percentage points, and Dukakis won the women's vote by four points. In 1984 Reagan's victory over Mondale was largely attributable to his enormous 28-point lead among male voters, a margin Bush was unable to sustain.

On election night, George Bush, still on edge, watched as the returns rolled in. It became clear early that he had swept the South, as expected. But not until the monitors showed him victorious in Connecticut, Maine and Missouri did the Vice President find it possible to relax. Ronald Reagan had not had that problem. At 10 p.m. a cheery Reagan was on the telephone, congratulating his successor-to-be. At 10:10 p.m., Michael Dukakis called to concede in what Bush described as a "gracious" manner.

When he appeared at his victory celebration in Houston that night, Bush—the first sitting Vice President to advance to the presidency by election since Martin Van Buren in 1836—seemed strangely subdued, as if the enormous burden he had sought so long to assume was weighing on him already. His first comment indicated he had been troubled by criticism of the tone of his campaign. "A campaign is a disagreement, and disagreements divide," Bush declared, somewhat solemnly. "But an election is a decision, and decisions clear the way for harmony and peace. And I mean to be a President of all the people. And I want to work for the hopes and interests not only of my supporters, but of the Governor's and those who didn't vote at all. To those who supported me, I will try to be worthy of your trust, and to those who did not, I will try to earn it, and my hand is out to you, and I want to be your President too." His hand is also out, Bush implied, to the Democratic Congress.

For his part, Dukakis expectably asked that the country unite behind the man who will be its President for the next four years. But Lloyd Bentsen, re-elected to the Senate that night but unable to deliver Texas to the national Democratic ticket, left no doubt that some bitterness over Bush's negative campaign will linger. Bentsen said he and Dukakis had "waged a campaign that is worthy of the American people." A large stretch of the imagination was not required to ascertain who, in Bentsen's mind, did not. "We told you the truth," Bentsen continued, "and we stepped up to those issues." Euterpe Dukakis, more emotional and outspoken than her son, observed that "we have not compromised our honor."

Election '88, then, was a triumph of experience, of issues successfully ducked, of negativism, of a surreal and no doubt evanescent avoidance of reality. Bush's sneering references to the word liberal also carried an undertone of racism. They reminded voters of the turbulent 1960s, of street riots, of softness toward crime, of children bused to schools far from their homes for the sake of court-ordered integration, of affirmative action whereby black police or fire fighters or secretaries may get the promotion ahead of whites with more seniority. These ills were all considered to be the result of woolly-headed liberal thinking, as were "the elimination of God from the classroom" and the burning of the American flag. America knows it cannot and indeed does not wish to turn back the clock. It does not want re-segregation, but it yearns for a tranquillity that disappeared in the civil rights struggles of the '60s. Only the subtlest reminders are required to awaken fears of who those "liberals" are and what they might do next.

The election established that the Democrats' problem is not themselves but liberals. That the two words are no longer synonymous, if indeed they ever were, was reaffirmed by increased Democratic margins in both the House and Senate, in governorships and in the makeup of state legislatures, despite another decisive Republican victory in the presidential race. "The only thing wrong with the Democratic Party is that they can't elect a President," said political scientist Nelson Polsby. "Everything else they're doing is right. The Senate, the House, party ID—they're all fine." Yet voters were keenly aware that George Bush said Michael Dukakis was a liberal who coddled murderer-rapists (the most infamous of whom, the whole world now knew, was black), and so they wanted no part of him. In a sense the Democrats were still doing penance for the 1960s, when too many voters considered them to be the party of militant blacks, meddlesome social workers, uppity feminists and draft-card-burning protesters.

The problem is part of the dilemma facing Democrats who wonder when, if ever, they will regain the White House. Unless they develop effective counterparts to Ailes and Atwater, no Democrat will be receiving his mail at 1600 Pennsylvania Avenue for many elections to come—barring a severe recession or other crisis that topples a Republican President. Although there is some hyperbole in the contention of Gerald Austin, Jesse Jackson's onetime campaign manager, that the Republican handlers could have guided even the post–Donna Rice Gary Hart to victory this year, their combination of skill and ruthlessness in presenting to the nation a candidate it does not know should not be underestimated. A number of Democrats—Sam Nunn, Lloyd Bentsen, Howell Heflin, Ernest Hollings—are immune from the pejorative meaning of "liberal," but they are also among the unlikeliest of Democrats to emerge from a party convention as the presidential nominee. Unless the rules are changed, nominees will continue to be determined by the small contingents of liberal Democrats who control the Iowa caucuses and the New Hampshire primary. If by some quirk a conservative Democrat should be nominated, the Republican image-makers, who have no equals on the Democratic side, probably would find other ways to savage him.

Of course, George Bush, as he is painfully aware, will quickly confront realities that could smooth the path to the White House for a member of the other party. Bush painted himself into a corner on the most urgent problem he will face, the deficit. His vow of "no new taxes" was a vote getter, but it was irresponsible. When Ronald Reagan in 1980 vowed to cut taxes, increase military spending and balance the budget, Bush called it "voodoo economics," and he was right. But in a disturbing triumph of opportunism over principle, Bush embraced what he had so recently condemned. He emerged from the 1988 election still committed to what has become known as Reaganomics; thus he left himself without flexibility. If he were to remain true to his campaign pledges, he could not raise taxes; neither could he significantly reduce military spending.

He also vowed to leave Social Security alone. Soon after he takes the oath of office, Bush will be presented with a proposal for cutting the deficit, assuming that a bipartisan commission appointed for that purpose can come up with a plan. The co-chairman of that commission, Democrat Robert Strauss, had already declared that defense and entitlements (i.e., Social Security, veterans' benefits, etc.) must both be looked at for cuts because "that's where the money is." Thus George Bush may find himself in the most painful of quandaries even before he takes office: whether to repudiate a commission that both parties had agreed to support, or to default on one or more of his most frequently proclaimed campaign pledges.

Some of Bush's advisers have confided that if the nation should face a crisis that the public can see requires emergency action, Bush could win broad support by explaining the changed circumstances compelling him to raise taxes, cut military spending or delay Social Security cost-of-living increases. It is an out that Bush could have left for himself and probably still would have won the election. After all, Michael Dukakis would go no further than to declare that raising taxes would be a last resort. But Bush slammed the door on new taxes, emphatically and repeatedly. A combination of new user fees, tax-rate adjustments and other masking devices is the likely route Bush will have to take around his no-new-tax campaign pledge. He will also have to dream up a fresh euphemism for tax increases to replace the "revenue enhancers" of the early Reagan days.

Bush is not likely to have an easy time with Congress. It will be even more Democratic and more partisan than the recently adjourned 100th Congress, which managed to force down Ronald Reagan's throat legislation calling for clean water, new highways, new civil rights and mandatory 60-day notification of plant closings. The 101st Congress surely will not be any more tender toward George Bush. Many congressional Democrats resent the manner in which Bush won the office, questioning the patriotism and character of his opponent and continuing the denigration of what to many was and to some still is a proud word, liberalism.

Pressures for new spending are likely to be immense, including outlays of perhaps $100 billion in taxpayers' money to bail out the collapsing savings and loan industry. Bush himself, by James Baker's count, has proposed $40 billion over the next five years in additional spending for new domestic initiatives, including a child-care program that would cost at least $2 billion, and more than $6 billion in oil and capital-gains tax breaks. Perhaps to placate the right wing, Bush committed himself to the costly Strategic Defense Initiative (Star Wars) and to the continued development of MX and Midgetman missile programs. The

Pentagon will need a total of $475 billion in added spending over the next five years merely to finish projects started under Reagan, and that does not include various expensive weapons—the Stealth bomber, *Seawolf* submarine, D5 Trident missile—soon to be out of development and ready for production.

A large number of indictments in the Pentagon procurement scandals seem certain. Bush may also face an emotionally charged situation if Oliver North and other key figures in the Iran-*contra* mess are convicted. Could he allow North and another guest at his 1987 Christmas party, former National Security Adviser John Poindexter, to go to prison, particularly in the face of demands by his party's right wing that they be pardoned?

Theodore Roosevelt proclaimed the presidency a "bully pulpit," and on the day after his election George Bush used that term to describe, though vaguely, his vision of the job. When he referred during the campaign to a "kinder, gentler nation," he meant it, Bush declared. But Presidents from Washington to Carter have confirmed that the office is also an awesome burden. Bush seems to have discovered that fact already from the vantage point of one who was only a single step removed for eight years. On election eve, Bush quoted Lincoln as having said that whatever role God had for him in the troubled times sure to come, he was ready. The implication was that George Bush was ready too. But he was sure to find, as have countless Presidents before him, that winning the White House is not the same as living in it. After a long, costly and bitter campaign, Bush will face the most difficult challenge of his career, the most trying assignment a democracy has to offer: being the President of all the people.

11

The Media: Tools and Targets

Huntington, Ind.—Republican vice-presidential nominee Dan Quayle today defended using family connections to get into the National Guard during the Viet Nam War at an extraordinary news conference staged amid thousands of chanting hometown supporters who angrily booed reporters . . . As thousands of hometown backers chanted, "Quayle, Quayle" . . . the new G.O.P. nominee said, "I asked no one to break any rules, and as far as my knowledge [goes] no rules were broken at all."

—Washington *Post*, Aug. 19, 1988

FOR VOTERS WITH EVEN SEMILONG MEMORIES, MUCH OF THE 1988 campaign fit into the category of clichés revisited: the turbulent contest of 1968 reverberated anew in the Republican emphases on flag-waving patriotism and the horrors of urban crime, and in the not-so-subtle linking of crime to blacks; the last Democratic victory, in 1976, echoed in this year's denunciations of corruption in Washington and the call for a new broom to sweep clean. The themes in the speeches and ad campaigns of both candidates—and many of the people who put them together—were drawn from past candidacies of Ronald Reagan and Richard Nixon on one side, Walter Mondale and Jimmy Carter on the other. The campaigns' allegedly new strategies for media manipulation dated back at least a generation. So did complaints about purported bias, ineptitude or issuelessness in news coverage.

Yet if the nightly newscasts and morning headlines generally had the familiar sound of a fable recollected from childhood, at least one customary litany about American politics was resoundingly disproved. Time-honored clichés about media power to the contrary, journalists in this election were almost never the conscious engines of change. They were less effective than ever at setting agendas, pursuing independent lines of inquiry, calling candidates to account. Time and again, the media were a story in the election, from the pre-primary skirmishing to the Election Day exit polling. But their power was passive or negative. Virtually without exception, the media made news by serving as a tool or as an outright target of some figure restoring his own credibility by debunking the bearers of bad tidings.

Consider these sequential media highlights—or nadirs—of the 1988 campaign:

▶ A still unidentified woman, pursuing still undisclosed aims, telephones the Miami *Herald* to reveal that a local resident is on her way to Washington to spend a weekend in the company of Senator Gary Hart. The *Herald* tracks two potential suspects for the alleged assignation on board a plane, then, losing the trail, stakes out Hart's Washington hideaway. Confronted, the Senator denies any adulterous intentions, although months later he fesses up to unspecified infidelities. His candidacy is in ashes, consumed in a fire storm of publicity—all of it engendered at the behest of an anonymous someone who knew just how to arouse reporters' competitive instincts, giving them enough information to be sure they could get a story, but not so much that they felt they had not tracked it down themselves.

▶ A campaign manager for Governor Michael Dukakis provides an "attack video" about a rival candidate, Senator Joseph Biden, to reporters for two big dailies. These papers then publish as news, in at least one case without adequately sourcing the story, exactly what the video purports to show: that Biden lifted words and imagery, without attribution, from a speech by British Labor Party leader Neil Kinnock. Never mind that Biden had acknowledged his source on other occasions, or that such borrowing is a political tradition. Beset by negative stories, which gradually expand to embrace other matters, Biden withdraws. The campaign manager who distributed the tape, John Sasso, is forced to emerge from the anonymity he initially negotiated with the media, and is thereby compelled to quit the Dukakis staff. But the tape achieves its purpose: with a formidable rival taken out of the race, Dukakis wins the nomination. Sasso eventually returns to direct the general election campaign.

▶ Vice President George Bush, who has been labeled a "wimp" on the cover of *Newsweek* and in countless newspaper columns, schedules a live interview on the CBS *Evening News*. His interlocutor is Dan Rather, in truth a solid and rather sentimental patriot, but a bugbear to the right-wing Republicans who most deeply doubt Bush's ferocity. When Rather asks a predictable question about Bush's involvement in controversial foreign policy matters, notably the Iran-*contra* scandal, Bush proclaims his indignation and, verbally, comes out swinging. In the written transcript, Rather has the better of the exchange. But on television, as Bush had hoped, the newsman seems rude and flustered and the Vice President appears as a macho man who stands up for his rights. For days after, Bush trumpets his triumph in what he calls "tension city," as though it had been a prizefight, and his problems with the conservative wing of his party all but vanish.

▶ Erstwhile televangelist Pat Robertson, who has just captured second place—stunningly, ahead of Bush—in the campaign-opening Iowa caucuses, appears in an interview with Tom Brokaw of NBC. Robertson expects the support of conservative Christians but fears that his background as a religious broadcaster may hinder him in reaching toward the mainstream, particularly in the wake of well-publicized misdeeds by other TV preachers. He reacts with calculated fury to a Brokaw question that labels him an evangelist; that phrasing, he says, reflects religious bigotry, and later he threatens never to do another interview with NBC. Soon afterward, other networks, understandably spooked by the controversy, bring Robertson on with maximum deference.

▶ Jesse Jackson, defeated at the ballot box but determined to wield power at the Democratic Convention, threatens to spurn the proffered time for a convention speech. If he walks out instead, he tells aides to Dukakis, then wherever he goes to orate, the network cameras will surely follow. From the way that the networks cover his mere threat, he is plainly right. So Jackson gets most of what he wants—although in hindsight many analysts, including New York *Times* columnist William Safire, believe the concessions cost front runner Dukakis his lead and his chance at the White House.

▶ Dan Quayle, within hours of being chosen as Bush's running mate, arouses a media onslaught of skepticism and scrutiny of the kind that, more often than not, ends in a public figure's forced departure to private life. The press has a seemingly endless list of questions about his academic background, family connections, military service record, indirect association with a sex scandal, and more. On some matters, the truth is bound to vindicate him; on others, there is plenty of potential for embarrassment. Rather than fight on the facts, Quayle is counseled, hammer away on the happier abstractions of fairness and due respect for public officials. So he holds a huge extended press conference—outdoors, in public, among friends and neighbors in his hometown of Huntington, Ind. Quayle's handlers have made sure that the exchange is amplified so that his backers can hear; the onlookers can be counted on to boo almost every tough question and to applaud nearly every earnest response. The use, or abuse, of the media is threefold: to shame or intimidate the campaign reporters who are present; to create a vivid scene that will have a similar effect on newspaper editors and broadcast-news directors around the country, impressing them with the general public's supposed hostility to tough reporting about Quayle; and to generate coverage nationwide that will implicitly persuade readers and viewers to disregard the whole run of questions raised about Quayle. Like Richard Nixon's 1952 Checkers speech, in which the then Republican vice-presidential candidate confronted questions about a "secret" slush fund set up on his behalf, the press-conference ploy works as a ritual purification: with the public convinced of Quayle's general decency and affability, the facts cease to matter much. Media rumblings about his background diminish quickly and soon all but disappear.

As these events point out, the 1988 campaign will likely go down in the annals of American journalism as the moment when reporters realized that the other side—the newsmakers and their handlers—had taken the upper hand. The notion of an adversary relationship between campaign reporters and candidates is, to be sure, a somewhat recent one. In his 1966 book *The Truman Presidency,* Cabell Phillips portrays a relatively chummy, poker-playing ease between the candidate's team and the press, sometimes involving the President himself. This was possible in large part because in those days campaign reporting consisted of synopsizing the candidate's speeches and estimating the size of crowds at rallies. Polling was in its infancy (indeed, pollsters almost unanimously predicted Dewey would win); other sociological techniques of assessing a campaign, such as intensive interviewing of small focus groups, were even more distant from general use. Moreover, the wartime spirit of collaboration between press and government had left a congenial residue. Reporters and politicians shared a fundamentally similar view of what the news was.

By the early 1950s, however, personal campaigning at rallies was already beginning to give way to campaigning via television, and Madison Avenue wizards were beginning to replace quondam journalists as politicians' principal advisers on how to reach the public. News people, unsurprisingly, resented anything that diminished their traditional role and mistrusted what they saw as attempts to bypass them. Meanwhile, throughout the news business were felt the first stirrings of a more aggressive, probing style of reportage. It would manifest itself in the 1960s in forms ranging from Theodore White's ground-breaking campaign books to the pseudo psychology and invented dialogue of the New Journalism.

In 1960 John Kennedy and Richard Nixon agreed to four debates (really, joint press conferences) on television, and those encounters became for millions of voters the decisive events of the campaign. Thereafter, whenever candidates agreed to debate—in 1976, 1980, 1984 and 1988—the candidate generally perceived as having won those meetings also won the general election. Nixon, burned in 1960 by television that he did not control, opted in 1968 for TV that he could. As Joe McGinniss recounted in his 1969 book *The Selling of the President,* the Republican candidate's advisers invented a series of pseudo press conferences, heavily scripted mock news events at which Nixon could appear spontaneous and at ease while delivering safe, canned corn.

The next phase in the struggle was a renewed effort by politicians to control the content of the news, which they label "free media," and to manipulate the themes of its stories so they would parallel what the candidate was arguing in his TV ads, or "paid media."

The very notion of discussing issues was supplanted by the ad industry approach of enunciating themes or displaying concerns. If Bush were to be concerned, as he apparently was, that voters might regard him or his party as insufficiently committed to cleaning up the environment, he need not actually call for more Government spending to do the job or for sanctions against corporate polluters. He could, and did, instead walk shorefronts and ride a boat through a befouled Boston harbor, extolling innocuously the joys of nature or, alternatively, displaying his meaningless personal revulsion at filth that nobody sane would support. If Michael Dukakis were to fret, as he did, that he and his party were perceived as soft on national defense, he need not actually pledge higher defense spending or endorse a battery of new weapons systems. He could, and did, put on a helmet and ride in a tank to show that he shares Everyman's little-boy fascination with gunnery and other hardware.

The news visuals generated by candidates are meant to be, if not identical, certainly complementary to the imagery in their commercials. By staging colorful events at carefully chosen intervals amid the endless look-alike glimpses of the candidate at a microphone—preferably with only one such attractive photo opportunity offered each day to foreclose editing-room discretion—the campaign staff can pretty much dictate what pictures will be used in nightly newscasts. Given the mind's supposedly superior retention of pictures over words, the handler-manipulators can thus determine what residual impression the broadcast stories will leave with viewers—and hence, indirectly but forcefully, also shape the context in which print reporters operate.

Some of this process of being turned into a mere megaphone, a passive conduit, was inadvertently aided by the press. The size of the campaign press corps increased more or less steadily during the 1970s and '80s, first to dozens and then to hundreds. Sometimes a single newspaper might have as many as four or five reporters encircling a nominee at big events, and increasingly they were joined by reporters for the larger local TV stations. As a result, logistics for managing this entourage became an ever more central function of the campaign staff. This in turn made reporters increasingly dependent on the candidate, or rather his aides, for everything from finding a hotel room at night to locating a telephone over which to file copy. Moreover, as the number of people yearning to question the candidate grew, it became easier and more reasonable looking to regulate access or deny it outright. Indeed, it evolved into a sort of dark joke among journalists that a candidate's availability for questions amounted to a confession that his campaign was in deep trouble. This sometimes applied even to Presidents. Gerald Ford, in fear of losing the New Hampshire primary to Ronald Reagan in 1976, invited editors and reporters from all but the single most right-wing of the state's dailies, some with circulations of less than 10,000, for a leisurely afternoon of White House chat. In 1984 early front runner Walter Mondale was often kept away from reporters, save perhaps for a few carefully planned minutes, day after day. He declined most offers of live interview time on network television, except for obligatory brief appearances on primary and caucus nights, reasoning that he had more to lose than to gain. Then, after he started losing primaries to Gary Hart, he was suddenly available for the morning talk shows. Asked by one interviewer why he was there in person, after months of lack of interest, he candidly replied, "Because I have to be."

Michael Dukakis displayed much the same sentiment in 1988. During the pre-primary season, when he was just one of a clutch of candidates, he was easy to reach, if not always vividly quotable: what he said off the record was almost exactly the same as what he said on the record, which in turn was almost exactly the same as what he said in his speeches. Later he became harder to buttonhole, yet was still relatively open, until he was persuaded by his staff that responding to reporters' concerns and agendas consistently clashed with his own and frequently made him appear to be on the defensive. One key campaign aide acknowledged the change, telling reporters, "You guys and your organizations have only yourselves to blame."

That observation came from Michael McCurry, press secretary to Lloyd Bentsen and formerly to candidates John Glenn in 1984 and Bruce Babbitt earlier in 1988. "You reward candidates who are inaccessible," McCurry said, "and you punish candidates who want to be accessible." His reasoning: accessible candidates frequently face embarrassing questions and other inconvenient coverage; they leave themselves open to slips and gaffes; moreover, they almost always sacrifice the political advantage of getting out a simple, coherent message that coordinates with their advertising. In short, accessible candidates wind up with blurry communication. Inaccessible candidates, by contrast, come across as crisp and clear. McCurry reflected the prevailing wisdom both of his trade and of the news business; when he launched his late-night salvo, few reporters disagreed.

Dukakis shifted back toward openness, however, in the final few weeks, as he continued to trail in polls. When ABC News president Roone Arledge offered to air a true, open-ended debate if both men accepted, and proffered a 90-minute interview with Ted Koppel on *Nightline* as an alternative if only one said yes, Dukakis eagerly agreed. Soon after, he said yes to a batch of other proposals, embracing virtually every major broadcast venue.

Front runner Bush, by contrast, was far more sparing in his press appearances, and toward the end was almost completely unavailable to beat reporters covering his campaign. He evoked groans from the frustrated press corps during a gag ceremony aboard the campaign plane, in which he gave away a Notre Dame football and sweatshirt, when he referred to the newsless nonevent as "my 209th press conference."

Taking a leaf from Ronald Reagan, Bush often placed himself in situations where he could feign being too distant to hear a reporter's question or too busy, despite the best of intentions, to pause and reply. In one of the more sardonically funny moments of the campaign, Bush aides led reporters into a Goya food plant in New Jersey to observe the candidate sampling

Hispanic dishes. When they tried to turn the appearance into an impromptu press conference, Bush waved off all questions because he was engaged in food tasting at the moment. He explained, "We gotta get the message out." The message, he was frankly admitting, had nothing to do with ideas. It had to do with, in the phrase of advertising people, concerns. Bush, the quintessential Wasp, was trying to convey to the nation's Hispanic voters that he was one of them, esteeming their culture and downing their chow. The message was something to be left unspoken. The picture would be worth a thousand words.

Why didn't reporters protest? Why didn't they refuse to write the stories the candidates wanted? Why didn't the networks, individually or collectively, resist being manipulated into airing the desired visuals? The answer has been expressed obliquely by the turn-of-the-century American essayist Finley Peter Dunne, whose comedic creation, the wise bartender Martin Dooley, uttered the aphorism "The Supreme Court follows the election returns." The phrase, rendered in broad Irish-immigrant dialect by Dunne, meant that the Justices, however Olympian their posture, recognized that they could count on enjoying society's deference only so long as the court's findings fell somewhere within the boundaries of acceptable mainstream opinion.

The same might be said of newspaper editors and broadcast-news directors: they tell the truth as they find it, but with an eye to the marketplace. If news people's methods and mannerisms are unpalatable to the public, they do not survive. Subdued behavior is wise during elections, when citizens' emotions tend to be aroused already, and it seemed particularly prudent after eight years of Ronald Reagan. When reporters had challenged Jimmy Carter, the public often agreed; but when they challenged Ronald Reagan, the surrogate national grandfather, the news people found themselves vilified. Reagan had, albeit in a more gentlemanly way, taken up the cudgel of Spiro Agnew. He had effectively dismissed the notion that journalists had any special constitutional standing, any right to claim to speak in behalf of the public. Reagan had held fewer press conferences than any recent predecessor; he had granted scarcely any one-on-one interviews, particularly not for broadcast; he had barred reporters from the invasion of Grenada. As political scientist James David Barber of Duke University has written, "Reagan is the first modern President whose contempt for the facts is treated as a charming idiosyncrasy."

At umpteen industry panels and symposiums on journalism ethics during the Reagan years, however, the same cry has been heard again and again from senior media managers: the news business must rein itself in, not because it is producing bad or improper stories, but because it is engendering the wrath of the paying customers. Like the President, the public has not been instantaneously ready to accept the idea that journalists speak in behalf of all, that resistance to the manipulations of candidates is an act for the public good. ABC's Jeff Greenfield, perhaps the shrewdest broadcast political analyst throughout the campaign, observed off-camera in its waning days, "The public does not see the limitation of access as an attack on its rights. You could say that the most ominous sign for the press in this campaign is that the lack of access is not felt to be an outrage. The public does not see the press as its tribunes."

Beyond any market-motivated reportorial hesitancy, was there something awry in the chemistry of the campaign—between the candidates themselves, or between them and the press—that made it so negative, issueless, trivial and mean? Was there something askew in the reportage, some passing fault, or had American politics truly and enduringly reached the state of vapidity envisioned in, say, *The Candidate,* Robert Redford's wryly cynical 1972 movie about a fictional U.S. Senate race in California. Journalists and political scientists would doubtless gather after the election in various forums to ponder that question. But by Election Day some answers were clear.

One is that, as was first said of French generals in the 19th century and has validly been observed of political journalists in most recent campaigns, they are invariably fighting the previous war. In 1980, for example, journalists underestimated the ideological element in Reagan's impending victory, and were thus thunderstruck when he swept twelve new Republican Senators into office with him, giving his party control of that body for the first time in a quarter-century. Then in 1982 election-night analysts were determined to spot the ideological trends, when in fact there were none: the Democrats gained substantially in House elections, which could be taken as a rebuke to Reaganism, while the Republicans held steady in the Senate, which could just as easily be read as a reaffirmation of Reagan's presidency. In 1984 Walter Mondale proved during the primaries the fragility of front-runner status, and during the general election demonstrated that the New Deal no longer struck a responsive cord in many voters. That left political reporters unprepared for, first, the midterm elections of 1986, which swept the Republicans out of control of the Senate and presumably marked an end to conservative hegemony, and then 1988, when George Bush successfully turned "liberal" into a term of scorn, invoking the euphemism "the L word." As for the tactics and the atmospherics of politics, reporters who had watched Mondale suffer a stomach-shaking roller-coaster ride through the spring of 1984 predicted the same bumpy course to the convention for Bush, his counterpart as front runner and Vice President—only to watch Bush's frail-looking front-runnerdom transmute by early March's Super Tuesday into a universally acknowledged victory.

In addition, reporters committed anew many of the sins of campaigns past. Once again they played the expectations game, in which a candidate is judged less by how he performs than by how the press guesses he would do in advance. The most conspicuous victim in 1988 was Republican hopeful Robert Dole, who after winning the Iowa caucuses managed to trim Bush's sizable lead in New Hampshire by fully half in just one week. A

lot of bullish reporters, however, implausibly predicted that
Dole would win New Hampshire outright, despite Bush's considerable organizational advantages; when Dole came in second, they declared him a loser, and his candidacy never recov-
ered. A similar mistake during the Democratic primary season
was the consistent underestimation of Jesse Jackson. Because
he won few white liberal votes in 1984, reporters wrongly expected he would remain unable to do so in 1988.

In the general election, reporters erred by succumbing to
the mania for a mechanical kind of balance, whereby every implicit criticism of a candidate—for example, noting that Bush
was waging a primarily negative campaign—must be offset by
tit-for-tat enumeration of comparable misdeeds by his opponent, regardless of whether the moral scales between the two
candidates are actually in equilibrium on any particular topic.
Fairness might better have been attained through deeper dig-
ging. But when Dukakis attacked Bush for inadequate commitment to social problems, for instance, reporters rarely leaned
hard on the Democrat to explain how he would pay for the programs he advocated; when Bush attacked Dukakis for giving
weekend furloughs to felons, reporters rarely noted that the furlough program had been instituted by Dukakis' Republican predecessor, that its most controversial features had already been
shut down and that a number of states had similar programs.

Pack journalism, the convergence of hundreds of reporters
on a story, was seen at its most virulent, particularly in the
hounding of Quayle. Reporters appeared ready to pursue almost
any accusation, no matter how wild, against a man who had after all occupied a Senate seat for more than seven years and had
survived, four times in all, the scrutiny of voters and and the
press to win elections to Congress. In fact, the Cleveland *Plain
Dealer*, which broke a number of legitimate stories about
Quayle's questionable past, reported receiving countless telephone calls from other major media asking if the paper was
working on other items, allegedly including a rumor that

Quayle had had someone else take his bar examination for him. The way reporters handled Quayle reflected journalists' misguided fondness for seeking "the smoking gun," the piece of conclusive evidence about a career, such as proof of outright fraud on the bar exam. In the absence of such melodramatic material, reporters tended to set aside altogether the serious question of Quayle's preparedness for high office, avoiding the need to undertake a less sexy, more considered look at his record.

Pack journalism of a subtler sort was evident throughout September and October as reporters tended to cluster, partly in reaction to one another, around a few big themes, each successively dominating campaign coverage. Some of the themes were quadrennial, others particular to this year. None had much to do with matters of substance, such as the federal budget deficit, the trade deficit, arms control or the environment. It was not that there were no definable differences between candidates. The ideological differences were stark enough, not only on emotional matters such as abortion, but also on harder-to-grasp ones such as taxation of capital gains. Seemingly disheartened by the candidates' successful manipulation of the visuals, however, the TV networks in particular failed to make ideology central to their coverage of the campaign. Perhaps as a result, media outlets were still reporting the weekend before the election that up to a fifth of all probable voters were either undecided or capable of switching sides at the last minute.

Among these overarching stories, the most predictable was the quadrennial reminder that there is not one election but 51—that is, the popular vote is a mere beauty contest, while the Electoral College, representing states and the District of Columbia, does the deciding. This in turn led to the customary stories defining key swing states and explaining how the candidates were focusing their strategies, even tailoring their talk, to appeal to these particular constituencies. The New York *Times* rather dispassionately noted that in contrast to conventional

wisdom, both sides were getting away with sending contradic-
tory messages in ads targeted at different regions of the country—Dukakis, as the allegedly more egregious example, emphasizing urban crime in ads for big-city black radio stations yet
opposing gun control in commercials for Texas.

Almost equally predictable, because it depended only on
the candidates' making the by now inevitable decision to debate
before TV cameras, was coverage of debate atmospherics. The
basic question, who must do what to win, tends to be answered
via an expectations game run amuck. What a candidate says is
often treated as far less important than whether he displays
such intangibles as strength, charm and the power to inspire
and how his display measures up against the electorate's and the
media's advance guesses of how he might behave. In 1988,
seemingly more than ever before, the press judged the candidates as potential television personalities and presumed that the
voters were doing the same. Knowing that one of these men
would be an almost inescapable presence for at least the next
four years, and gauging from polls and intuition that neither
was captivating the public, even the prestige press talked about
the debates largely in terms of "charisma" or at least
"likability."

Of all the questions asked in either debate, and all the other, weightier questions that might have been asked instead, the
one that drew the most press attention was a hypothetical pos-
tulate to Dukakis, an opponent of capital punishment, about
how he would react if his wife were raped and murdered. Dukakis, by common consent, bobbled the topic but did not dispute
its legitimacy. In fact, in a subsequent live interview with the
questioner, Bernard Shaw of Cable News Network, Dukakis
not only validated the question but also offered a more elaborate
answer that he said he should have made initially. Capital punishment, indeed law enforcement in general, is in truth not
much of a presidential issue. Constitutionally, the subject belongs primarily to the states. Moreover, Dukakis' personal emo-

tional response to a family tragedy, imaginary or otherwise, has little relevance to public policy; nor does the fact, which he liked to point out, that his father and brother had been actual victims of violent crime. Yet what seemed to strike most reporters was not the substance or appropriateness of the question, but rather an absence of evident passion in Dukakis' response. What was wrong about his performance, they suggested, was not so much his answer as his lack of strong emotion. In this analysis, Dukakis failed by not showing a normal enough response, not echoing the vengeful rhetoric of the common man.

Coverage of the vice-presidential debate was almost as trivial. The sound bite on virtually every broadcast report, the featured quote in virtually every newspaper story, was Lloyd Bentsen's remark to Dan Quayle that he was "no Jack Kennedy." It summed up, in a phrase, the prevalent charge that Quayle was a lightweight. Yet hardly any report about the vice-presidential debate thereupon proceeded to make the case, citing examples and evidence, that Quayle had overall proved himself uninformed or unfit. At worst, on the evidence offered by reporters, he had unwittingly set up his opponent's shrewd quip.

What happened to him echoed what happened in the debates of 1984. In the first, Walter Mondale lay in wait for Ronald Reagan to use again his debunking line of 1980, "There you go again." Mondale then stunned Reagan by pointing out that Reagan had last used the line in a presidential debate back in 1980, to disavow any plan to cut Medicare—an attempt that he had nonetheless undertaken soon after entering office. Because Reagan's poor performance during that first debate prompted much talk about his mental and physical health, expressed in the phrase "the age issue," he in turn lay in wait in the second meeting. Listening for any reference to age, he took his first opportunity to assure the public that he would "not exploit for political purposes my opponent's youth and inexperience." When the chuckles were over, so was all serious public attention to the debate. It mattered little what was said the rest of the night. Each of these cracks, from Mondale, Reagan and this year Bentsen, became the catchphrase in the media and hence in collective public memory. Not one of them had more than the vaguest connection to any philosophical differences being discussed.

Curiously, there was little reporting, and also little editorializing, about the most striking aspects of the debates: their timing. All three—two presidential and one vice-presidential—took place before the election had the public's undivided attention. The first presidential debate came in the middle of another great patriotic event, the Olympics. Only at the last minute, in fact, did NBC pre-empt coverage of the Seoul Games in an attempt to enhance the debate's total viewership. The vice-presidential encounter and the second presidential debate cropped up in the middle of major league baseball's championship series: the very dates and timing of both were kept fluid until the last minute to accommodate the contingencies of the sport. The timing was at the insistence of Bush and his team, who believed their side was ahead and therefore wanted the debates to attract only passing attention. Dukakis, for whatever reasons, chose not to make an issue of the schedule. Other than mild tut-tutting on a few editorial pages, neither did the news media.

The biggest theme of October coverage was the genesis, prevalence and effectiveness of negative campaign advertising. Although negative ads, particularly on TV, had become more and more commonplace in congressional and gubernatorial campaigns, 1988 marked the first time that attacks on an opponent, rather than promotion of one's own agenda, became the primary thrust of a presidential campaign. Bush fit the classic definition of a candidate who would benefit from negative advertising: he was himself well known but not well liked, with just as many voters viewing him unfavorably as favorably. Meanwhile, the much publicized but as yet largely unscrutinized Dukakis enjoyed an overwhelmingly favorable public opinion and a sizable, if soft, lead in opinion polls. Making use of what a focus group indicated about how to reach Democrats, particularly those who had voted for Reagan in 1984, the Bush team shaped negative ads that were intended as interim measures but that proved so potent they were kept running long after their scheduled stop date.

Several were inflammatory. Some were taken to be racist. At least one, run at the behest of an ostensibly independent Republican organization, was disavowed by Bush's campaign chairman, James Baker, although not by the candidate. The most successful of the Republicans' negative ads concerned furloughs, and the key example, mentioned over and over by Bush himself, involved the case of Willie Horton, who raped a Maryland woman while on prison furlough. A particularly controversial fund-raising letter for the G.O.P. showed pictures of Dukakis and Horton, asking whether this was "your pro-family team for 1988."

The notion that the references to Horton were tacit appeals to racism was reinforced, in a sense, by another quasi-independent ad campaign in North Dakota. There party officials distributed literature that linked Dukakis to Jesse Jackson, and speculated, as many right-wing Republicans had throughout the year, on the role Jackson might play in a Democratic Administration. "Imagine life," the text read, "with Jesse Jackson as Secretary of State." The North Dakota officials disingenuously claimed that they meant only to connect Dukakis to Jackson's liberalism and that thoughts of race had never entered their minds.

Closely tied to the reproving stories about negative campaigning was a theme of indulgence and forgiveness, heard especially in editorials although also on news pages. Never mind that both candidates sound shrill, shallow and unpresidential, the stories said, because the two men do not really mean what they are saying. Normally the assertion that a politician is insincere or deceptive is the height of journalistic denunciation. But in 1988 both the New York *Times,* which weakly endorsed Dukakis, and the Washington *Post,* which declined to back either man, acknowledged a widespread assumption among journalists that both candidates' assertions might best be gently overlooked as mere expedience.

Editorial endorsements in general turned out to be fewer in number than in 1984. According to the trade weekly *Editor & Publisher,* 55% of U.S. newspapers either chose not to endorse a candidate or remained undecided as the campaign neared its close, up from 32% in 1984. Of the 772 papers polled by *E&P,* 241 were for Bush, 103 for Dukakis and 428 on the fence. Among the minority of papers that did back a candidate, the endorsements were often strikingly tepid. The editorial-page editor of the Charlotte *Observer,* for example, called his paper's embrace of Dukakis "unenthusiastic." The Governor's hometown Boston *Globe* bluntly said it had been tempted to sit this one out. On the Republican side, pro-Bush papers such as the Chicago *Tribune* and the New York *Daily News* often appeared to base their backing on the peace and prosperity of the Reagan era rather than any specific expectations about Bush. Some all but disavowed Quayle even as they urged the election of his ticket.

Amid these big-theme stories of the campaign's final weeks, however, there was almost no high-profile attempt to write what seemed to be the biggest story of all. Although news organizations generated the usual plethora of polls and reported on them extensively to the effect that Dukakis' cause was hopeless, journalists stopped short of the obvious implication. Whether from fear of the appearance of unfairness, or simply from worry about being premature, political reporters did not put together the definitive description of how Dukakis blew a 15-point lead in polls, going from an apparent shoo-in during the early summer to a long-shot in the fall. By tradition, such chronicles are left for the morning after the election at the earliest. Yet surely it would have said something illuminating about both the candidate and the voters, something helpful to the unsettled fifth of the electorate, to assess why the pendulum of opinion swung on so wide an arc.

Undistinguished as the performance of the American press was during the campaign of 1988, the nation's journalists may have done both their audiences and their own profession a favor in the long run. Former Vice President Spiro Agnew's charge that the news media are "elected by no one," yet hugely influential, struck a still resonating cord in the society. Every time the course of national politics is affected by an event like the Washington *Post's* coverage of Watergate, or in a lesser key the Miami *Herald's* exposure of the peccadilloes of Gary Hart, people across ideological lines renew the call for some sort of restraint, voluntary or otherwise, on the workings of the free press. The consummate power of the news media has become a totem of conventional wisdom.

In 1988, however, the press was powerful only when used or acted upon. No big-league reporter or major news organization was visibly and consistently at odds with either candidate. No news story made a discernible difference in the outcome of the final campaign. Given the opportunity to be probing yet abrasive or to be superficial and benign, journalists mostly chose the latter. If inadequately informed and insufficiently challenged to think about the hard issues facing the nation, the electorate was at least left demonstrably free to form its own opinion.

Index

AFL-CIO, 188-189

Ailes, Roger, 5-6, 10-11, 51, 198, 218, 219, 223

American Civil Liberties Union (ACLU), 5, 11, 12, 224

Anderson, Martin, 43

Atwater, Lee, 6, 59-61, 62, 67, 70, 71, 74, 75, 76, 198, 218, 219, 223

Austin, Gerald, 154, 160, 163, 167, 176, 240

Babbitt, Bruce, 1-2, 14, 17, 122-123

Baker, Howard, 17, 61-62

Baker, James, 62, 90, 99, 198-199, 214, 227, 242, 261

Bell, Griffin, 116

Bentsen, Lloyd, 94, 175, 183, 184-186, 195, 216, 227, 229, 234, 239, 240, 259, 260

Biden, Joseph, 1, 7, 17, 33, 38, 123-124, 246

Blacks: Democratic Party and, 6, 7, 106-107, 118, 217; Jackson and, 154, 156, 159; Reagan and, 22-23; voting patterns, 238

Bloom, Alan, 21

Bork, Robert, 7-8, 67, 123

Bradley, Bill, 113, 184

Brady, Nicholas, 59, 98, 219

Brock, Bill, 67, 75

Broder, David, 230

Brountas, Paul, 175, 183, 218, 225, 227

Brown, Ron, 176

Brown, Willie, 164

Buchanan, Patrick, 4, 55

Buckley, John, 55

Buckley, William, 1-2, 67

Bush, Barbara, 88, 96

Bush, Dorothy, 80, 81, 82, 83, 91

Bush, George, 2, 4, 5, 29, 33, 41, 131-132, 182, 195; ADA rating, 92-93; announces candidacy, 50-53; convention speech, 209-212; education of, 83-86, 88; experience, 86-96, 92-93, 98-102; factors favoring, 213-215; family and friends, 80-86, 88-91; foreign policy, 37; Goldwater and, 72; heros, 84-85; image, 33, 53, 58, 79, 82, 83, 93-94, 100-101, 218, 225; Iran-contra scandal and, 101; issues, 47, 236-237, 241-243; likability, 228, 228-229; media and, 253, 256, 262; negative campaign, 10-12, 39, 63, 71, 208-209, 215-225, 260-261; negative image, 60-61, 215-218;

nomination of, 25; primaries, 66-76; Quayle and, 200-205, 229; Rather and, 10, 246; Reagan and, 33-35, 46-48, 61, 78, 100-102, 213-214; Robertson and, 5-6, 13; strategy, 16, 233-238; support, 57-58; weaknesses, 56, 57, 59, 59-60, 63-64; victory, 238-239

Bush, George Walker, 88, 91

Bush, Prescott, 80-82, 86, 95

Carter, Jimmy, 24, 30, 36, 41, 97, 104, 108, 118, 119, 176, 179, 253

Champion, Hale, 116

Cheney, Dick, 36-37

Civil rights, 99-100, 106-107

Clinton, Bill, 150-151

Cohen, Beryl, 139, 144-145

Connally, John, 94, 104

Cuomo, Mario, 16, 17, 113, 121, 150, 189, 192, 230

Darman, Richard, 198-201, 219

Debates, 227-231, 258-260

Democratic Leadership Council, 6, 109-111, 125

Democratic National Convention, 179-196, 197-212

Democratic Party: Congress and, 108; losses of, 103-104; liberalism and, 6-7, 106-112, 240-241; platform, 173, 187-188; South and, 105-106, 118-120, 128-129, 159-160, 185; special interests and, 6-8, 108-110, 187-188, 217

Dewey, Thomas E., 103, 233

Dole, Robert, 4, 17, 37, 53, 200, 203, 209, 216, 255-256; announces candidacy, 51-53; Bush and, 62-63; primaries, 68-73, 75-76; strategies, 64-67; support for, 56-57, 59; weaknesses, 64-67

Domenici, Pete, 203

Dukakis, Euterpe, 135-138, 147, 239

Dukakis, Kitty, 142-144, 193

Dukakis, Michael, 2, 14, 33, 119, 121, 124, 152-153, 155, 159, 161, 166-167, 167, 169, 182, 183, 205, 208; Bush and, 11-12, 208-209, 224-225; campaign issues, 224, 226, 236-237; campaign strategies, 217-219, 225-230, 227, 234-238; candidacy of, 7, 126-132;

concession of, 238-239; convention speech, 189-190, 192-195; education, 138-139, 141-142; experience, 126, 142, 144-150; factors favoring, 215-218; family, 134-141; final surge, 231-232, 233; image, 6, 48, 133-134, 136, 139, 143, 146, 148-151, 223; Jackson and, 5, 6, 9, 12, 13, 170-176, 226-227, 247, 261; liberalism of, 5, 6, 12-13, 230; likability, 133-134, 228; media and, 251, 252, 256, 257-258, 258-259, 262; national security and, 37-39, 127; Pledge of Allegiance and, 5, 11-12; prison furlough and, 5, 11, 12, 261; vice-presidential choice, 183-186

Dukakis, Panos, 134-138, 142
Dukakis, Stelian, 135, 139-141, 223
Dunne, Finley Peter, 253
Du Pont, Pete, 2, 17, 55, 58, 76

Economic policy: Bush and, 213-214; Jackson and, 8-9, 156-157; Reagan and, 19-20, 28, 40-45, 48, 241
Eisenhower, Dwight, 32, 103, 118
Election, 232-233, 237-238
Ellsworth, Robert, 64-65, 66-67
Estrich, Susan, 175, 218, 225

Farmer, Robert, 127, 129, 130
Federal deficit, 19, 44, 236-237
Ferguson, Joel, 163
Ferraro, Geraldine, 17, 119, 149
Ford, Gerald, 56, 92, 96, 108, 251
Foreign policy, 35-40
Fuller, Craig, 59, 62, 74, 198, 220
Futrell, Mary Hatwood, 188

Gephardt, Richard, 2, 14, 17, 109, 110, 125, 155, 158, 163, 184-185
Glenn, John, 184-185
Goldwater, Barry, 43, 72, 118
Gore, Albert, 2, 17, 38, 109, 118-121, 128, 131, 161, 167-169, 184-185, 222
Grassley, Chuck, 57, 68, 70
Greenberg, Stanley B., 40
Greenfield, Jeff, 254
Greenwood, Lee, 30-31, 34

Haig, Alexander, 3, 36, 55-56, 60, 72-73, 100
Harrington, Kevin, 146
Hart, Gary, 1, 7, 16, 33, 61, 109, 116-117, 245, 251, 263
Healy, Robert, 220
Heflin, Howell, 7, 240
Hollings, Ernest, 240
Horton, Willie, 5, 11, 12, 261
Humphrey, Hubert, 104, 107, 112

INF Treaty, 3, 36-38

Iran-*contra* affair, 26, 56, 59-61, 243

Jackson, Jesse, 2-4, 17, 33, 119-121, 130, 131, 189, 195, 216; candidacy, 114-115; Democrats and, 6-9, 182-184, 190-192, 247; Dukakis and, 6, 9, 12, 13, 170-176, 185-187, 217, 226-227, 261; economic populism, 8-9; funding, 160-161; issues, 155, 157-158; Jews and, 168; media and, 256; national security and, 38; popularity, 152-154, 158-161, 164-165; primaries, 152-153, 159-164, 166-170; problems, 165-171; vice-presidential bid, 170-176, 183-184
Johnson, Lyndon, 63, 93-94, 104, 105, 107, 118

Kean, Tom, 209
Keene, David, 63, 73, 75
Kemp, Jack, 4, 5, 16, 16-17, 33, 37, 38, 54-55, 73, 74, 76, 203
Kennedy, Edward (Ted), 9, 17, 113, 189, 189-190, 192
Kennedy, John, 32, 105, 107, 112, 118
Kennedy, Joseph P., II, 225
Kennedy, Paul, 20
Kimmitt, Robert, 198-201
Kirk, Paul, 110-111, 167, 185, 187-188, 218
Kirkland, Lane, 188
Kirkpatrick, Jeanne, 4, 17, 55
Koch, Ed, 121, 131, 168, 169
Kostmayer, Peter, 112
Kristol, Irving, 36, 44

Lance, Bert, 9, 164, 172, 174
LaRouche, Lyndon, 223
Laxalt, Paul, 17, 55
Liberalism, 4-5, 11-12, 214-215, 218-220, 230, 239-241
Loeb, William, 58, 93

McCurry, Michael, 251-252
McGinniss, Joe, 249
McGovern, George, 104, 107
Manatt, Charles, 195
Manchester *Union Leader*, 58
Martin, Lynn, 51
Media coverage: candidates and, 250-253; of debates, 258-260; Democratic Convention, 183; free, 249-253; highlights, 245-248; negative campaign and, 254-263; Quayle and, 204-205; role of, 245, 248, 263
Meese, Edwin, 26, 216-217
Miami *Herald*, 117, 245, 263
Mitropoulos, Nick, 220-221
Mondale, Walter, 6, 10, 46, 104, 108, 109, 111, 116, 119, 156, 255, 259
Moral Majority, 27-28

Mosbacher, Robert, 72, 90

National security, 27-28, 37-39, 127, 242-243
Newspaper endorsements, 261-262
New York Times, 117, 257, 261-262
Nixon, Richard, 59, 65, 93, 94, 95, 103, 104, 108, 112, 189, 248, 249
Noriega, Manuel, 35-36, 165-166
Nunn, Sam, 7, 9, 17, 108, 109, 110, 113, 119, 184, 240
Nyhan, David, 125-126

O'Claireacain, Carol, 8
Organized labor, 111, 187-189
Overbey, John, 89

Parks, Rosa, 191
Peace issue, 38-39, 213, 214
Phillips, Cabell, 248
Polsby, Nelson, 240
Poverty, 22-23, 41, 42
Public opinion polls, 37, 40, 72, 233

Quayle, J. Danforth (Dan), 2, 5, 11, 29, 198-205, 209, 227, 229, 234, 235, 247-248, 256-257, 259, 262

Racism, 4, 239-240
Rather, Dan, 10, 218, 246
Reagan, Nancy, 61, 101
Reagan, Ronald, 2-3, 10, 18, 28-31, 43, 83, 103, 108, 112-113, 223, 234, 235, 251, 259; 1980 Iowa caucuses, 67-68; Bush and, 33-35, 78, 98-102; convention speech, 25-26, 31; economic policies, 28, 40-45, 48, 241; foreign policy, 27-28, 35-40; as "Gipper," 32; Gorbachev and, 36-37; legacy, 26-29, 213-214; "luck," 29-30, 49; media and, 253-255; sleaze factor and, 30, 217; state of country under, 18-24
Reed, Clarke, 207-208
Regan, Donald, 44, 61
Republican National Convention, 5, 25-26, 31, 205, 206
Republican Party, 2-3, 17, 67; image of, 107; platform, 206-208
Richards, Ann, 189-190, 192
Robb, Charles, 108-109, 110, 119
Robertson, Pat, 3-6, 13, 17, 28-29, 38, 55, 68-70, 74-76, 209, 246-247
Rockefeller, Nelson, 54, 96, 99
Rogers, Ed, 59, 61, 70, 74
Roosevelt, Franklin D., 106, 118
Roosevelt, Theodore, 213, 243

Safire, William, 195, 247
Sanford, Terry, 110
Sasso, John, 124, 148-150, 217-218, 226-227, 231, 246
Schlesinger, Arthur M., Jr., 26-27
SDI, 38-39
Sears, John, 65
Shaw, Bernard, 230, 258
Shultz, George, 4-5
Simon, Jeanne, 167
Simon, Paul, 1, 124, 130-131, 162
Sleaze factor, 30, 217
Social Security, 241
Sorensen, Theodore, 173, 193
"Special interests," 6-8, 108-110, 187-188, 217
Spencer, Stuart, 204
Standard of living, 21, 44
Stevenson, Adlai, 103, 118
Stock-market crash (1987), 18
Strauss, Robert, 215-216, 231, 241
Sununu, John, 71, 207, 219
Super-delegates, 181
Supply-side economics, 40-45, 54-55, 100
Supreme Court, Reagan and, 29
Synhorst, Tom, 68, 70

Taxes, 44-47, 71-72, 236-237, 241
Teeley, Peter, 74
Teeter, Robert, 58, 59, 62, 74, 75, 198, 219, 235
Thomas, Tommy, 57-58
Thurmond, Strom, 7, 75
Trudeau, Gary, 58
Truman, Harry S, 103, 106, 112, 118, 233

Van Deerlin, Lionel, 122
Van Dyk, Ted, 225-226
Viguerie, Richard, 93, 203
"Voodoo economics," 46, 74, 100, 241

Wage stagnation, 43-44
Walker, George Herbert, 80
Walker, G. Herbert, Jr., 89
Washington Post, 117, 261-262, 263
Wattenberg, Ben J., 20
Weicker, Lowell, 206
Welfare, Reagan and, 23-24, 41-42
White, Theodore H., 15
Will, George, 58
Wirthlin, Richard, 30, 67, 71-72, 75
Women, 6, 8, 22, 223-224, 238
Woodward, Bill, 192-193
Wright, Jim, 176, 181-182

Yarborough, Ralph, 92, 94

ABOUT THE AUTHORS

Garry Wills, who wrote the introduction, is a historian at Northwestern University and a frequent contributor to TIME and other publications. He is the author of *The Kennedy Imprisonment*, *Nixon Agonistes* and *Reagan's America*.

Robert Ajemian, who wrote the chapters on George Bush and Michael Dukakis, has covered every presidential election since 1952. He graduated from Harvard University in 1948 and worked for three years as a sportswriter for the old Boston *Evening American* before joining LIFE magazine in 1952. At LIFE he was political editor and assistant managing editor in charge of news. He came to TIME in 1972 and was the magazine's Washington bureau chief during the Carter years and the first Reagan term. He is currently TIME's Boston bureau chief.

Laurence I. Barrett, who wrote the chapters on the Reagan legacy, the Republicans and the New Orleans convention, is TIME's national political correspondent. A New Yorker educated at New York and Columbia universities, he started his career with the old New York *Herald Tribune* in 1958. He headed the newspaper's city hall bureau, wrote a weekly column and worked in the Washington bureau, covering his first presidential campaign in 1964. Barrett's novel *The Mayor of New York* was published in 1965, the year he joined TIME as a national affairs writer. He later served as a senior editor, New York bureau chief and, from 1980 through 1985, as the magazine's main reporter covering candidate and then President Ronald Reagan. His book *Gambling with History: Ronald Reagan in the White House* was published in 1984.

Michael Duffy, who wrote the chapter on Jesse Jackson, covers the White House for TIME. Born in 1958 in Columbus, Duffy received an A.B. degree in English from Oberlin College in 1980. He joined TIME as a Pentagon correspondent in 1985 and later covered Congress. He reported on Democratic candidates during the 1988 campaign.

Hays Gorey, who wrote the chapters on the Democrats, the Atlanta convention and the general election campaign, is a TIME senior correspondent based in Washington. He has covered national politics since 1967 and is the author or co-author of three books, as well as numerous articles for publications besides TIME. He was co-author, along with the late Theodore H. White, of *The Making of the President, 1984*, which was never completed. Gorey was a Nieman Fellow at Harvard University in 1950 and an Eisenhower Fellow in Tehran in 1963. Before joining TIME, he was city editor and news editor of the Salt Lake City *Tribune*.

William A. Henry III, an associate editor of TIME, has covered aspects of the past five presidential campaigns for several publications and broadcast media, including LIFE, GQ, the Boston *Globe* and the New York *Daily News*, and, in frequent guest commentary, for CBS News, ABC News, PBS and Cable News Network. He has taught a course on the media and presidential politics at Yale and has lectured extensively on the subject. Henry is the author of the book *Visions of America: How We Saw the 1984 Election*, which was praised by the New York *Times* Book Review for "elegant prose and . . . an intelligent effort to place the campaign in a broader sociological context." In 1980, at age 30, he won a Pulitzer Prize in Distinguished Criticism for his coverage of television at the Boston *Globe*.

Donald Morrison, who edited the book and wrote the chapter on the nation's mood, is special projects editor at TIME. He joined the magazine in 1968 to cover that year's presidential election and has since written and edited in virtually every department. Born in Alton, Ill., he received a bachelor's degree in political science from the University of Pennsylvania in 1968 and a master's degree in comparative government from the London School of Economics in 1970. He is the editor and a co-author of *Mikhail S. Gorbachev: An Intimate Biography*, a TIME book published in 1988.

RESEARCH STAFF

Ursula Nadasdy de Gallo, director of research for the project, came to the U.S. from Hungary in the wake of that country's 1956 revolution. She graduated from Manhattanville College in 1965 with a B.A. degree in political science. She joined TIME's World section as a researcher and became head researcher of the department in 1973. Since 1985 she has been the department head of reporter-researchers in the Nation section.

Audrey J. Ball, a senior reporter-researcher in TIME's Nation section, was a reporter and associate editor at LIFE and a member of that magazine's investigative reporting team. Educated at Columbia University, she joined TIME in 1972 and has covered politics since 1976.

Bernard Baumohl is a senior reporter-researcher in the Business section of TIME. Educated at Columbia University, he received an M.A. in international economics before joining TIME in 1980.

Barbara Burke is a reporter-researcher in TIME's Nation section. She worked for *Newsweek* for twelve years and covered the 1976 and 1980 elections. She has a B.A. in English literature from Columbia University and has lived and worked in Guatemala.

Tom Curry, a reporter-researcher in the Nation section, has a B.A. in history from Haverford College and an M.A. in teaching from Reed College. He came to TIME after six years as a history teacher at high schools in the suburbs of New York City. He has written political articles for *Commonweal* and *Student Life*.

David Ellis, a reporter-researcher in the Nation section, was born in New York City and educated at Boston University and Trinity College, Dublin. He has written news broadcasts for National Public Radio in Boston and reported from London for the *Economist*. He joined TIME in 1985, and has specialized in urban and political affairs for the magazine.

Susan Harrington, a free-lance writer and editor, is the author of *Today's Jungle Peoples* and co-author of *Finding Facts*, second edition.

Naushad Mehta is a senior reporter-researcher in TIME's Press section. Before that she was a free-lance writer and worked for five years as a reporter-researcher for the magazine's international editions. Born and raised in Bombay, she has a bachelor's degree in English and philosophy from the University of Bombay and a master's degree in journalism from Syracuse.

Katherine Mihok is a senior reporter-researcher in the Nation section of TIME. She received a B.A. in English from Bryn Mawr College and an M.A. from Columbia University's Teachers College.

David Seideman's work has appeared in the *New Republic*, the New York *Times* Book Review and the London *Times* Literary Supplement, among other publications. A reporter-researcher in the Nation section, he is the author of *The New Republic: A Voice of Modern Liberalism* and was editor of the *New Republic's* 70th-anniversary book volume in 1984.

William Tynan, a senior reporter-researcher for TIME, covers the television and home-video beat. A graduate of Harvard University, he has been a reporter for *Money* magazine; an editor of magazines, filmstrips and teachers' guides for the multimedia Genesis Project; and a contributor to the reference book *Notable Names in the American Theatre*.

Sidney Urquhart is a senior reporter-researcher in the Nation section. A native New Yorker, she has a B.A. in modern history from Smith College and an M.S. from the Columbia School of Journalism. She has written fashion copy for *Vogue*, worked for various New York book publishers and taught at a boys' elementary school. In her eight years at TIME, she has worked on both national and international news stories, in addition to reporting for the Education and Design sections.